THE GLAS[illegible] GUIDE FOR PARENTS AND CARERS

2004 edition

A HANDBOOK FOR PARENTS, GRANDPARENTS AND CARERS

Edited by Irene Laird

DISCLAIMER

The information provided in *The Glasgow Guide for Parents and Carers* was to our knowledge, correct, when going to print. Glasgow Under 6's Ltd cannot be held responsible for any errors or omissions.

Published 2004 by Glasgow Under 6's Ltd, 48 Flenders Avenue, Glasgow, G76 7XZ

Design and project management by The Partnership Publishing Solutions Ltd, Glasgow, G77 5UN
www.the-pps.co.uk

Printed and bound in Great Britain by The Bath Press Ltd, CPI Group (UK)

Contents

Editor's Letter

Hello, and welcome to the 2004 (2nd) edition of *The Glasgow Guide for Parents and Carers* and thank you for buying your copy.

We aim to provide parents, grandparents and carers with a comprehensively researched guide for everyday use.

Listings within the guide are free and advertisers have paid to be included. The guide contains valuable information on many specialist facilities and services for parents with babies and young children.

We hope you enjoy *The Glasgow Guide for Parents and Carers* and we would welcome your comments by post or email to:

Glasgow Under 6's Ltd
48 Flenders Avenue
Clarkston
Glasgow, G76 7XZ
Tel/Fax: 0141 616 3661
Email: glasgowunder6s@fsmail.net

THE GLASGOW GUIDE

FOR PARENTS AND CARERS

2005 edition

NOTE TO ADVERTISERS

If you were not listed in ***The Glasgow Guide for Parents and Carers*** 2004 (2nd) edition, don't worry. Have your business or service listed in ***The Glasgow Guide for Parents and Carers*** 2005 (3rd) edition. Fill in your details below and return by the 30th September 2004 to:

Glasgow Under 6's Ltd
48 Flenders Avenue
Clarkston
Glasgow, G76 7XZ
Tel/Fax 0141 616 3661
E: glasgowunder6s@fsmail.net

Name of Business & Contact Name . . . .

Address . . . .

. . . .

Postcode . . . . Tel/Fax No. . . . .

Email . . . . www . . . .

PLEASE TICK BELOW

Free Listing ☐

Request advertising details ☐

NOTE TO READERS

We would like to hear your comments and suggestions for our 2005 edition. These should be sent to **Glasgow Under 6's Ltd** at the address above.

Activities for Children

Please find included in the following section listings of:

- **Dancing Schools**
- **Golf**
- **Horse Riding Schools**
- **Martial Arts Academy/Schools**
- **Music, Drama & Exercise**
- **Language & Maths**

Dancing Schools

Please find in the following section listings of Dancing Schools available for children in and around the Glasgow area. For Dancewear *see* SHOPPING (DANCEWEAR).

- **Audrey Clark**
  School of Dance
  ☎ 01236 840166

  Classes from $2^1/_2$ yrs in ballet, tap, modern & jazz. Classes held in Clelland (Tues & Wed), Carnbroe (Wed)

- **The Bonnie & Sharon Barr School of Dance, Music & Drama**
  ☎ 01324 623007

  Classes from $2^1/_2$ yrs in Paisley (YMCA), Bishopton (Community Centre) & Laurieston (old folks hall)

- **The Dance Factory**
  142 Calder Street
  Govanhill
  Glasgow
  G42 7QP
  ☎ 0141 423 9430

  Dancing classes from 3 yrs in ballet, tap, modern, jazz, highland & rock & roll
  Classes available daily at the address opposite

- **The Dance Foundation**
  ☎ 0141 638 4199

  Classes from $2^1/_2$ yrs in Clarkston, Giffnock & Netherlee
  Ballet, modern, theatre, acro/gymnastics & jazz, R.A.D. & I.S.T.D.

- **The Dance House**
  ☎ 0141 334 0716

  Creative movement classes for 3–5 yrs and 6–9 yrs in Hillhead High School, Oakfield Avenue, Hillhead
  Dance classes available for 14yrs plus
  For details and times of classes please contact the Dance House

- **Dees Dance Classes**
  PO Box 5456, G77 5LN
  ☎ 0141 639 8300
  www.deesdancing.co.uk

  Classes from 4 yrs in Newlands & Paisley
  Freestyle disco, Latin American & salsa

- **Dorothy Kemp**
  ☎ 0141 641 3432

  Classes from $2^1/_2$ yrs in tap, ballet, modern & disco
  Classes held in Cambuslang Masonic Hall on Saturdays

- **Eileen Degnan Stage School**
☎ 0141 942 2518

Classes from $2^1/_2$ yrs to adult in tap, ballet, modern & jazz. Classes held in Westerton Hall (Bearsden) Sat 10am–4pm & The Scout Hall (Milngavie) Thurs from 2.15pm

- **Elizabeth Henderson**
☎ 0141 339 8116

Classes from $2^1/_2$ yrs in ballet, tap & modern. Classes in Hyndland Community Hall (Mon) & Maryhill Community Central Hall (Thurs)

- **Garrowhill School of Dance**
☎ 07751 848190

Classes from 3 yrs in tap, ballet, modern, highland, majorettes, cheerleading & acrobatics. Classes available Mon–Sat in Garrowhill Masonic Halls

- **J & D School of Dance & Drama**
☎ 01505 351058

Classes from 2–16 yrs in tap, ballet, modern, highland & disco. Classes held in Elderslie Village Hall (Tues & Wed 6–9pm) & Howood Community Hall (Tues 6–9pm)

- **Lillian McNeill**
School of Dancing
☎ 0141 423 0931

Classes from 2 yrs in tap, ballet, modern & jazz
Classes held at The Studio, 29 Marywoord Square, Strathbungo, Glasgow G41 2BW
Classes available Tues, Wed & Sat

- **Linda Lowry**
School of Ballet
☎ 01505 705287

Ballet classes from 3 yrs in Hillhead (Hutchesons' Grammar School) & Bearsden (New Kilpatrick Old Halls)

- **Lynn Duncan**
School of Dance
☎ 01698 320964

Classes from 2 yrs in tap, modern, disco, majorettes & cheerleading
Classes in Blantyre (Fri), Bridgeton (Tues), Burnside (Thurs), Cranhill (Mon), Easterhouse (Thurs), Hamilton (Wed) & Toryglen (Mon)

- **Margaret MacBain**
School of Dance
☎ 0141 956 3388

Classes from 3 yrs
Classes in Cairns Church Hall, Buchanan Street, Milngavie (Mon, Tues & Thurs) and Scout Hall, Main Street, Milngavie (Wed)

- **M A Gilbride**
  ☎ 0141 639 4485

  Classes from $2^1/_2$ yrs in ballet, tap, modern, jazz, acro/gymnastics, disco & cheerleading
  Classes available Mon – Thurs in Crookfur Pavilion, Newton Mearns.

- **Sandra Harrington School of Dancing**
  ☎ 0141 639 7789

  Classes from 2 yrs in tap, ballet, modern, disco, cheerleading & majorettes
  Classes held in The Couper Institute, Cathcart (Fri), Blantyre (Mon) & Cambuslang (Thurs).

- **Supreme School of Dancing**
  ☎ 0141 632 6427

  Classes from $2^1/_2$ yrs for boys & girls at Rhuallan House on Mondays from 4.00pm in tap, ballet & modern

- **The Studio**
  19 Westbourne Gardens
  Glasgow
  G12 9UL
  ☎ 0141 339 9637 / 7783

  Classes available from 3 yrs in music & movement and from 5yrs in ballet
  Classes held 5 days/week at the address opposite

- **The Uddingston School of Theatre Dance**
  ☎ 01698 817424

  Classes from 3 yrs in tap, ballet, modern, hip hop & jazz
  Studios in Tannochside (Sat) & Uddingston (Mon & Wed)

- **Yvonne Clark School of Dance**
  The Dance Studio
  2 Carlisle Road
  Airdrie
  ML6 8AA
  ☎ 01236 766505

  Classes from 3 yrs in Airdrie & Glenmavis
  Tap, ballet, modern & jazz

Golf

Please find in the following section details of golfing facilities in the Glasgow area.

Opening Times:
7 days 9.00am–10.00pm (last balls 9.00pm) Closed 25th & 26th December, 1st & 2nd January
Mearns Castle Golf Academy, Scotland's newest and best dedicated facility for improving your game of golf. The Academy represents the result of three years work in planning and developing a combination of the most modern facilities with a dedicated programme of instruction to allow players of all levels to improve their game. We are now open and when we say open we mean it. One of our aims is to break down the barriers of golf but maintain the traditions and dedication to the sport. As such we offer full public access and are not limited to membership lists. Juniors, Seniors and Ladies can enjoy our facilities on an equal footing.

Our nine hole golf course opened in May 2003 and has been a huge success with our registered players. The challenge that this Par 33 course will offer players, belies the fact that the object is to offer a game which takes less time. Being more accessible doesn't mean lower standards. We maintain high codes of dress, behaviour and etiquette – and will offer to teach anybody who doesn't understand the importance of the rules of golf.

Our Billy Birdie Kids Club has now been extended to cater for the demand of our junior golfers. The club runs throughout the year and summer schools are in addition to the block sessions. Most of all though is our desire for you to improve your game and as a result improve your enjoyment!

- **Mearns Castle Golf Academy**
  Waterfoot Road
  Newton Mearns
  Glasgow
  G77 5RR
  ☎ 0141 644 4008
  www.am2pro.co.uk

Horse Riding Schools

Please find below listings of Horse Riding Schools in and around the Glasgow area.

Riding school from 5 yrs Open all year	**Bankend House Stables** Bankend House Craigmaddie Milngavie G62 ☎ 0141 956 3798
Riding school from 5 yrs Pony rides for under 5's Summer courses available Open all year	**Busby Equestrian Centre** Wester Farm Westerton Avenue Clarkston G76 8JU ☎ 0141 644 1347
Open all year Riding school from 5 yrs Pony walks from 5 yrs & pony camp during summer holidays available from 8 yrs	**Dumbreck Riding School** 82 Dumbreck Road Glasgow G41 4SN ☎ 0141 427 0660
Riding lessons from nursery age Pony days during school holidays, 10.00am–3.30pm Caters for special needs Residential camps available during holidays	**Fordbank Equestrian Centre** Beith Road Johnstone PA10 2NS ☎ 01505 705829
Riding school from 4 yrs	**Glasgow Easterton Riding School** Easterton Stables Mugdock Milngavie G62 8LG ☎ 0141 956 1518
Riding school from 5 yrs	**Hazelden Equestrian Centre** Hazelden Road Mearnskirk Newton Mearns G77 6RR ☎ 0141 639 3011

- **Hillhead Equestrian Centre**
  South Hillhead Farm
  Milton Road
  Braidwood
  Carluke
  ☎ 01555 772151

  Open all year
  Riding school from 5 yrs

- **Jumps Equestrian Centre**
  Eastside Farm
  Yieldshields Road
  Carluke
  ML8 4QY
  ☎ 01555 773206

  Open all year
  Walkabout from 4 yrs
  Lessons from 5 yrs
  Own-a-Pony days & summer camp

- **Kenmure Riding School**
  Kenmure Farm
  Kenmure Avenue
  Bishopbriggs
  G64 2QN
  ☎ 0141 772 3041

  Open all year
  Riding school from 6 yrs

- **Lethame House Equestrian Centre**
  Lethame Road
  Strathaven
  ML10 6RW
  ☎ 01357 521108

  Riding school from 4 yrs
  Pony Club available.
  Open all year

- **Linn Park Equestrian Centre**
  Linn Park
  Simshill Road
  Glasgow
  G44 1TA
  ☎ 0141 637 3096

  Riding school from 5 yrs
  Own-a-Pony days available; please contact Riding School directly for further details
  Open all year

- **Meadowhead Trekking Centre**
  Auldhouse
  East Kilbride
  G75 0QL
  ☎ 0795 7749846

  Open all year
  Riding school from 4 yrs
  Pony days available during summer holidays

- **Scottish Equi Complex**
  Lanark Moor Country Park
  ☎ 01555 661853

  Children's residential riding holidays available
  Riding school open all year from 8 yrs
  Own-a-Pony days available throughout the year

- **Strathkelvin Riding Centre**
  Wester Muckcroft Road
  Chryston
  G69 0JJ
  ☎ 0141 775 2675

  Riding school from 4 yrs
  Open all year

MARTIAL ARTS ACADEMY/SCHOOLS

Please find below listings of Martial Arts Schools and Teachers in and around the Glasgow area.

- **KRAUSEWORLD**
  International Martial Arts Academy
  1 Hill Street
  Glasgow
  ☎ 0141 333 1817

  Classes from 6 yrs to adult
  Childrens classes available Mon, Wed, Fri, Sat & Sun

- **Martial Arts Training**
  For beginners with Kupso
  ☎ 01383 820770
  www.kupso.com

  Classes from 5 yrs
  Classes available in Scotstoun, Charing Cross, Pollok, Rutherglen & Cumbernauld

- **Taekwon-Do**
  ☎ 0131 443 2730

  Korean Art of Self Defence classes from 5 yrs throughout Glasgow.
  Classes available in The Couper Institute, Cathcart (Tues), Netherlee Primary School (Fri), Eastwood High School (Wed), Thornliebank, Thorntreehall (Mon), St Ninian's Sports Hall, Eastwood Park (Tues & Fri), Shettleston Community Centre (Wed), Scotstoun Leisure Centre (Fri & Sun), Carolside Primary School (Mon)

- **Tae Kwon/Do**
  ☎ 01236 735 177
  www.tagb-scotland.co.uk

  Classes from 6 yrs
  Classes available in Cumbernauld, Hamilton, Blantyre & Larkhall

Music, Drama & Exercise

Please find below listings of Music and Drama classes in and around the Glasgow area.

Musical activity groups for all ages
Birthday parties available for children age 3–6 yrs

- **Annamaetion**
  ☎ 0141 585 3287
  ☎ 01465 861 233

Music fun for pre-school children aged 6 mnths to 5 yrs
Classes held at The Annexe, Healthy Living Centre, 9A Stewartville Street, Partick, Glasgow

- **Colourstrings Songbirds Music Kindergarten**
  ☎ 0141 427 7965

The Drama Workshop

The aim of **The Drama Workshop** is to provide a friendly and creative atmosphere in which children of all ages are encouraged to develop their personalities and confidence, as well as social skills. The classes cover a wide range of theatre skills and dramatic technique and include movement and mime, improvisation (which stimulates the child's own imagination) and enjoyable games and exercises to promote clarity of speech and vocal expression.

Drama is a performing art and so we provide an opportunity for every child in the Workshop to perform in front of an audience at our end-of-year show, which is written by us each year for the children. We endeavour to stretch each individual child, and everyone is given a chance to shine – bearing in mind that each pupil may have a different starting point and a different challenge to overcome. We hope this is a thoroughly enjoyable experience for all the students.

- **The Drama Workshop**
  ☎ 01505 614077
  ☎ 0141 647 6222

The Drama Workshop has served the communities of Glasgow for over 18 years. It is run by Debbie Garson and Janice McKenna, both graduates of the Royal Scottish Academy of Music and Drama and Jordanhill College of Education. For further information ☎ **01505 614077** or **0141 647 6222**

■ **Glasgow Academy of Musical Theatre Arts**
Possil Road
Glasgow
G4 9SY
☎ 0141 354 0483

Opening Times
Daily 10.00am–10.00pm
Clases from 5 yrs in drama, dance and singing
Infant classes are held on Sundays

■ **Gymboree Play & Music**
(Gym, Music and Art)
Opening soon in the West End of Glasgow
☎ 0800 0920911
www.gymboreeplayuk.com

Classes for newborn to under 5s featuring play, music and movement.
Also art classes from 18 months. Available Mon – Sun, all year round. Free trial classes. Birthday party bookings available.

Gymboree offers exciting **play** classes featuring movement, exploration, songs and age-appropriate activities. They are designed to build confidence, imagination, social skills, physical abilities and early language skills. But most of all they are designed for fun!

Gymboree **music** is unique in its exploration of over 18 different musical styles from around the world. Exposing children to sounds and rhythms, children sing, dance and play instuments to a medley of musical styles with a new style introduced every fortnight. Styles include jazz, classical, latin. Rock 'n' roll, rhythm and blues, country, folk, celtic, polka, African and more!

Gymboree **art** classes explore the fun and creative world of colour, texture, composition, imagination and tactile stimulation. Children and parents engage in a wide variety of artistic activities such as painting, sculpting, cutting, pasting, building, puppetry, fancy dress, drama and imaginary play.

Designed by experts in early childhood development, Gymboree's curriculum-based classes feature a child's parent or carer as an active participant and play partner.

Call us to book your free trial class and discover why thousands of families consider Gymboree Play & Music to be the UK's pre-eminent programme for children under 5.

Pre-school music & movement classes available for children age 9 mnths – 5 yrs Classes in Newton Mearns, East Kilbride, Strathaven, Hamilton & Bothwell

- **Jo Jingles**
  ☎ 01357 522 603

- **Little Maestros**
  New Kilpatrick Church Halls
  Bearsden
  G61 3RT
  ☎ 0141 558 6555

  Opening Times: Thurs 2.30pm–3.10pm
  Fun and music for 1–4 yrs

- **Live & Loud Stage School & Agency**
  188 St Vincent Street
  Glasgow G2 5SB
  ☎ 0141 222 2942

  Drama classes from 5 yrs
  The Stage School has weekly classes and The Agency promotes and represents in professional acting work

- **macrobert**
  Scotland's arts centre for families
  University of Stirling
  FK9 4LA
  Tickets and information
  ☎ 01786 466666
  www.macrobert.org

macrobert offers an exciting, quality programme to offer you and your family – everything from film, theatre, dance, music and comedy.

macrobert is located on the stunning campus of the University of Stirling and is easily accessible to all areas of Scotland. We are unique in Scotland – offering facilities, which have been designed by young people themselves and include a dedicated theatre for children – **play**house; a state of the art cinema – **film**house; children's art gallery – **art**house; creche – **tree**house; a workshop rehearsal space – **work**house as well as a stylish café-bar and medium scale theatre space – **main**house.

If you would like a brochure or would like to be included in our monthly mailings, either by email or post, please inform a staff member from **Tickets and Information – 01786 466666**. Check out our main website for regular updates or click to our children's website www.macrobert-wow.org

- **Music Box**
  ☎ 0141 649 0002

  Fun and educational music classes for children from 18 mnths–6 yrs

- **Music Now**
  ☎ Office 0141 955 1676

  Music classes in Helensburgh, Anniesland & Milngavie
  Milngavie: 1 yr to Primary 2
  Helensburgh: 1–5 yrs, Anniesland: 1–5 yrs

- **The Music School**
  ☎ 01505 613113

  Keyboard and recorder from 5 yrs
  Teacher of 52 instruments and voice lessons which can be provided in your own home for fun or for exams

- **Music Stars Production**
  Strathclyde Business Centre
  120 Carstairs Street
  Glasgow G40 4JD
  ☎ 0141 556 5888

  The ultimate gift or experience for anyone who enjoys singing

- **Pace Youth Theatre**
School Wynd
Paisley
PA1 2DB
☎ 0845 130 5218

Drama classes held on Sat & Sun for 3–18 yrs

- **Rhythm Time**
Music for babies, toddlers & pre-school children
☎ 0141 880 6539

Classes available from 0–18 mnths, 18mnths–3 yrs, 3–5 yrs
Classes held in St John's Chapel, Barrhead (Mon am & Fri pm) and in Glasgow New Synagogue (Thurs am)

- **Scottish Mask and Puppet Centre**
8–10 Balcarres Avenue
Kelvindale
G12 0QF
☎ 0141 339 6185
www.scottishmaskandpuppetcentre.co.uk

Different shows every Saturday
Birthday Parties available, please book early to avoid disappointment
Suitable from 3–8yrs

Sat 24th January **Jack and the Beanstalk & Billy Goats Gruff** * CLYDEBUILT 2.00pm
Reach for the stars and find out how Jack defeats the Giant who has stolen all his family treasures.

Sat 31st January **Jabberwocky** * FOLDING THEATRE COMPANY 2.00pm
And so begins the riotous story of Lewis Carroll's 'The Jabberwocky.'

Sat 7th February **The Kidgloves Puppet Show** * KIDGLOVES PUPPETS 2.00pm & 3.30pm
A varied mixture of fables and folk tales. 2.00pm in English, 3.30pm in French.

Sat 14th February **Rainbow Magic** * SYLVIA TROON KENSPECKLE PUPPETS 2.00pm
Can the children help the elves to paint a magic rainbow? An adventure full of sights, sounds and colour.

Sat 28th February **A Magpie's Nest of Memories** * COLLABORATORS THEATRE CO. 2.00pm
The story unfolds, one for sorrow, two for joy ... but what is the secret that has never been told?

Sat 6th March **Henny Penny Chicken Licken** * IAN TURBITT'S PUPPET THEATRE 2.00pm
A traditional tale told with songs, stories and audience participation.

Sat 13th March **Anansi the Magic Spider** * JACK 'O' LANTERN 2.00pm
Africa's folk hero takes on a quest to bring all the stories of the world to children everywhere.

Sat 20th March **A Witch's Tail!** * TALKING HEADS 2.00pm
Little Rosie wants to learn to be a good Witch. Is there a twist in this tale?

Sat 27th March **Anchors Away** * MR GIGGLES 2.00pm
Pirate Pete's in search of a fresh crew for an adventure aboard the high seas!

Sat 3rd April **The Hot Cross Bunny** * MR AMAZING BONES 2.00pm
PC Parrot flies in to save the day. Puppets, songs, games and prizes for the best Easter Bonnet.

Sat 10th April **Easter Magic Egg–stravaganza** * MAGIC BOB 2.00pm
Fast funny and full of close-up magic in a mix n' mingle style just for you. How does he do it?

Sat 24th April **Guard of the Night** * A TARUMBA (TEATRO DE MARIONETAS) 2.00pm & 3.30pm
The Keeper of the Night takes care of all children. We welcome A Tarumba from Portugal.

Sat 1st May **Oscar's Amazing Space Adventure** * MOUSETALE PUPPETS 2.00pm & 3.30pm
Oscar the Mouse, investigates when a mysterious object lands in the garden shed.

Sat 8th May **The Blue Dress Show** * FLOTSAM & JETSAM THEATRE 2.00pm
Pockets full of puppets. Adults £4.00 Children £6.50 - show & workshop inclusive of materials.

Sat 15th May **The Witch The Wizard and Little Red Riding Hood** * TALKING HEADS 2.00pm
Red Riding Hood is going to visit Granny Smith, but the witch has other plans for the little girl.

Sat 22nd May **Travels in a Wash Basket** * SYLVIA TROON'S KENSPECKLE PUPPETS 2.00pm
Baby Binkleburp travels afar to summon help. A colourful new show with songs and music.

CREATE AND TAKE FOR FAMILIES AND CHILDREN

Due to popular demand, parents took part in last season's workshops at the Puppet Centre together with their children. This season we are offering family workshops, where the adult (who may really be a child at heart) can join in and make a puppet or learn a magic trick or two (optional). There will also be a short break half way through the two-hour workshops for tea, coffee, juice and biscuits – included in the workshop price.

Sat 13 March **Junk Puppets with Malcolm Knight**
Back by popular request you can discover how to turn your junk into fun puppets. We have plenty of our own junk, but if you would also like bring along some of your own for re-cycling, please start collecting now.. 5 yrs – adult, 3.00pm–5.00pm, all places £6.00 incl. materials and refreshment.

Sat 3 April **Noisy Puppets with the Amazing Mr Bones**
Come and join in some Easter fun and make noisy puppets at Mr. Bones' family workshop. What else could it be, with the Amazing Mr. Bones running this workshop? Book now (to avoid disappointment) for snappy crocodiles, basking dogs and puppets that whistle and toot!
5 yrs – adult, 10.00am–12.00pm, all places £6.00 incl. materials and refreshment.

Sat 10 April **Magic Bob's School of Magic with Magic Bob**
Come and meet Magic Bob. He will teach you a series of magic tricks in a one-hour workshop that will keep you amused and confused for the rest of the Easter holidays. Keep practising and take away some notes on magic dealers, magic books, and web-sites to further your research.
7 yrs – adult, 12.00pm–1.00pm, all places £6.00

Sat 24 April **Jumping Jacks with A Tarumba**
A Jumping Jack is an articulated toy puppet. It takes a specific form in Portugal as well as being a mainstay in popular European folk culture. In this workshop you will learn how to design, cut, build and manipulate your own jumping jack. This workshop is being run by the company A Tarumba from Portugal as part of the Portuguese Festival 23–25th April organised and promoted by the Caledonian Portuguese Association.
6 yrs – adult, 10.00am–12.00pm, all places £6.00 incl. materials and refreshment

SHOWS AND WORKSHOPS SUPPORTED BY GLASGOW CITY COUNCIL

Language & Maths

Please find below listings of Language and Maths classes in and around the Glasgow area.

- **Alliance Français de Glasgow**
  7 Bowmont Gardens
  Glasgow
  G12 9LR
  ☎ 0141 339 4281
  www.afglasgow.org.uk

French Language and Cultural Centre
Established in 135 countries and through almost 1200 centres, the aim of the Alliance Française is to spread a knowledge of French language and culture. As such, our centre attracts a wide range of people with very different needs. The Alliance Française de Glasgow is officially recognised and sponsored by the French government.

French courses for children
We offer classes from Monday to Saturday, tailored to the age and needs of the youngest and the not so young. Children aged 3–6 can develop an awareness of French through stories, songs, handicraft, games and dance in our playgroup. Primary and secondary pupils can also enhance their knowledge of the language with fun activities for children aged 6–14, and exam support classes for Standard Grade and above.

We also run classes for French-speaking children from the age of 4.

- **French Connections**
  East Kilbride
  ☎ 01355 222925

Classes from 5yrs to adult

- **Kumon Educational (Maths & English)**
  Ground Floor Landmark House
  Station Road
  Cheadle Hulme
  Stockport, Chesire
  SK8 7GE
  ☎ 0161 488 4988

Kumon is the world's most successful after-school **maths** programme and has over **35,000 children** studying at the 500 study centres in the UK. The Kumon programme ranges from counting to calculus and **complements the school curriculum**.

The Kumon programme meets each student's individual needs and improves confidence, concentration, accuracy and speed.

The Kumon **English** programme is also available at the study centres.

- **Spanish Classes**
  Central Chamber
  93 Hope Street Level 2
  G26 6LD
  ☎ 0141 221 8806

Spanish classes for children age 3yrs to senior
Contact directlly for class venues

THE GLASGOW GUIDE

FOR PARENTS AND CARERS

2005 edition

NOTE TO ADVERTISERS

If you were not listed in ***The Glasgow Guide for Parents and Carers*** 2004 (2nd) edition, don't worry. Have your business or service listed in ***The Glasgow Guide for Parents and Carers*** 2005 (3rd) edition. Fill in your details below and return by the 30th September 2004 to:

Glasgow Under 6's Ltd
48 Flenders Avenue
Clarkston
Glasgow, G76 7XZ
Tel/Fax 0141 616 3661
E: glasgowunder6s@fsmail.net

Name of Business & Contact Name . . . .

Address . . . .

. . . .

Postcode . . . . Tel/Fax No. . . . .

Email . . . . www . . . .

PLEASE TICK BELOW

Free Listing ❑

Request advertising details ❑

NOTE TO READERS

We would like to hear your comments and suggestions for our 2005 edition. These should be sent to **Glasgow Under 6's Ltd** at the address above.

Birthday Parties

Please find included in the following section listings of:

- **Bowling & Entertainment Centres**
- **Bouncy Castles & Inflatables**
- **Cake Shops**
- **Children's Activity & Adventure Centres**
- **Children's Entertainers**
- **Stationery**

For more Birthday Party ideas & venues *see* Restaurants (coffee & family eating out) Days Out (places to visit), Community & Leisure (local authority)

BOWLING & ENTERTAINMENT CENTRES

Please find in the following section listings of bowling and entertainment centres in and around the Glasgow area.

- **AMF Bowling**
  10 Elliot Street
  Glasgow
  G3 8DZ
  ☎ 0141 248 4478

  Opening Times:
  Sun – Thurs 10.00am–12.00pm
  Fri & Sat 10.00am–1.00 am
  Diner, childrens parties
  Disabled facilities

- **Buttlecamp Paintball Scotland**
  ☎ 01292 610097

  Age 12 yrs +
  Birthday party bookings available

- **The Garage**
  36–40 Grange Street
  Kilmarnock
  ☎ 01563 573355

  Opening Times:
  7 days from 10.00am–midnight
  10 pin bowling, go-karts, children's soft play (toddlers to 13 yrs) and restaurant facilities
  Disabled facilities
  Can cater for children's parties

- **Hotshots**
  The Quay, off Paisley Road
  Glasgow
  G5 8NP
  ☎ 0141 418 0088

  Opening Times:
  From 4.00pm daily, Sat & Sun from 12.00pm
  Times vary during school holidays
  Ten-pin bowling, American pool, interactive video games & arcade games
  Diner and disabled facilities
  Can cater for children's parties

- **Megazone (laser games)**
  104 Grahams Road
  Falkirk
  ☎ 01324 634828

  Opening Times:
  Mon 4.00pm–10.00pm
  Tues – Fri 12.00pm–10.00 pm
  Sat & Sun 10.00am–10.00pm
  Laser games from 5 yrs

- **Pro Bowl**
  Milton Road
  Kirkintilloch
  Glasgow
  G66 1SY
  ☎ 0141 777 8588

  Opening Times:
  7 days 11.00am–11.00pm
  Restaurant facilities
  Disabled facilities
  Can cater for children's birthday parties

- **Pro-Lane Bowl**
  1 The Boardwalk
  Stroud Road, Kelvin Industrial Area
  East Kilbride
  Glasgow
  G75 0YW
  ☎ 01355 902902

Opening Times: From 10.00am daily
Restaurant facilities
Disabled facilities
Can cater for children's birthday parties
New soft play now open (Buckaroo Jaxx) from 10.00am daily

- **Scalliwags**
  215 Main Street
  Alexandria
  G83
  ☎ 01389 601234

Opening Times:
From 11.00am daily
Children's soft play centre

- **Scottish Paintball Centre**
  Rowallan Activity Centre
  Fenwick
  ☎ 0141 423 9199

Age 10 yrs +
Outdoor laser games and paintball
Birthday party facilities

- **Swings & Roundabouts**
  ☎ 0141 332 0740

Suppliers of fairground rides, bouncy castles, fun stalls, face painting, snack bars and children's entertainers

- **XS Superbowl**
  21–3 Wallneuk Road
  Paisley
  Renfrewshire
  PA3 4BT
  ☎ 0141 848 1442

Opening Times: 11am–late (daily)
Wimpy restaurant
Can cater for children's birthday parties
Disabled facilities

BOUNCY CASTLES & INFLATABLES

Please find in the following section listings of bouncy castles and inflatables for hire in and around the Glasgow area.

- **Bounce Along**
  44 Greenwood Road
  Clarkston
  Glasgow
  G76 7JN
  ☎ 0141 571 3180

  Outdoor bouncy castle hire

- **Bounce Around Bouncy Castle Hire**
  ☎ 01355 260237

  Hire of bouncy castles, giant garden games and softplay

- **Bounce Busters**
  ☎ 0141 634 4925

  Bouncy castles for hire
  All ages

- **Bounce Higher**
  ☎ 0141 950 6009
  www.bounce-higher.co.uk

  Hire of bouncy castles, face painting and children's entertainers

- **Bounce Till You Drop**
  ☎ 0141 613 3957

  Hire of bouncy castles for children up to 14 yrs

- **Bouncy Castles**
  ☎ 0141 637 4241

  Hire of bouncy castles for children up to 12 yrs

- **Bouncy Castles** (for lease/hire)
  ☎ 0141 620 1051

  Hire of bouncy castles, soft play equipment, popcorn & candyfloss machines
  All ages

- **CE Bouncy Castles**
  City Eats
  ☎ 01560 600444

  Bouncy castle hire and outside catering

- **Douglas the Magic Clown**
  Bouncy Castle Hire
  ☎ 01671 402451

  For Douglas the Magic Clown *see* BIRTHDAY PARTIES (CHILDREN'S ENTERTAINERS)

- **Fun & Games**
  Inflatables for all events
  ☎ 0800 0735250

  Bouncy castles & giant slides for hire

- **JK Entertainment**
  ☎ 01236 606491

  Bouncy castle hire
  For JK Entertainment *see* BIRTHDAY PARTIES (CHILDREN'S ENTERTAINERS)

- **Mini Bouncy Castles**
  17 Hillend Road
  Clarkston
  Glasgow
  ☎ 0141 577 6604

  Bouncy castles for hire
  For Michael Breck magic & puppet shows *see* BIRTHDAY PARTIES (CHILDREN'S ENTERTAINERS)

- **Neil Drover Agency**
  Bouncy Castle Hire
  ☎ 0141 357 3377

  For Neil Drover Agency *see* BIRTHDAY PARTIES (CHILDREN'S ENTERTAINERS)

- **T's Bouncy Castles**
  19 Burnbrae Road
  Blantyre
  Glasgow
  G72 0QU
  ☎ 01698 826040

  Bouncy castle hire for all ages

CAKE SHOPS

Please find in the following section listings of cake shops in and around the Glasgow area. All the cake shops listed supply christening cakes and children's birthday cakes.

- **The Cake Box**
  199 Knightswood Road
  Glasgow
  ☎ 0141 576 0040

  Opening Times:
  Mon – Fri 8.00am–4.45pm,
  Sat 8.00am–1.00pm, Sun – closed
  Can supply christening cakes, children's birthday cakes, photo and 3-dimensional children's cakes

- **Cakes & Flowers By Gillian**
  2337 Dumbarton Road
  Glasgow
  ☎ 0141 434 1130

  Opening Times:
  Mon, Tues, Thurs, Fri 9.30am–5.00pm,
  Sat 9.30am–2.00 pm
  Wed & Sun – closed

- **Classic Touch Celebration Cakes**
  202 Caldonian Road
  Wishaw
  MI2 OHT
  ☎ 01698 357700

  Opening Times:
  Mon – Sat 9.30am–5.00pm, Sun – closed
  Large range of children's birthday cakes and christening cakes

- **Creative Cakes**
  379 Clarkston Road
  Glasgow
  ☎ 0141 633 0392

  Opening Times:
  Mon – Sat 9.00am–5.00pm, Sun – closed
  Can supply 3-dimensional children's cakes and free-hand artwork on children's cakes

- **Speciality Cakes**
  236 Hamilton Road
  Cambuslang
  Glasgow
  G72 7PF
  ☎ 0141 646 2054

  Opening Times:
  Mon – Sat 9.00am–5.00pm, Sun – closed
  Can supply children's photo cakes, 3-dimensional cakes and free-hand artwork cakes

CHILDREN'S ACTIVITY & ADVENTURE CENTRES

Please find in the following section listings of Children's Activity & Adventure Centres in and around the Glasgow Area.

- **The Apollo**
  Winton Circus
  Esplanade
  Saltcoats
  KA21 5DA
  ☎ 01294 471777

Opening Times:
From 10.00am daily
Soft play area, 2 cinemas, family restaurant, amusement arcade and birthday party facilities available

- **Bearsden Ski + Board Club**
  The Mound
  Stockiemuir Road
  Bearsden
  Glasgow
  G61 3RS
  ☎ 0141 943 1500

For skiing, snowboarding and curling
Open all year except Xmas Day & New Year's Day
Birthday boarding, ski or sledging parties available

- **The Big Adventure** (soft play)
  2 Napier Street
  Linwood
  PA3 3AJ
  ☎ 01505 336655

Opening Times:
7 days 10.00am–8.00pm
Height restriction 5ft 2 or 12yrs
Birthday parties & group bookings available
Café, (non-smoking)
Disabled and baby changing facilities

- **Brewster's** (Fun Factory & Soft Play)

For **Brewster's (Fun Factory & Soft Play)** *see* Restaurants (Coffee & Family Eating Out)

- **Buckaroo Jaxx** (soft play)
  ☎ 01355 902902

For **Buckaroo Jaxx** *see* Birthday Parties (Bowling & Entertainment Centres)

- **The Ceramic Experience**
  24 Albion Way
  East Kilbride
  Glasgow
  ☎ 01355 263194

Opening Times:
10.00am–5.00pm daily
Birthday party bookings available minimum 6 children

■ **Caperhouse Playbarn** (soft play)
5 MacNeish Way
East Kilbride
Glasgow
G74 4TT
☎ 01355 579836

Open 7 days a week 10.00am–6.00pm
Mon – Fri: £2.60 for 1 hour,
£3.10 for 1 hour & 30 mins, £3. 60 for 2 hours.
Public Holidays & weekends: £3.50 for 1 hour & 30 mins.
Height restriction of 4 feet 6 inches.

Hassle-free parties for height restriction & under!

Kids have 1 hour and 15 mins on the structure:
Bouncy Castle, Slides, Rope Swings, Soft Toys, Ball Pool, Ghost House and Tunnels.
And for the Toddler & Baby: Ball Pool and a Soft Play Area with Soft Toys.
Afterwards children will be taken to a private room with a play leader.
They will play two party games and then will be provided with a meal of their choice:
Hamburger/Cheeseburger/Hotdogs/Fish fingers/Chicken nuggets/Vegiburger.
All served with chips and a drink. (Drinks are provided while downstairs at the structure).
You bring two prizes (1 prize wrapped 3 times for Pass the Parcel), birthday cake and extra sweets and/or toys for the lucky bags. We provide invitations and lucky bags (toy, sweets and game)
Weekdays: Minimum 10 kids if possible. Cost £7.50 per child
Weekends: Minimum 15 kids if possible.
Payment: only accept cash or cheque (with guarantee card).
Special Needs Night is 1st Monday of every month from 6.00–8.00pm. £3.00 for 2 hours play.
School groups and nurseries etc £3.00 each including jugs of juice for children.
All trips to be paid on day of visit unless otherwise arranged. Deposit of £20.00 secures booking.

■ **Cheeky Monkeys Play Centre**
93–97 High Street
Falkirk
FK1 1ED
☎ 01324 636660

Opening Times:
Mon – Sat 9.30am–6.00pm
Sun 10.00am – 6.00pm, last session 4.30pm Height restriction 4ft 6ins
Cafe, birthday party facilities, Halloween & Christmas parties

■ **Craftzone 1**
Pottery Painting Studio
62c Rannoch Drive
Bearsden
G61 2HH
☎ 0141 943 1186

Birthday parties, max 12 children

■ **Funasaurus**
Buchanan Galleries
220 Buchanan Street
Glasgow
G1 2FF
☎ 0141 332 4353

Opening Times:
Mon, Tues, Wed, Fri 10.00am–5.00pm, Thurs 10.00am–6.00pm, Sat 9.00am–6.00pm, Sun 11.00am–5.00pm
Shopper's crèche, a pager will be provided while you are shopping Max 2hr stay, approx £3.50 per hour, age 2–8 yrs

■ **Geronimos Playcentre**
273 Duke Street
Dennistoun
Glasgow
G31 1HX
☎ 0141 556 4314

Opening Times: 10.00am–8.00pm daily
Height restriction 4ft 10 ins
Cafe, toddler area, birthday party facilities
Disabled toilets

■ **Girl Heaven**

See SHOPPING (BABY & CHILDREN'S CLOTHES SHOPS)

■ **Glasgow Climbing Centre**
534 Paisley Road West
Glasgow
G53
☎ 0141 427 9550

Opening Times:
Mon – Fri 12.00pm–10.00pm
Sat & Sun 10.00am–8.00pm
Located on the south side of Glasgow, just off the M8 at Ibrox. Birthday party facilities from 6 yrs Cafe facilities available for birthday parties at an extra charge

- **Glasgow Ski and Snowboard Centre**
  Bellahousten Park
  16 Dumbreck Road
  Glasgow
  G41 5BW
  ☎ 0141 427 4991

  Birthday party bookings available
  Open all year

- **Goals Glasgow South**
  941 Pollokshaws Road
  Glasgow
  G41 2EW
  ☎ 0141 636 5334

  Opening Times: 9.00am–11.00pm daily
  Kids birthday party facilities available

- **Goals Glasgow West**
  2650 Great Western Road
  Glasgow
  G81 2XT
  ☎ 0141 944 2020

  Opening Times: 9.00am–11.00pm daily
  Kids birthday party facilities available

- **Gogglebox (soft play)**
  17 Maitland Street
  Helensburgh
  G84 7PD
  ☎ 01436 670909

  Opening Times: 10.00am–6.00pm 7 days
  0–12 yrs
  Birthday party facilities
  Cafe and disabled facilities

- **Hilton Coylumbridge**
  The Funhouse
  ☎ 01479 813081

  Great for children's parties
  For **Hilton Coylumbridge** *see* FAMILY BREAKS
  See advert on page 260–261

- **Jungle Mania**
  181 Shawbridge Street
  Pollokshaws
  Glasgow
  ☎ 0781 4572613

  Opening Times:
  Tues – Sun 10.00am–6.00pm
  Children's soft play centre
  Birthday party facilities

- **K7X**
  Five- & Seven-a-side Football
  Rouken Glen Park
  Rouken Glen Road
  Giffnock G46 6UG
  ☎ 0141 621 4459

  Opening Times:
  9.00am–11.00pm 7 days
  Kids coaching available on Sat & Sun mornings
  Birthday parties from 5 yrs

- **Kid-A-Mania** (soft play)
  At Parklands Country Club
  Crookfur Park
  Ayr Road
  Newton Mearns
  G77 6DT
  ☎ 0141 639 9222

Opening Times:
Mon – Sun 9.30am–5.30pm
The crèche within the soft play area is for member use only, although the general public can hire the use of it for Birthday Parties. Food, decorated balloons and party bags can also be provided. Hall hire within the Country Club is also available for Birthday Parties.

- **Kidzplay**
  The Esplanade
  Prestwick
  ☎ 01292 475215

Opening Times:
Sun–Thurs 9.30am–7.00pm
Fri & Sat 9.30am–7.30pm
Children's indoor adventure play centre
Birthday party bookings available

- **Knockhill Karting Centre**
  Knockhill Racing Circuit
  Dumfermline
  KY12 9TF
  ☎ 01383 626264

Opening Times:
Open all year, 7 days from 10.00am–6.00pm
Birthday parties from 8 yrs
Book in advance

- **KOKOS** (children's activity centre)
  87 Paisley Road
  Renfrew
  PA4 8LH
  ☎ 0141 885 1274

Opening Times:
7 days from 11.00am, closing time varies depending on party bookings
Please phone to avoid disappointment
Birthday Party bookings – 7 days a week
Height Restriction: 4ft 7inches or 55 inches
Maximum age 10 yrs. Café facilities available

- **KOKOS** (children's activity centre)
  1 Muiryhall Street
  Coatbridge
  Lanarkshire
  ML5 3HB
  ☎ 01236 436516

Opening Times:
7 days from 11.00am, closing time varies depending on Party Bookings
Please phone to avoid disappointment
Birthday Party bookings – 7 days a week
Height Restriction: 4ft 7inches or 55 inches
Maximum age 10 years
Café facilities available

KOKOS also have branches in:
Dundee, Aberdeen, Kirkcaldy, North Shields, Ashington & Newcastle

KOKO's

- **Lagoon Leisure Centre**
  Mill Street
  Paisley
  Renfrewshire
  PA1 1LZ
  ☎ 0141 889 4000

Opening Times:
Swimming Mon – Fri 10.00am–8.45pm,
Sat & Sun 9.30am–5.00pm
Ice Rink (contact centre directly)
This leisure centre has swimming pools, an ice rink, a soft play area and a cafeteria. Birthday party bookings available in skating, swimming, (or swimming & skating combined) & soft play.

- **Langside College**
  50 Prospecthill Road
  Glasgow
  G42 9LB
  ☎ 0141 272 3770

Langside College Glasgow offers opportunities for children through our summer activities programme and children's parties. The summer club runs throughout the summer holidays and is for 8–16 yrs. Children can attend 8.30am–5pm Mon–Fri or for half a day (am or pm).

Activities vary but are mainly of a sports nature and day trips are organised every Fri to a leisure centre.

Our parties are available on Sat pm and run throughout the year for 5 yrs +. Use of the pool is included and qualified staff are on hand to organise the fun and games.
Contact Clare Cairns for booking and further information.

- **Mega Mania Play Space**
  22–26 Campbell Street
  Kilmarnock
  ☎ 01563 570424

Opening Times:
7 days, 9.30am–7.00pm Approx age to 8 yrs
Birthday party bookings available
Cafeteria facilities available

- **Noiseland** (within Agenda)
  15 Millbrae Road
  Glasgow
  G42 9UA
  ☎ 0141 649 6861

Birthday Party bookings available 7 days
Generally for children from 2yrs to approx 10yrs but there is a height restriction
Food will be supplied
For Agenda *see* RESTAURANTS (COFFEE & FAMILY EATING OUT)

- **Pirate Petes**
  Indoor Adventure Play Centre
  The Pavilion
  Ayr
  ☎ 01292 265300

Opening Times:
Sun – Thurs 9.30am–6.30pm,
Fri & Sat 9.30am–7.00pm
Admission price per 2hr session
Weekdays £2.75, weekends £3.50, school holidays £3.50, last hour £1.50, adults & babes-in-arms free.
Birthday party bookings available

■ **The Play Drome**
2 Abbotsford Road
Clydebank
Glasgow
G81 1PA
☎ 0141 951 4321

Opening Times:
Mon & Thurs 7.00am–9.00pm,
Tues, Wed, Fri 9.00am–9.00pm,
Sat 9.00am–6.30pm, Sun 9.00am–7.00pm
Chutes open weekdays from 3.30pm, Sat & Sun from 10.30am
The Play Drome has 3 swimming pools, wave machine, teaching pool & sports hall.
Birthday party bookings available in soft play, football, swimming & roller skating (summer only)

■ **Scottish Football Museum**
☎ 0141 616 6139

For Scottish Football Museum *see* DAYS OUT (Places to Visit)

■ **The Tall Ship**
☎ 0141 222 2513

Birthday party bookings available
You can get the use of a section of the middle deck, minimum 10 children and you must provide your own entertainment & food.
For The Tall Ship *see* DAYS OUT (PLACES TO VISIT)

■ **Whale of a Time** (soft play)
1273 Pollokshaws Road
Shawlands
Glasgow
G41
☎ 0141 649 5455

Opening Times:
7 days, from 10.00am
Birthday party bookings available
Café

CHILDREN'S ENTERTAINERS

Please find in the following section listings of children's entertainers in and around the Glasgow area.

Children's entertainer Magic parties from 3 yrs	**Abracadabra** Douglas Cameron ☎ 0141 778 8391
Children's entertainer Magic shows, game shows & music shows Face painting available on request	**Absolutely Fab** ☎ 0141 882 0080
Children's entertainer Magic parties from nursery age	**Alex the Magician** ☎ 0141 644 4418
Children's magician	**Amazing Mark Lawrence** 54a Evan Drive Giffnock Glasgow G46 6NL ☎ 0141 638 6843
Children's entertainer For Balloons N Parties *see* SHOPPING (Balloons & Fancy Dress)	**Animal Man & Pickles the Clown** ☎ 0141 649 7181
Children's entertainer, magic, music & games	**Auntie Margaret** 131 Muirdrum Avenue Cardonald Glasgow G52 3AW ☎ 0141 882 6983
Children's entertainment	**Best in the West** Stars of Magic & TV ☎ 0141 889 7672
Children's entertainers For The Big Top *see* SHOPPING (TOY SHOPS)	**The Big Top** Tel 0141 332 3300

Bubbles the Clown ☎ 01236 768 395	Children's entertainer
Cheeko the Clown 15 South Street Greenock PA16 8UA ☎ 01475 791414	Children's entertainer, bubble workshops, competitions & games
Cheezee Choonz ☎ 0141 616 0466	Children's entertainer, disco's & children's interactive games
Douglas the Magic Clown ☎ 01671 402451	Children's entertainer, magic shows, disco's & bouncy castle hire Distance no object For bouncy castle hire *see* BIRTHDAY PARTIES (bouncy castles & inflatables)
Dunno the Clown ☎ 01294 218808	Children's entertainer & magic shows
Fantastic Faces ☎ 01355 574951	Children's face painting & hair braids
Freckles the Party Clown 8 Charles Avenue Renfrew PA4 8RS ☎ 0141 562 6143	Children's entertainer clown parties, face painting, fairy parties & star make-over parties
Giggles Parties for Kids 21 Nethercliffe Avenue Netherlee Glasgow G44 ☎ 0141 585 7919	Children's entertainer, a musical & magical adventure
Jenny Jester ☎ 01355 303684	Children's entertainer, magic, puppets, balloon modelling, games and much more

■ **JK Entertainment**
153 Earlston Cresent
Coatbridge
ML5 4UJ
☎ 01236 606491
07801 354512

Magic shows, balloon modelling, discos, kids games, karaoke & giant games
Bouncy castles also available for hire

■ **The Magical Singing Chef**
☎ 0141 889 2468

Character birthday parties
Pizza-making parties

■ **Magic Den**
☎ 01236 765743

Children's entertainer, magic & games

■ **Michael Breck** (magic & puppet shows)
17 Hillend Road
Clarkston
Glasgow
☎ 0141 577 6604

For Michael Brecks Mini Bouncy Castles *see* BIRTHDAY PARTIES (BOUNCY CASTLES & INFLATABLES)

■ **MiniStars**
☎ 0141 571 8655 / 07963 017233

MINISTARS...2 hours of pure girlie delight
That's the ultimate party service offered by MINISTARS, the new and exciting way of entertaining girls aged 3–12 yrs.

Ministars supplies all the glitter, glamour and glitz for the magical makeovers and each mini party guest not only has a photograph taken dressed in a fairytale or popstars costume, they decorate photo frames to take home, both as a keepsake of their fantastic fun day.

Ministars provides all costumes and materials and comes to your chosen venue. Choose from painting, crafts, karaoke, or go for the full girlie glitz.

- **Moira Colvan**
  ☎ 0141 810 3543

  Magic Moira specialises in magic for children

- **Mr Bongo the Clown**
  ☎ 0141 347 1009

  Children's entertainer
  Juggling, balloon modelling, events & workshops

- **Nat Sanderson Entertainments**
  ☎ 0141 621 0194

  Children's entertainer, puppets, disco's & clowns

- **Neil Drover Agency**
  ☎ 0141 357 3377

  Children's entertainer, clowns, face painting, magicians & bouncy castle hire
  For Neil Drover bouncy castle hire *see* BIRTHDAY PARTIES (BOUNCY CASTLES & INFLATABLES)

- **Raymo T Clown**
  ☎ 0141 889 6034

  Children's entertainer
  Magic shows

- **Scott C Magic**
  20 Holehouse Brae
  Neilston
  Glasgow
  G78 3LY
  ☎ 0141 580 1997

  Children's entertainer
  Discos, magic shows & balloon modelling

- **Silly Billy**
  12 Greenlaw Avenue
  Paisley
  Renfrewshire
  PA1 3RA
  ☎ 0141 561 0000

  Children's entertainer
  A complete party with Silly Billy – games, singalong and magic

■ **Steve Lindsay**
20 Southern Avenue
Burnside
Glasgow
G73 4JN
☎ 0141 634 4720
07968 850691

Treat your children to a magical feast of fun with one of Scotland's leading entertainers, balloons, comedy and the madcap antics of Steve Lindsay.
Your children will be amazed as coins come out of their ears, hair, mouth and nose. They are lost in laughter as they learn about eating a healthy breakfast, and are in hysterics because Steve's breakfast banana just keeps reappearing. This along with many other items create the fastest moving and most action-packed show on the market today – this show really is the one to see.
Call today and make your birthday or event unforgettable!

■ **Talking Heads Puppets**
4 Duntarvie Place
Easterhouse
Glasgow
G34 9JB
☎ 0141 781 0721

Children's puppet shows

■ **Uncle Billy**
☎ 01292 261653

Children's entertainer, magic shows, Punch & Judy and Little Red Riding Hood shows

STATIONERY

Please find in the following section listings of stationery suppliers in and around the Glasgow area.

- **Precious Moments Stationery**
  ☎ 0141 639 0429
  www.preciousmomentsstationery.com

Family-based business specialising in printed card designs for all occasions. We create beautiful cards, which can include photo. We pride ourselves on personal attention to detail and our flexible approach to customer's requests. Christening and 1st birthdays a speciality.

Invitations for every occasion

Christenings a speciality and occasions such as First Communion.

1st birthdays and all other childhood/ teenage birthdays

Adult birthdays and special occasions

Thank You cards

New Baby Thank You – printed card with a personal message and photograph of the new baby. Christening Thank You – card to match your invitation design and sent to well wishers or used as favours on the day. Thank You cards for any occasion birthday, anniversary etc.

Birth Announcement cards

We can help you announce the birth of your new child with delightful cards that can include photographs. We also specialise in twins and multiple births.

Custom-designed greeting cards

Unique greeting cards completely custom designed according to your wishes with photograph, name and date on the cover if wished. Personal message printed inside. Beautiful for special occasions.

For more details or to order please visit our website and email us www.preciousmomentsstationery.com or phone 0141 639 0429

COMMUNITY & LEISURE (LOCAL AUTHORITY)

Please find included in the following section listings of Community and Leisure Facilities for all ages in:

- **East Dunbartonshire Council**
- **East Renfrewshire Council**
- **Glasgow City Council**
- **North Lanarkshire Council**
- **South Lanarkshire Leisure**

The amount, content and style of information will vary from council to council, but most of them include entries in Sports and Leisure Facilities, Children's Activities, Birthday Party Facilities, Libraries, Museums, Community Art and Parks and Country Parks.

East Dunbartonshire Council

Please find in the following section listings of Sports and Recreation Centres, Libraries and Museums, Art Galleries/Centres, Community Centres, Halls for Hire and Places to Visit in East Dunbartonshire.

Sports & Recreation Centres

- **Allander Sports Complex**
  ☎ 0141 942 2233
  ☎ 0141 943 1365 Booking Line

  Opening Times:
  Mon – Fri 9.00am–11.00pm,
  Sat, Sun 9.00am–10.00pm
  Facilities: Swimming Pool, Sports Hall, Indoor Pitches, Fitness Gym, Squash Courts & Bistro

- **Campsie Recreation Centre**
  Bencloich Road
  Lennoxtown
  ☎ 01360 313215
  ☎ 01360 313215 Booking Line

  Opening Times:
  Mon – Fri 3.00pm–10.00pm,
  Sat, Sun 9.30am–5.00pm
  Facilities: Indoor Games Hall, Table Tennis, Badminton, Conditioning Gym, Free Weights Area, Sauna, Indoor Bowls, Outdoor Pitches, Outdoor Tennis Court & Cafeteria.

- **Huntershill Outdoor Centre**
  ☎ 0141 772 5907

- **Merkland Outdoor Recreation Centre**
  ☎ 0141 776 6871

- **The Leisuredrome**
  147 Balmuildy Road
  Bishopbriggs
  G64 3HD
  ☎ 0141 772 6391
  ☎ 0141 772 8080 Booking Line

  Opening Times:
  Mon – Fri 9.00am–11.00pm,
  Sat, Sun 9.00am–10.00pm
  Facilities: Swimming Pool, Sports Hall, Outdoor Pitches, Charlie's Big Adventure, Fitness World, Squash Courts & Bistro

Libraries / Museums

Opening Times: Tues – Sat 10.00am–1.00pm, 2.00pm–5.00pm	**Auld Kirk Museum** The Cross, Kirkintilloch ☎ 0141 578 0144
Opening Times: Mon – Thurs 10.00am–8.00pm	**Bishopbriggs Library** ☎ 0141 772 4513
Opening Times: Mon – Thurs 10.00am–8.00pm, Fri & Sat 10.00am–5.00pm	**Brookwood Library** ☎ 0141 942 6811
Opening Times: Mon & Thurs 1.00pm–8.00pm, Tues, Wed & Fri 10.00am–5.00pm	**Craighead Library** ☎ 01360 311925
Opening Times: Mon & Thurs 1.00pm–8.00pm, Tues, Wed & Fri 10.00am–5.00pm	**Lennoxtown Library** ☎ 01360 311436
Opening Times: Mon & Thurs 1.00pm–8.00pm, Tues, Wed & Fri 10.00am–5.00pm	**Lenzie Library** ☎ 0141 776 3021
Opening Times: Mon – Thurs 10.00am–8.00pm, Fri & Sat 10.00am–5.00pm	**Milngavie Library** ☎ 0141 956 2776
Opening Times: Mon & Thurs 1.00pm–8.00pm, Tues, Wed & Fri 10.00am–5.00pm	**Westerton Library** ☎ 0141 943 0780
Opening Times: Mon – Thurs 10.00am–8.00pm, Fri & Sat 10.00am–5.00pm	**William Patrick Library** ☎ 0141 776 7484 (lending) ☎ 0141 776 8090 (reference)

Art Galleries / Centres

- **Kilmardinny Arts Centre**
  50 Kilmardinny Avenue
  Bearsden
  ☎ 0141 931 5083

  Please contact directly for information on events

- **Lillie Art Gallery**
  71 Station Road
  Milngavie
  ☎ 0141 578 8846

  Opening Times:
  Tues – Sat 10.00am–1.00pm, 2.00pm–5.00pm

Community Centres

Auchinairn Community Centre	☎ 0141 563 5015
Craighead Community Centre	☎ 01360 311884
Hillhead Community Centre	☎ 0141 578 6011
Kirkintilloch Learning Centre	☎ 0141 777 2077
Kirkintilloch Resource Centre	☎ 0141 776 7330
Milngavie Community Centre	☎ 0141 570 1522
Torrance Community Centre	☎ 01360 620748
Woodhead Community Centre	☎ 0141 578 0060

Halls for Hire

Auchinairn Hall	☎ 0141 772 6888
Bearsden Hall	☎ 0141 942 0860
Booking Office	☎ 0141 574 5730

- **Brackenbrae House** ☎ 0141 772 4947
- **Caldwell Hall** ☎ 01360 620776
- **Campsie Memorial Hall** ☎ 01360 310123
- **Kessington Hall** ☎ 0141 942 7266
- **Kirkintilloch Town Hall** ☎ 0141 776 2266
- **Lenzie Public Hall** ☎ 0141 775 2902
- **Milngavie Town Hall** ☎ 0141 956 3132
- **Milton of Campsie Hall** ☎ 01360 310046
- **War Memorial Hall** ☎ 0141 772 6884
- **Westerton Hall** ☎ 0141 942 2679

Places to Visit

- **Mugdock Country Park**
  ☎ 0141 956 6100
  www.mugdock-country-park.org.uk

Mugdock Country Park – 260 hectares of unspoilt countryside with contrasting landscapes and wealth of wildlife – rich in history, with Mugdock and Craigend Castles, reminders of a bygone age.

Whether you want to make a willow basket or listen to the dawn chorus, there is a countryside event to suit everyone.

Within Mugdock Country Park there is a small theatre, a cinema with a small program is also available throughout the year.

Visit the garden centre & activity rooms. Tea room

East Renfrewshire Council

Please find in the following section listings of Swimming Pools and Recreation Centres, Theatres, Libraries, Community Facilities (available for hire) in East Renfrewshire

Community Facilities available for Hire

There are 21 halls/community facilities with a range of accommodation available for hire. Many organisations already use our halls to provide a variety of activities including out of school care clubs, toddlers groups, dance classes and sports activities. Several of the halls are used on a regular basis for childrens and family parties and celebrations.

For further information on the range of activities and accommodation available in the facilities listed, our staff will be able to assist. Please contact Community Facilities Letting Section on 0141 577 3900.

- **Albertslund Hall**
  Westacres Road
  Newton Mearns
  ☎ 0141 639 8817

- **Arthurlie House**
  Springhill Road
  Barrhead
  ☎ 0141 881 1265

- **Auchenback Community Centre**
  Blackburn Square
  Barrhead
  ☎ 0141 876 1032

- **Carmichael Hall**
  Eastwood Park
  Giffnock
  ☎ 0141 621 1760

- **Clarkston Hall**
  Clarkston Road
  Clarkston
  ☎ 0141 638 4050

- **Crookfur Pavilion**
  Ayr Road
  Newton Mearns
  ☎ 0141 639 2235

- **Dalmeny Community Centre**
  Barnes Street
  Barrhead
  ☎ 0141 876 1034

- **Duff Memorial Hall**
  Main Street
  Busby
  ☎ 0141 644 2034

- **Dunterlie Centre**
  Stewart Street
  Barrhead
  ☎ 0141 881 1717

- **Eastwood House**
  Eastwood Park
  Giffnock
  ☎ 0141 638 0231

- **Fairweather Hall**
  Barrhead Road
  Newton Mearns
  ☎ 0141 639 2081

- **Glen Hall**
  Main Street
  Neilston
  ☎ 0141 881 2020

- **McGuire Centre**
  124 Main Street
  Barrhead
  ☎ 0141 876 4258

- **Montgomerie Hall**
  Gilmour Street
  Eaglesham
  ☎ 01355 302648

- **Muirend Pavilion**
  Hazeldean Gardens
  Muirend
  ☎ 0141 637 9562

- **Mure Hall**
  Tannoch Road
  Uplawmoor
  ☎ 01505 850581

- **Netherlee Pavilion**
  Linn Park Avenue
  Netherlee
  ☎ 0141 637 1301

- **Overlee Pavilion**
  Moray Drive
  Clarkston
  ☎ 0141 644 4157

- **Rhuallan House**
  Montgomerie Drive
  Giffnock
  ☎ 0141 638 5018

- **Thorntree Hall**
  Main Street
  Thornliebank
  ☎ 0141 638 4844

- **Woodfarm Pavilion**
  Berryhill Drive
  Giffnock
  ☎ 0141 638 3609

LIBRARIES

- **Barrhead Community Library**
Glen Street
Barrhead
☎ 0141 577 3518
E-mail:
barrhead.library@eastrenfrewshire.gov.uk

Opening Times:
Mon & Wed 10.00am–8.00pm
Tues & Thurs 10.00 am–6.00pm
Fri 10.00am–6.00pm
Sat 10.00am–5.00pm
Facilities – Learndirect Scotland Learning Centre/ Children's library/ Electronic Catalogue/ Talking Books/ CDs/ Video Collection/ DVDs/ CD ROM Multimedia/ Photocopier/ Free Internet Access/ Word processing facilities/ Email/ Scanning/ Local History/ In-Touch Electronic Community Information/ IT Classes/ ECDL

- **Busby Community Library**
Duff Memorial Hall
Main Street
Busby
☎ 0141 577 4971
E-mail:
busby.library@eastrenfrewshire.gov.uk

Opening Times:
Mon 1.30pm–5.00pm, 6.00pm–8.00pm
Tues & Fri 10.00am–1.00pm, 2.00pm–6.00pm
Wed 2.00pm–5.00pm, 6.00pm–8.00pm
Thurs – closed
Sat 10.00am–1.00pm, 2.00pm–5.00pm
Facilities – Learndirect Scotland Learning Centre/ Children's Corner/ Electronic Catalogue/ Talking Books/ CDs/ Video Collection/ Local History/ In-Touch electronic Community Information/ Storytimes for under 5s/ Free Internet Access/ Word processing facilities/ Email/ IT Classes/ ECDL

- **Clarkston Community Library**
Clarkston Road
Clarkston
☎ 0141 577 4972
🖹 0141 577 4973
E-mail –
clarkston.library@eastrenfrewshire.gov.uk

Mon & Wed 10.00am–8.00pm
Tues, Thurs 10.00am–6.00pm
Fri 10.00am–6.00pm
Sat 10.00am–5.00pm
Facilities – Learning Centre/ Children's Library/ Electronic Catalogue/ Talking Books/ CDs/ Video Collection/ DVDs/ Photocopier/ Local History/ Community Access Point/ Storytime for under 5s/ Free Internet Access/ Word Processing/ Email/ Scanning/ Self Service issue and return point/ IT Classes

Eaglesham Community Library
Montgomerie Hall
Eaglesham
☎ 01355 302649
🖹 01355 302649
Email – eaglesham.library@
eastrenfrewshire.gov.uk

Opening Times
Mon 1.30pm–5.00pm, 6.00pm–8.00pm
Tues & Fri 10.00am–1.00pm,
2.00pm–6.00pm
Wed 2.00pm–5.00pm, 6.00pm–8.00pm
Thurs closed
Sat 10.00am–1.00pm, 2.00–5.00pm
Facilities – Electronic Catalogue/ Children's Corner/ Fax/ Talking Books/ CDs/ Video Collection/ Local History/ In-Touch Electronic Community Information/ Photocopier/ Internet Access/ CDROMs/ Word Processing/ Email

Giffnock Community Library
Station Road
Giffnock
☎ 0141 577 4976
🖹 0141 577 4978
E-mail –
giffnock.library@eastrenfrewshire.gov.uk

Opening Times
Mon & Wed 10.00am–8.00pm
Tues, Thurs & Fri 10.00am–6.00pm
Sat 10.00am–5.00pm
Facilities – Electronic Catalogue/ Children's Library/ Talking Books/ CDs/ Video Collection/ CD ROM Multimedia/ Photocopier/ Study Room/ Internet Access/ Word processing facilities/ Email/ Ethnic Minority Language Collection/ Local History Collection/ In-Touch Electronic Community Information/ IT Classes

Mearns Community Library
MacKinlay Place
Newton Mearns
☎ 0141 577 4979
🖹 0141 577 4980
E-mail –
mearns.library@eastrenfrewshire.gov.uk

Opening Times
Mon & Fri 10.00am–8.00pm
Tues, Wed, Thurs 10.00am–6.00pm
Saturday 10.00am–5.00pm
Facilities – Learndirect Scotland Learning Centre/ Children's library/ Electronic Catalogue/ Talking Books/ CDs/ Video Collection/ DVDs/ Storytime for under 5s/ CD ROM Multimedia/ Photocopier/ Study Room/ Internet Access/ Word processing/ Email/ Local History/ In-Touch Electronic Community Information/ IT Classes/ ECDL

Library	Opening hours and facilities
Neilston Community Library Main Street Neilston ☎ 0141 577 4981 🖹 0141 477 4982 E-mail – neilston.library@eastrenfrewshire.gov.uk	Mon 1.30pm–5.00pm, 6.00pm–8.00pm Tues & Fri 10.00am–1.00pm, 2.00pm–6.00pm Wed 2.00pm–5.00pm, 6.00pm–8.00pm Thurs closed Sat10.00am–1.00pm, 2.00pm–5 .00pm Facilities – Learning Centre/ Children's library/ Electronic Catalogue/ Talking Books/ CDs/ Video Collection/ CD ROM Multimedia/ Photocopier/ Internet Access/ Word processing facilities/ Email/ Local History/ Exhibition Room/ In-Touch Electronic Community Information/ IT Classes
Netherlee Library Centre Netherlee Pavilion Linn Park Avenue Netherlee ☎ 0141 637 1301	Mon, Tues & Thurs 10.00am–1.00pm, 2.00pm–5.00pm Facilities – Talking Books/ CDs
Thornliebank Community Library 1 Spiersbridge Road Thornliebank ☎ 0141 577 4983 🖹 0141 577 4816 E-mail – thornliebank.library@ eastrenfrewshire.gov.uk	Mon 1.30pm–5.00pm, 6.00pm–8.00pm Tues & Fri 10.00am–1.00pm, 2.00pm–6.00pm Wed 2.00pm–5.00pm, 6.00pm–8.00pm Thurs closed Sat 10.00am–1.00pm, 2.00pm–5.00pm Facilities – Learning Centre/ Electronic Catalogue/ Talking Books/ CDs/ Video Collection/ Internet Access/ Word processing facilities/ Email/ Local History/ In-Touch Electronic Community Information/ IT Classes/ Fax/ Storytime for under 5s
Uplawmoor Library Centre Mure Hall Tannoch Road Uplawmoor ☎ 0141 577 3508	Tues & Fri 2.30pm–4.30pm Wed 6.00pm–8.00pm Facilities – Children's Corner/ Talking Books/ CDs/ Internet Access/ Word processing facilities/ Email/ Fortnightly storytime for under 5s

Did you know you could learn at your local library?

While the kids are busy, why not take the chance to learn something new? Your local library offers a variety of subjects including basic computer skills. European Computer Driving Licence (ECDL) and foreign languages. Your library offers access to learning at a time that suits you, whether that is morning, noon or night! If you would like further information contact Caroline Thompson on 577 4992.

STORYTIMES

Regular storytimes are held during term time, in Community Libraries throughout East Renfrewshire. Why not check if there is one on near you and come along – staff and children are always happy to welcome new faces.

Mon 2.30pm–3.00pm	**Mearns Community Library** ☎ 0141 577 4979
Tues 2.00pm–2.30pm	**Clarkston Community Library** ☎ 0141 577 4972
Alternate Tues 3.00pm–3.30pm	**Uplawmoor Library Centre** ☎ 0141 577 3513 for details
Wed 2.00pm–2.30pm	**Busby Community Library** ☎ 0141 577 4971
Wed 2.15pm–2.45pm	**Thornliebank Community Library** ☎ 0141 577 4983

Please note: pre-fives must be accompanied by an adult at all times

Swimming Pools & Recreation Centres

For opening times please call the appropriate sports centre.

- **Barrhead Sports Centre**
  Main Street
  Barrhead
  ☎ 0141 580 1174

  25 mtr swimming pool
  Tending pool, sports hall
  2 squash courts, stage area
  Cafeteria, sauna suite
  Sports Injury Clinic
  Action Zone Fitness Suite
  Amenity Hall

- **Eastwood Recreation Centre**
  Eastwood Park
  Rouken Glen Road
  Giffnock
  ☎ 0141 577 4956

  25 mtr swimming pool
  Tending pool, spa pool
  Bubble pool, Action Zone Fitness Suite
  Sauna suite, vending area
  Spectator gallery

- **Neilston Leisure Centre**
  Factory Road
  Neilston
  ☎ 0141 577 4970

  25 mtr swimming pool
  Sauna suite, fitness suite
  Vending area

Theatres

- **Eastwood Theatre**
  Eastwood Park
  Giffnock
  East Renfrewshire
  Glasgow
  G46 6UG
  ☎ 0141 577 4970

GLASGOW CITY COUNCIL

Please find in the following section listings of Museums and Galleries, Performing Arts Venues, Swimming Pools, Libraries and Lifelong Learning Centres in Glasgow City.

For **The Burrell Collection** *see* DAYS OUT (PLACES TO VISIT)

For **Fossil Grove** *see* DAYS OUT (PLACES TO VISIT)

For **Gallery of Modern Art** *see* DAYS OUT (PLACES TO VISIT)

For **Kelvingrove Art Gallery and Museum** *see* DAYS OUT (PLACES TO VISIT)

For **Martyrs' School/Open Museum** *see* DAYS OUT (PLACES TO VISIT)

For **McLellan Galleries** *see* DAYS OUT (PLACES TO VISIT)

For **Museum of Transport** *see* DAYS OUT (PLACES TO VISIT)

For **St Mungo Museum of Religious Life and Art** *see* DAYS OUT (PLACES TO VISIT)

For **People's Palace** *see* DAYS OUT (PLACES TO VISIT)

MUSEUMS AND GALLERIES

- **The Burrell Collection**
  ☎ 0141 287 2550
  Fax 0141 287 2597
- **Fossil Grove**
  ☎ 0141 287 2000
- **Gallery of Modern Art**
  ☎ 0141 229 1996
  Fax 0141 204 5316
- **Kelvingrove Art Gallery and Museum**
  ☎ 0141 287 2699
  Fax 0141 287 2690
- **Martyrs' School/Open Museum**
  ☎ 0141 552 2356
- **McLellan Galleries**
  ☎ 0141 331 1854
  Fax 0141 332 9957
- **Museum of Transport**
  ☎ 0141 287 2720
  Fax 0141 287 2692
- **St Mungo Museum of Religious Life and Art**
  ☎ 0141 553 2557
  Fax 0141 552 4744
- **People's Palace**
  ☎ 0141 554 0223
  Fax 0141 550 0892

- **Pollok House**
  ☎ 0141 616 6410
  🖹 0141 552 4744

For **Pollok House**
see DAYS OUT (PLACES TO VISIT)

- **Provand's Lordship**
  ☎ 0141 552 8819
  🖹 0141 552 4744

For **Provand's Lordship**
see DAYS OUT (PLACES TO VISIT)

- **Scotland Street School Museum**
  ☎ 0141 287 0500
  🖹 0141 287 0515

For **Scotland Street School Museum**
see DAYS OUT (PLACES TO VISIT)

PERFORMING ARTS VENUES

- **The Mitchell Theatre**
  3 Granville St
  Glasgow
  G3
  ☎ 0141 287 5008/9

The Mitchell Theatre complex comprises a 400 seat auditorium and the James Moir Hall, together with café and bar facilities. Its programme spans a wide repertoire encompassing dance, drama, alternative comedy and pantomime. The James Moir Hall is in demand for lectures, musical events, weddings and social functions.

- **Tramway**
  25 Albert Drive
  Glasgow
  G41 2PE
  ☎ 0141 287 5429

Tramway is one of the leading contemporary visual and performing arts venues in Europe. Situated in Pollokshields in Glasgow's Southside, it reopened in June 2000 as a multi-functional arts venue, following a major Lottery-funded refurbishment programme.

In addition to its ground-breaking visual art and performance programme, Tramway houses a range of workshop spaces offering regular classes in music, dance, drama and visual arts, as well as major community events. Visitors, artists, performers, producers and collaborators seek out Tramway's unique spaces as a place to create and engage, challenge and question, and have a good time.

During 2002, Nva organisation are developing the Hidden Gardens project, which will transform the derelict site to the rear of Tramway into a contemporary garden. This visionary new landmark will offer a public contemplative green space in a busy urban environment for Glasgow's communities and visitors.

Facility information:
- 25m Pool
- Fitness Suite
- Health Suite with sauna and steam room
- Function Suite

Opening Times:
Mon 10.00am–9.00pm
Tues, Wed, Thurs & Fri 9.30am–9.00pm
Sat & Sun 10.00am–4.00pm

Facility information:
- 25m Pool
- Small Teaching Pool
- 200+ seated Spectator Gallery
- Fitness Suite
- Health Suite
- Disabled access to centre & pool
- Massaging service
- Baby changing facilities

Opening Times:
Mon – Fri 7.45am–9.00pm
Saturday 8.30am–2.00pm
Sunday 8.30am–2.00pm

ALL GLASGOW SWIMMING POOLS

Children and young people under 18 enjoy 'Free Swimming' with their Glasgow Kidz Card or Glasgow Young Scot Card.

- **Drumchapel Swimming Pool**
  199 Drumry Road East
  Glasgow
  G15
  ☎ 0141 944 5812

- **Whitehill Pool**
  240 Onslow Drive
  Dennistoun
  Glasgow
  G31
  ☎ 0141 551 9969

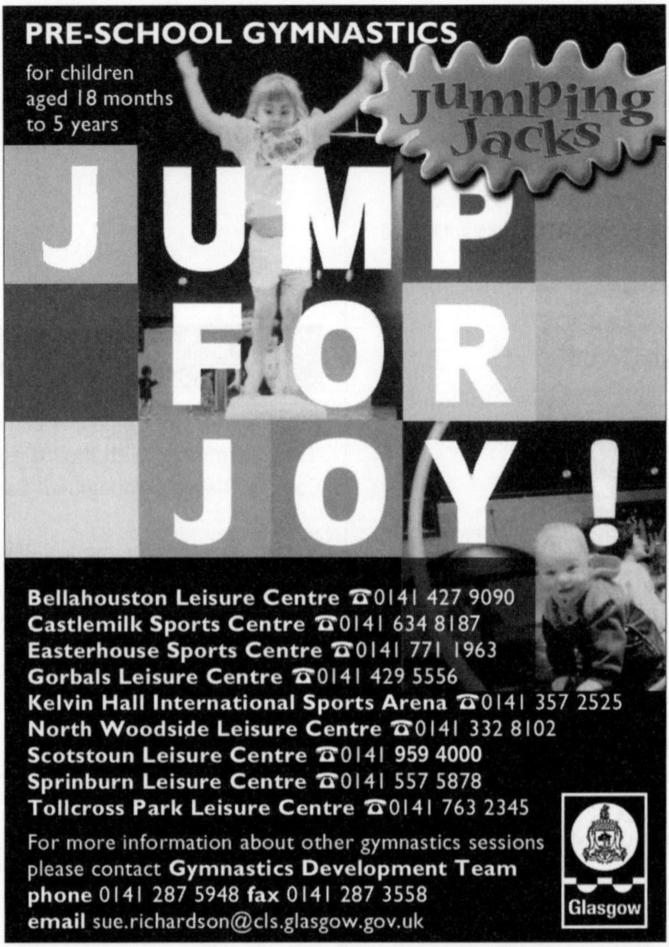

- **Easterhouse Pool**
  6 Bogbain Road
  Glasgow
  G34
  ☎ 0141 771 7978

A major refurbishment of this facility is planned which will integrate it with a unique new Arts Factory and Cultural Campus in Easterhouse.

Facility information:

- 33m Pool
- Separate Teaching Pool
- Large Spectator Gallery
- Sauna Suite
- General purpose room

Opening Times:
Mon, Thurs & Fri 8.00am–9.00pm
Tues 7.30am–9.00pm
Wed 10.00am–9.00pm
Sat 8.30am–3.00pm
Sun 9.30am–4.00pm

■ **Easterhouse Sports Centre**
Auchinlea Road
Easterhouse
Glasgow
G34
☎ 0141 771 1963

Facility information:
- 2 four court Sports Halls (8 badminton courts)
- Fitness Suite with free weights area
- General purpose room
- Crèche
- Jumping Jacks pre-school gynamstic classes for children aged 18 mnth–5 yrs available at this centre

Opening Times:
Mon, Tues, Thurs & Fri 9.00am–10.00pm
Wed 10.00am–10.00pm
Sat & Sun 10.00am–5.00pm

■ **Stepford Road Sports Park**
Edinburgh Road
Easterhouse
Glasgow
G34
☎ 0141 773 2363

Facility information:
- Full size floodlit artificial grass pitch
- Can operate as four 7-a-side pitches (all floodlit)
- Two full size natural grass pitches
- Modern team changing facilities

Opening TImes:
Mon – Fri 1.00pm–10.00pm
Sat 10.00am–6.00pm
Sun 10.00am–7.00pm

- **Alexandra Sports Hall**
  Alexandra Parade
  Glasgow
  G31
  ☎ 0141 556 1695

Facility information:
- Four large Badminton Courts
- Large Sports Hall
- 2 Blaes Outdoor Football Pitches
- Changing Facilities

Opening Times:
Mon & Tues 4.00pm–10.00pm
Wed 5.00pm–10.00pm
Thurs & Fri 2.00pm–10.00pm
Sat & Sun 10.00am–5.00pm

- **Tollcross Park Leisure Centre**
  350 Wellshot Road
  Tollcross
  Glasgow
  G32
  ☎ 0141 763 2345

Facility information:
- 50m Swimming Pool
- 25m Teaching Pool/Children's Splash Pool
- Poolside Spa (Pool)
- Health Suite with 2 Saunas and Steam Room
- Double Court Sports Hall
- Dance Studio
- Split level hi-tech Fitness Suite
- Function Rooms and Café
- Jumping Jacks pre-school gynamstic classes for children aged 18 mnth–5 yrs available at this centre

Opening Times:
Mon – Fri 7.00am–10.00pm
Sat 9.00am–5.00pm
Sun 9.00am–9.00pm

- **Crownpoint Sports Park**
  183 Crownpoint Road
  Bridgeton
  Glasgow
  G40
  ☎ 0141 554 8274

Facility information:
- 400m Outdoor Track
- 2 Outdoor 11-a-side Football Parks consisting of one grass pitch and one blaes pitch
- Fitness Suite with free weights and cardio-vascular equipment
- Function Rooms

Opening Times:
Mon – Fri 3.00pm–10.00pm
Sat & Sun 10.00am–5.00pm

- **Gorbals Leisure Centre**
  275 Ballater Street
  Glasgow
  G5
  ☎ 0141 429 5556

Facility information:
- 25m Pool
- Children's Splash Pool and Poolside Spa Pool
- Health Suite with 3 Saunas, Steam Room
- Double Court Sports Hall
- Four Court Tennis Hall
- Dance Studio
- Hi-tech Fitness Suite
- Meeting Room/Crèche
- Café
- Jumping Jacks pre-school gynamstic classes for children aged 18 mnth–5 yrs available at this centre

Opening TImes:
Mon, Wed, Thurs & Fri 7.00am–10.00pm
Tue 10.00am–10.00pm
Sat 9.00am–6.00pm
Sun 9.00am–10.00pm

■ **North Woodside Leisure Centre**
10 Braid Square
Glasgow
G4
☎ 0141 332 8102

Facility information:
- Beautifully restored Victorian Swimming Pool
- Spa Pool
- Health Suite
- Dance Studio
- Fitness Suite
- Jumping Jacks pre-school gynamstic classes for children aged 18 mnth–5 yrs available at this centre

Opening Times:
Mon 10.00am–9.00pm
Tue & Thurs 9.30am–9.00pm
Wed & Fri 7.30am–9.00pm
Sat & Sun 10.00am–4.00pm
(Gym opens at 9.00am)

■ **Bellahouston Leisure Centre**
Bellahouston Drive
Glasgow
G52
☎ 0141 427 9090

Facility information:
- 25m Pool
- Leisure Pool
- Toddler Splash Pool
- Outdoor Pool/Lagoon
- 90m Flume Ride
- Health Suite with Sauna, Sanarium, Steam Room, Spa Pool and Relaxation Lounge
- Purpose-built Gymnastics Centre
- Hi-tech Fitness Suite with entertainment system
- Sports Hall
- 2 Squash Courts
- Dance Studio
- Function Room
- Childrens' Play Centre with Crèche, Soft Play Area and Baby Soft Play Corner
- Café
- Jumping Jacks pre-school gynamstic classes for children aged 18 mnth–5 yrs available at this centre

Opening Times:
Mon – Fri 9.00am*–10.00pm
Sat 9.00am**–6.00pm
Sun 9.00am–10.00pm***

* 25m Pool and Fitness Suite open 6.30am
** Swimming Pools open 10.00am
*** Swimming Pools close at 4.00pm

- **Castlemilk Sports Centre and Indoor Bowling Club**
  Dougrie Road
  Castlemilk
  Glasgow
  G45
  ☎ 0141 634 8187

Facility information:

- Double Court Sports Hall
- Fitness Suite
- 8 Lane Indoor Bowling Arena
- Multi-purpose area
- Crèche
- Jumping Jacks pre-school gynamstic classes for children aged 18 mnth–5 yrs available at this centre

Opening Times:
Mon – Thurs 8.30am–10.30pm
Fri 10.00am–10.30pm
Sat & Sun 9.30am–8.30pm

- **Barlia Sports Complex**
  Barlia Drive
  Castlemilk
  Glasgow
  G45
  ☎ 0141 634 5474

Facility information:

- Full-size 11-a-side floodlit Astro-turf Football Pitch (can adapt to hockey pitch or 4, 7-a-side football pitches)
- 2. 5-a-side football pitches (can adapt to four tennis courts)
- Pavilion with changing facilities

Opening Times:
Mon – Thurs 10.00am–10.30pm
Friday 10.00am–9.30pm
Saturday 9.00am–3.30pm
Sunday 10.00am–4.30pm

- **Springburn Leisure Centre**
  Kay Street
  Glasgow
  G21
  ☎ 0141 557 5878

Facility information:
- Swimming/Leisure Pool
- Spa, Sauna and Steam facilities
- Sports Hall
- Dance Studio
- Fitness Suites and Weight Room
- Play Area
- Jumping Jacks pre-school gynamstic classes for children aged 18 mnth–5 yrs available at this centre

Opening Times:
Mon 10.00am–10.30pm
Tues & Thurs 7.30am–10.00pm
Wed & Fri 9.00am–10.00pm
Sat & Sun 9.00am–5.00pm

- **Castlemilk Swimming Pool**
  137 Castlemilk Drive
  Glasgow
  G45
  ☎ 0141 634 8254

Facility information:
- 25m main pool
- Boom pool with disabled lift
- Teaching Pool
- 2 Flumes
- Spectator Gallery
- Health Suite with Sauna and Steam Room
- 2 general purpose/meeting rooms

Opening Times:
Mon & Wed 8.30am–9.00pm
Tues & Thurs 7.00am–9.00pm
Fri 10.00am–9.00pm
Sat 9.00am–3.30pm
Sun 9.00am–3.00pm

■ **Pollok Leisure Centre**
27 Cowglen Road
Glasgow
G53
☎ 0141 881 3313

Facility information:

- Leisure Pool
- Flumes
- Gym
- Fitness Studio
- Changing Village (including disabled)
- Library with internet access facilities

Opening Times:
Mon – Fri 9.30am–9.00pm
Sat & Sun 10.00am–4.00pm

■ **Holyrood Sports Centre**
60 Aikenhead Road
Glasgow
G42
☎ 0141 423 9431

Holyrood Sports Centre is a joint use building with Holyrood Secondary School. Between the hours of 9.00am–4.00pm the School has sole use of the building. After 4.00pm, the building is open for public use, with the School using some areas until 5.30pm.

Facility information:

- Fitness Suite
- Dance Studio
- Sports Halls
- Outdoor Synthetic Pitch
- Internet Café

Opening Times:
Mon – Fri & Sun 9.00am–10.00pm
Saturday 9.00am–6.00pm

- **Glasgow Green Football Centre**
  Kings Drive
  Glasgow
  G40
  ☎ 0141 554 7547

Facility information:
- Floodlit synthetic grass pitch (new generation turf)
- Floodlit reinforced grass pitch
- 4 adult size Grass Pitches
- Juvenile Grass Pitch
- 3 Soccer 7 Grass Pitches (under 12s)
- 8 Five-a-side Synthetic Pitches (new generation turf)
- Changing facilities
- Multi purpose room suitable for meetings and seminars
- Lounge/Café with licensed bar

Opening Times:
Mon – Fri & Sun 9.00am–10.00pm
Sat 9.00am–5.00pm

- **Kelvin Hall International Sports Arena**
  Argyle Street
  Glasgow
  G3
  ☎ 0141 357 2525

Facility information:
- Athletics Track
- Sports Medicine Clinic
- 5 multi-purpose Sports Halls
- Climbing Wall
- Spectator Gallery
- Fitness Suite
- Conditioning Suite
- Conference Room
- Function Suite
- Club Room
- Jumping Jacks pre-school gynamstic classes for children aged 18 mnth–5 yrs available at this centre

Opening Times:
Mon – Fri & Sun 9.00am–10.30pm
Sat 9.00am–6.30pm

Facility information:

- Main Hall suitable for full range of racquet sports and team games
- Outdoor Floodlit Blaes Football Pitch with separate changing facilities
- Fitness Suite with free weights
- Personal Training facility available
- Main Hall also available for birthday parties, accommodating up to 25 children aged 3 to 15

Opening Times:
Mon & Thurs 10.00am–9.00pm
Tues 9.30am–9.00pm
Wed & Fri 9.00am–9.00pm
Sat 9.00am–4.00pm
Sun 10.00am–4.00pm

■ **Yoker Sports Centre**
2 Speirshall Terrace
Glasgow
G14
☎ 0141 959 8386

■ **Scotstoun Leisure Centre**
72 Danes Drive
Glasgow
G14
☎ 0141 959 4000

Facility information:

Indoor

- 25m Pool
- Teaching & Splash Pool
- Sports Hall (can adapt to 8 Badminton Courts)
- Tennis Hall with 8 Courts
- National Badminton Academy
- Volleyball/Netball Centre
- Fitness Suite with Resistance and Cardio Zones
- Health Suite with sauna, steam room and solarium
- Dance Studio
- Crèche with soft play area
- Café & Lounge Bar
- Jumping Jacks pre-school gynamstic classes for children aged 18 mnth–5 yrs available at this centre

Outdoor

- 400m International Running Track
- 2 Rugby Pitches
- 5-a-side Football Pitches x 4
- 7-a-side Footballs Pitches x 4
- 3 Tennis Courts
- Grandstand Seating for 900 spectators
- Children's Play Area

Opening Times:
Mon, Wed & Fri 7.30am–10.00pm
Tues & Sun 9.00am–10.00pm
Thursday 10.00am–10.00pm
Saturday 9.00am– 6.00pm

Libraries and Lifelong Learning Centres

In addition to the usual library facilities, most of Glasgow's libraries have a *REAL Learning Centre* on site, providing members with free access to computers, including a range of software, internet and email facilities. The *REAL Learning Centres* are in partnership with **Scottish Enterprise Glasgow** and within the next year, it is expected that each of the 33 libraries in Glasgow's Community Network will have a R*EAL Learning Centre* open.

Libraries marked * do **not** currently have a *REAL Learning Centre*.

- **Anderston***
  Berkeley Street
  Glasgow
  G3 7DN
  ☎ 0141 287 2872

Opening Times:
Monday 10.00am–8.00pm
Tuesday 10.00am–8.00pm
Wednesday 10.00am–5.00pm
Thursday 12.00pm–8.00pm
Friday 9.00am–5.00pm
Saturday 9.00am–5.00pm
Sunday Closed

- **Anniesland Library & Learning Centre**
  833 Crow Road
  Glasgow
  G13
  ☎ 0141 954 5265

Opening Times:
Monday 10.00am–8.00pm
Tuesday 10.00am–8.00pm
Wednesday 10.00am–5.00pm
Thursday 12.00pm–8.00pm
Friday 9.00am–5.00pm
Saturday 9.00am–5.00pm
Sunday Closed

- **Baillieston**
  141 Main Street
  Glasgow
  G69 6AA
  ☎ 0141 771 2433

Opening Times:
Monday 10.00am–8.00pm
Tuesday 10.00am–8.00pm
Wednesday 10.00am–5.00pm
Thursday 12.00pm–8.00pm
Friday 9.00am–5.00pm
Saturday 9.00am–5.00pm
Sunday Closed

- **Barmulloch**
  99 Rockfield Road
  Glasgow
  G21 3DY
  ☎ 0141 558 6185

Opening Times:
Monday 10.00am–8.00pm
Tuesday 10.00am–8.00pm
Wednesday 10.00am–5.00pm
Thursday 12.00pm–8.00pm
Friday 9.00am–5.00pm
Saturday 9.00am–5.00pm
Sunday Closed

- **Bridgeton**
  23 Landressy Street
  Glasgow
  G40 1BP
  ☎ 0141 554 0217

Opening Times:
Monday 10.00am–8.00pm
Tuesday 10.00am–8.00pm
Wednesday 10.00am–5.00pm
Thursday 12.00pm–8.00pm
Friday 9.00am–5.00pm
Saturday 9.00am–5.00pm
Sunday Closed

- **Cardonald**
  1113 Mosspark Drive
  Glasgow
  G52 3BU
  ☎ 0141 882 1381

Opening Times:
Monday 10.00am–8.00pm
Tuesday 10.00am–8.00pm
Wednesday 10.00am–5.00pm
Thursday 12.00pm–8.00pm
Friday 9.00am–5.00pm
Saturday 9.00am–5.00pm
Sunday Closed

- **Castlemilk**
  100 Castlemilk Drive
  Glasgow
  G45 9TN
  ☎ 0141 634 2066

Opening Times:
Monday 10.00am–8.00pm
Tuesday 10.00am–8.00pm
Wednesday 10.00am–5.00pm
Thursday 12.00pm–8.00pm
Friday 9.00am–5.00pm
Saturday 9.00am–5.00pm
Sunday Closed

- **Couper Institute**
  84 Clarkston Road
  Glasgow
  G44 3DA
  ☎ 0141 637 1544

Opening Times:
Monday 10.00am–8.00pm
Tuesday 10.00am–8.00pm
Wednesday 10.00am–5.00pm
Thursday 12.00pm–8.00pm
Friday 9.00am–5.00pm
Saturday 9.00am–5.00pm
Sunday Closed

- **Dennistoun**
  2a Craigpark
  Glasgow
  G31 2NA
  ☎ 0141 554 0055

Opening Times:
Monday 10.00am–8.00pm
Tuesday 10.00am–8.00pm
Wednesday 10.00am–5.00pm
Thursday 12.00pm–8.00pm
Friday 9.00am–5.00pm
Saturday 9.00am–5.00pm
Sunday Closed

- **Drumchapel**
  65 Hecla Avenue
  Glasgow
  G15 8LX
  ☎ 0141 944 5698

Opening Times:
Monday 10.00am–8.00pm
Tuesday 10.00am–8.00pm
Wednesday 10.00am–5.00pm
Thursday 12.00pm–8.00pm
Friday 9.00am–5.00pm
Saturday 9.00am–5.00pm
Sunday Closed

- **Easterhouse**
  65 Shandwick Street
  Glasgow
  G34 9DP
  ☎ 0141 771 5986

Opening Times:
Monday 10.00am–8.00pm
Tuesday 10.00am–8.00pm
Wednesday 10.00am–5.00pm
Thursday 12.00pm–8.00pm
Friday 9.00am–5.00pm
Saturday 9.00am–5.00pm
Sunday Closed

- **Elder Park**
  228a Langlands Road
  Glasgow
  G51 3TZ
  ☎ 0141 445 1047

Opening Times:
Monday 10.00am–8.00pm
Tuesday 10.00am–8.00pm
Wednesday 10.00am–5.00pm
Thursday 12.00pm–8.00pm
Friday 9.00am–5.00pm
Saturday 9.00am–5.00pm
Sunday Closed

- **Govanhill**
  170 Langside Road
  Glasgow
  G42 7JU
  ☎ 0141 423 0335

Opening Times:
Monday 10.00am–8.00pm
Tuesday 10.00am–8.00pm
Wednesday 10.00am–5.00pm
Thursday 12.00pm–8.00pm
Friday 9.00am–5.00pm
Saturday 9.00am–5.00pm
Sunday Closed

- **Hillhead**
  348 Byres Road
  Glasgow
  G12 8AP
  ☎ 0141 339 7223

Opening Times:
Monday 10.00am–8.00pm
Tuesday 10.00am–8.00pm
Wednesday 10.00am–5.00pm
Thursday 12.00pm–8.00pm
Friday 9.00am–5.00pm
Saturday 9.00am–5.00pm
Sunday Closed

- **Ibrox**
  1 Midlock Street
  Glasgow
  G51 1SL
  ☎ 0141 427 5831

Opening Times:
Monday 10.00am–8.00pm
Tuesday 10.00am–8.00pm
Wednesday 10.00am–5.00pm
Thursday 12.00pm–8.00pm
Friday 9.00am–5.00pm
Saturday 9.00am–5.00pm
Sunday Closed

■ **Knightswood**
27 Dunterlie Avenue
Glasgow
G13 3BB
☎ 0141 959 2041

Opening Times:
Monday 10.00am–8.00pm
Tuesday 10.00am–8.00pm
Wednesday 10.00am–5.00pm
Thursday 12.00pm–8.00pm
Friday 9.00am–5.00pm
Saturday 9.00am–5.00pm
Sunday Closed

■ **Langside***
2 Sinclair Drive
Glasgow
G42 9QE
☎ 0141 632 0810

Opening Times:
Monday 10.00am–8.00pm
Tuesday 10.00am–8.00pm
Wednesday 10.00am–5.00pm
Thursday 12.00pm–8.00pm
Friday 9.00am–5.00pm
Saturday 9.00am–5.00pm
Sunday Closed

■ **The Mitchell Library**
North Street
Glasgow
G3 7DN
☎ 0141 287 2999

The Mitchell Library is the largest public reference library in western Europe. It provides a wide range of reference, information and archive resources, including many rare and unique items and collections. The Mitchell Library was founded in 1877 from the bequest of Stephen Mitchell, a tobacco merchant.

The Mitchell Library now has a Real Learning Centre on level 3 of the building with 50 multimedia PCs

Opening Times:
Monday – Thursday 9.00am–8.00pm
Friday – Saturday 9.00am–5.00pm
Closed Sunday

- **Maryhill**
  1508 Maryhill Road
  Glasgow
  G20 9AD
  ☎ 0141 946 2348

Opening Times:
Monday 10.00am–8.00pm
Tuesday 10.00am–8.00pm
Wednesday 10.00am–5.00pm
Thursday 12.00pm–8.00pm
Friday 9.00am–5.00pm
Saturday 9.00am–5.00pm
Sunday Closed

- **Milton**
  163 Ronaldsay St
  Glasgow
  G22 7AP
  ☎ 0141 772 1410

Opening Times:
Monday 10.00am–8.00pm
Tuesday 10.00am–8.00pm
Wednesday 10.00am–5.00pm
Thursday 12.00pm–8.00pm
Friday 9.00am–5.00pm
Saturday 9.00am–5.00pm
Sunday Closed

- **Parkhead**
  64 Tollcross Road
  Glasgow
  G31 4XA
  ☎ 0141 554 0198

Opening Times:
Monday 10.00am–8.00pm
Tuesday 10.00am–8.00pm
Wednesday 10.00am–5.00pm
Thursday 12.00pm–8.00pm
Friday 9.00am–5.00pm
Saturday 9.00am–5.00pm
Sunday Closed

- **Partick**
  305 Dumbarton Road
  Glasgow
  G11 6AB
  ☎ 0141 339 1303

Opening Times:
Monday 10.00am–8.00pm
Tuesday 10.00am–8.00pm
Wednesday 10.00am–5.00pm
Thursday 12.00pm–8.00pm
Friday 9.00am–5.00pm
Saturday 9.00am–5.00pm
Sunday Closed

- **Pollok Leisure Pool and Library**
  Cowglen Road
  Glasgow
  G53 6EW
  ☎ 0141 881 3540

Opening Times:
Monday 10.00am–8.00pm
Tuesday 10.00am–8.00pm
Wednesday 10.00am–5.00pm
Thursday 12.00pm–8.00pm
Friday 9.00am–5.00pm
Saturday 9.00am–5.00pm
Sunday Closed

- **Pollokshaws**
  50/60 Shawbridge Street
  Glasgow
  G43 1RW
  ☎ 0141 632 3544

Opening Times:
Monday 10.00am–8.00pm
Tuesday 10.00am–8.00pm
Wednesday 10.00am–5.00pm
Thursday 12.00pm–8.00pm
Friday 9.00am–5.00pm
Saturday 9.00am–5.00pm
Sunday Closed

- **Pollokshields**
  30 Leslie Street
  Glasgow
  G41 2LF
  ☎ 0141 423 1460

Opening Times:
Monday 10.00am–8.00pm
Tuesday 10.00am–8.00pm
Wednesday 10.00am–5.00pm
Thursday 12.00pm–8.00pm
Friday 9.00am–5.00pm
Saturday 9.00am–5.00pm
Sunday Closed

- **Possilpark**
  127 Allander Street
  Glasgow
  G22 5JJ
  ☎ 0141 336 8110

Opening Times:
Monday 10.00am–8.00pm
Tuesday 10.00am–8.00pm
Wednesday 10.00am–5.00pm
Thursday 12.00pm–8.00pm
Friday 9.00am–5.00pm
Saturday 9.00am–5.00pm
Sunday Closed

- **Riddrie**
  1020 Cumbernauld Road
  Glasgow
  G33 2QS
  ☎ 0141 770 4043

Opening Times:
Monday 10.00am–8.00pm
Tuesday 10.00am–8.00pm
Wednesday 10.00am–5.00pm
Thursday 12.00pm–8.00pm
Friday 9.00am–5.00pm
Saturday 9.00am–5.00pm
Sunday Closed

- **Royston**
  67 Royston Road
  Glasgow
  G21 2QW
  ☎ 0141 552 1657

Opening Times:
Monday 10.00am–8.00pm
Tuesday 10.00am–8.00pm
Wednesday 10.00am–5.00pm
Thursday 12.00pm–8.00pm
Friday 9.00am–5.00pm
Saturday 9.00am–5.00pm
Sunday Closed

- **Shettleston**
  154 Wellshot Road
  Glasgow
  G32 7AX
  ☎ 0141 778 1221

Opening Times:
Monday 10.00am–8.00pm
Tuesday 10.00am–8.00pm
Wednesday 10.00am–5.00pm
Thursday 12.00pm–8.00pm
Friday 9.00am–5.00pm
Saturday 9.00am–5.00pm
Sunday Closed

- **Sighthill**
  Fountainwell Square
  Glasgow
  G21 1RB
  ☎ 0141 558 6910

Opening Times:
Monday – Friday 10.00am–10.00pm
Saturday & Sunday 10.00am–5.00pm

Opening Times:
Monday 10.00am–8.00pm
Tuesday 10.00am–8.00pm
Wednesday 10.00am–5.00pm
Thursday 12.00pm–8.00pm
Friday 9.00am–5.00pm
Saturday 9.00am–5.00pm
Sunday Closed

The Library is situated in the marble-lined basement of the Gallery of Modern Art (GoMA), and offers a wide range of services to people living and working in Glasgow, including free book lending and a REAL Learning Centre with free internet access for members.

Library Services:

- REAL Learning Centre with access to internet, email, online learning, and an extensive library of software and learning materials
- Music CDs, video and DVD films for hire
- A visual art focus in the bookstock, in addition to a wide range of fiction and non-fiction
- A children's area and youth space
- Café with Costa Coffee
- A display area for artists' work for integrated use with the Gallery

Opening Times:
Monday 10.00am–8.00pm
Tuesday 10.00am–8.00pm
Wednesday 10.00am–5.00pm
Thursday 10.00am–8.00pm
Friday 11.00am–5.00pm
Saturday 10.00am–5.00pm
Sunday 11.00am–5.00pm

- **Springburn***
179 Ayr Street
Glasgow
G21 4BW
☎ 0141 558 5559

- **The Library at GoMA**
Gallery of Modern Art
Queen Street
Glasgow
G1 3AZ
☎ 0141 221 1876

- **Whiteinch**
  14 Victoria Park Drive South
  Glasgow
  G14 9RL
  ☎ 0141 959 1376

Opening Times:
Monday 10.00am–8.00pm
Tuesday 10.00am–8.00pm
Wednesday 10.00am–5.00pm
Thursday 12.00pm–8.00pm
Friday 9.00am–5.00pm
Saturday 9.00am–5.00pm
Sunday Closed

- **Woodside**
  343 St George's Road
  Glasgow
  G3 6JQ
  ☎ 0141 332 1808

Opening Times:
Monday 10.00am–8.00pm
Tuesday 10.00am–8.00pm
Wednesday 10.00am–5.00pm
Thursday 12.00pm–8.00pm
Friday 9.00am–5.00pm
Saturday 9.00am–5.00pm
Sunday Closed

North Lanarkshire Council

Please find in the following section listings of Country Parks, Libraries, Museums, Places to Visit, Sports and Leisure Facilities, Swimming Pools, Sports Centres and Community Arts Activities in North Lanarkshire.

For **Burngreen Recreation Park**
see Days Out (places to visit)

For **Drumpellier Country Park**
see Days Out (places to visit)

For **Palacerigg Country Park**
see Days Out (places to visit)

For **Strathclyde Country Park**
see Days Out (places to visit)

For **Viewpark Gardens**
see Days Out (places to visit)

Country Parks/Wildlife

- **Burngreen Recreation Park**

- **Drumpellier Country Park**
  ☎ 01236 422257

- **Palacerigg Country Park**
  ☎ 01236 720047

- **Strathclyde Country Park**
  ☎ 01698 266155

- **Viewpark Gardens**
  ☎ 01698 818269

passport to leisure

A concession scheme called **'Passport to Leisure'** is available to residents of North Lanarkshire who can fulfil certain criteria, such as being unemployed, over 60 or in receipt of a specified state benefit.

Holders are given a special card which entitles them to obtain entry to a number of leisure activities at **half** the normal adult charge. Annual membership of the scheme costs **£2.**

For further details please contact your local library or leisure centre, or write to the special freepost address below:

Creative Services
Department of Community Services
North Lanarkshire Council
FREEPOST SCO656
Glasgow G33 1BR

Tel: **0141 304 1956**
Fax: **0141 304 1839**

community services

North Lanarkshire Council

LIBRARIES

Modern libraries offer much more than the loan of books. North Lanarkshire's 24 local libraries provide books, CD's, cassettes, videos and instruments for loan.

Every library has a collection of books to suit every child. Our libraries provide a stimulating environment with an increasingly wide range of multimedia resources that encourage even the youngest reader to develop their reading skills and discover that learning can be fun. Most libraries have story tapes, comics, CD's, cassettes and computer software for young people. We also have regular special events for children including story times and competitions. Please check with your local library for up-to-date information and for individual opening hours.

Libraries within North Lanarkshire are as follows:-

- **Abronhill Library**
  17 Pine Road
  Cumbernauld
  G67 3BE
  ☎ 01236 731503
  🖹 01236 731503

Opening Times:
Mon, Tues, Thurs & Fri 9.30am–7.30pm
Wed 9.30am–12 noon
Sat 9.00am–12 noon
Sun closed

- **Airdrie Library**
  Wellwynd
  Airdrie
  ML6 0AG
  ☎ 01236 763221
  🖹 01236 766027

Opening Times:
Mon, Tues, Thurs & Fri 9.00am–7.30pm
Wed 9.00am–12 noon
Sat 9.00am–12 noon
Sun closed

- **Bellshill Cultural Centre**
  John Street
  Bellshill
  ML4 1RJ
  ☎ 01698 346770
  🖹 01698 843509

Opening Times:
Mon, Tues, Thurs & Fri 9.00am–7.30pm
Wed 9.00am–12 noon
Sat 9.00am–12 noon
Sun closed

- **Chapelhall Library**
  2 Honeywell Crescent
  Airdrie
  ML6 8XW
  ☎ 01236 750099
  🖹 01236 770055

Opening Times:
Mon, Tues & Thurs 9.30am–7.30pm
Wed 9.30am–12 noon
Fri 9.30am–5.00pm
Sat 9.00am–12 noon
Sun closed

- **Chryston Library**
  Chryston Valley Business Park
  Cloverhill Place
  Chryston
  Glasgow
  G69 9DH
  ☎ 0141 779 4720
  🖹 0141 779 4720

Opening Times:
Mon & Thurs 9.30am–1.00pm & 2.00–7.30pm
Tues & Fri 9.30am–1.00pm & 2.00–5.00pm
Wed 9.30am–12 noon
Sat 9.00am–12 noon
Sun closed

- **Cleland Library**
  Main Street
  Cleland
  ML1 5QW
  ☎ 01698 860487

Opening Times:
Mon, Tues & Thurs 9.30am–1.00pm & 2.00–7.30pm
Fri 9.30am–1.00pm & 2.00–5.00pm
Wed 9.30am–12 noon
Sat 9.00am–12 noon
Sun closed

- **Coatbridge Library**
  Academy Street
  Coatbridge
  ML5 3AW
  ☎ 01236 424150
  🖹 01236 437997

Opening Times:
Mon, Tues, Thurs & Fri 9.00am–7.30pm
Wed 9.00am–12 noon
Sat 9.00am–12 noon
Sun closed

- **Condorrat Library**
  North Road
  Condorrat
  G68 9AE
  ☎ 01236 736615
  🖹 01236 736615

Opening Times:
Mon, Tues, Thurs & Fri 9.30am–7.30pm
Wed 9.30am–12 noon
Sat 9.00am–12 noon
Sun closed

- **Craigneuk Library**
  Sheildmuir Street
  Craigneuk
  Wishaw
  ML2 7TJ
  ☎ 01698 376689

Opening Times:
Mon, Tues & Thurs 9.30am–1.00pm & 2.00–7.30pm
Fri 9.30am–1.00pm & 2.00–5.00pm
Wed 9.30am–12 noon
Sat 9.00am–12 noon
Sun closed

- **Cumbernauld Library**
  8 Allander Walk
  Cumbernauld
  G67 1AA
  ☎ 01236 725664
  🖹 01236 458350

Opening Times:
Mon, Tues, Thurs & Fri 9.00am–7.30pm
Wed 9.00am–12 noon
Sat 9.00–12 noon
Sun closed

- **Eastfield Library**
  8 Ben Lawlers Drive
  Eastfield
  Cumbernauld
  G68 9JH
  ☎ 01236 720032
  🖹 01236 720032

Opening Times:
Mon, Tues & Thurs 9.30am–1.00 & 2.00–7.30pm
Fri 9.30am–1.00pm & 2.00–5.00pm
Wed 9.30am–12 noon
Sat 9.00am–12 noon
Sun closed

- **Kilsyth Library**
  Burngreen
  Kilsyth
  G65 0HT
  ☎ 01236 823147
  🖹 01236 823147

Opening Times:
Mon, Tues, Thurs & Fri. 9.30am–7.30pm
Wed 9.30am–12 noon
Sat 9.00–12 noon
Sun closed

- **Moodiesburn Library**
  Glenmanor Avenue
  Moodiesburn
  G69 0LS
  ☎ 01236 874927
  🖹 01236 875024

Opening Times:
Mon, Tues, Thurs & Fri 9.30am–7.30pm
Wed 9.30am–12 noon
Sat 9.00am–12 noon
Sun closed

■ **Motherwell Library** 35 Hamilton Road Motherwell ML1 3BZ ☎ 01698 332619	Opening Times: Mon, Tues, Thurs & Fri 9.00am–7.30pm Wed 9.00am–12 noon (Information Section open till 5.00pm) Sat 9.00–12 noon Sun closed
Open Learning (Motherwell) 01698 230214	As above
■ **Newarthill Library** Kirkhall Road Newarthill ML1 5BB ☎ 01698 732033	Opening Times: Mon, Tues & Thurs 9.30am–1.00pm & 2.00–7.30pm Fri 9.30am–1.00pm & 2.00–5.00pm Wed 9.30am–12 noon Sat 9.00am–12 noon Sun closed
■ **Newmains Library** Manse Road Newmains ML2 9AX ☎ 01698 385325	Opening Times: Mon, Tues & Thurs 9.30am–1.00pm & 2.00–7.30pm Fri 9.30am–1.00pm & 2.00–5.00pm Wed 9.30am–12 noon Sat 9.00am–12 noon Sun closed
■ **New Stevenston Library** Clydesdale Street New Stevenston ML1 4JG ☎ 01698 732745	Opening Times: Mon, Tues & Thurs 9.30am–1.00pm & 2.00pm–7.30pm Fri 9.30am–1.00pm & 2.00–5.00pm Wed 9.30am–12 noon Sat 9.00–12 noon Sun closed
■ **Old Monkland Library** Marshall Street Coatbridge ML5 ☎ 01236 428018	Opening Times: Mon & Thurs 9.30am–1.00pm & 2.00pm–7.30pm Tues & Fri 9.30am–1.00pm & 2.00–5.00pm Wed 9.30am–12 noon Sat 9.00–12 noon Sun closed

- **Petersburn Library**
  Varnsdorf Way
  Petersburn
  Airdrie
  ML6 8EQ
  ☎ 01236 755008

Opening Times:
Mon, Tues & Thurs 9.30am–1.00pm & 2.00pm–7.30pm
Fri 9.30am–1.00pm & 2.00–5.00pm
Wed 9.30am–12 noon
Sat 9.00–12 noon, Sun closed

- **Shotts Library**
  Benhar Road
  Shotts
  ML7 5EN
  ☎ 01501 821556

Opening Times:
Mon, Tues, Thurs & Fri 9.30am–7.30pm
Wed 9.30am–12 noon
Sat 9.00–12 noon, Sun closed

- **Stepps Library**
  School Road
  Stepps
  G33 6HF
  ☎ 0141 779 1050
  🖹 0141 779 1050

Opening Times:
Mon & Thurs 9.30am–1.00pm & 2.00–7.30pm
Tues & Fri 9.30am–1.00pm & 2.00–5.00pm
Wed 9.30am–12 noon
Sat 9.00am–12 noon, Sun closed

- **Viewpark Library**
  Burnhead Street
  Viewpark
  G71 5RN
  ☎ 01698 812801
  🖹 01698 810311

Opening Times:
Mon, Tues, Thurs & Fri 9.30am–7.30pm
Wed 9.30am–12 noon
Sat 9.00am–12 noon, Sun closed

- **Whifflet Library**
  Easton Place
  Whifflet
  Coatbridge
  ML5 4EW
  ☎ 01236 429118

Opening Times:
Mon, Tues, Thurs & Fri 9.30am–7.30pm
Wed 9.30am–12 noon
Sat 9.00am–12 noon, Sun closed

- **Wishaw Library**
  Kenilworth Avenue
  Wishaw
  ML2 7LP
  ☎ 01698 372325
  🖹 01698 376462

Opening Times:
Mon, Tues, Thurs & Fri 9.30am–7.30pm
Wed 9.30am–12 noon
Sat 9.00–12 noon, Sun closed

Open Learning (Wishaw)
01698 357614

As above

Museums/Places to Visit

- **Airdrie Leisure Centre**
  Motherwell Street
  Airdrie
  ML6
  ☎ 01236 762871

Welcome to **Airdrie Leisure Centre** where an abundance of indoor and outdoor leisure facilities ensure that the centre is one of the busiest of its kind in Scotland. Easily accessible and with ample car parking, it is located in Airdrie beside the A73, within the grounds of Rawyards Park.

The centre runs a large amount of activities for all ages in the sports hall. There is also a Jungle Safari with an extensive and exciting soft play area. This is very popular for children's parties, please call reception to check availability.

The centre is open from Monday to Sunday from 8.30am–10.00pm.

- **Aquatec**
  ☎ 01698 276464

For **Aquatec**
see Days Out (places to visit)

- **John Smith Pool**
  Stirling Street
  Airdrie
  ML6
  ☎ 01236 750130

Not merely a 25 metre pool, at the touch of a button the moving floor turns one end into a shallow or deep area giving it the versatility to offer many different activities. The pool offers swimming lessons, children's fun time and much more.

The centre also features a Under 4's soft play area, a mini world of soft shapes, colours, textures and puzzles for all our younger customers. The centre is open Monday to Friday from 8.00am–10.00pm and Saturday and Sunday from 8.00am–5.00pm.

Kilsyth Swimming Pool has a four lane, 25 metre swimming pool where swimming is available for all ages and abilities. There is also a children's fun pool, a shallow pool which features it's own desert island, a water cannon and a baby slide.

The centre is open Monday from 9.00am–8.15pm, Tuesday to Friday from 7.30am–10.00pm and Saturday and Sunday from 8.00am–5.00pm.

- **Kilsyth Swimming Pool**
  1 Airdrie Road
  Kilsyth
  Glasgow
  G65
  ☎ 01236 828166

The **Sir Matt Busby Sports Complex** offers an excellent combination of indoor and outdoor sporting facilities, designed to suit the serious and recreational user alike. The centre boasts a 25 metre pool suited to both recreational swimming and competitive galas, plus a separate teaching pool, offering a comprehensive swimming programme. The "Learn to Swim" scheme can accommodate swimmers of all ages and abilities.

The centre is open from Monday to Friday from 8.00am–10.30pm and on Saturdays and Sundays from 9.00am–10.30pm.

- **Sir Matt Busby Sports Complex**
  50 Main Street
  Bellshill
  ML4
  ☎ 01236 747466

For **Motherwell Heritage Centre**
see Days Out (places to visit)

- **Motherwell Heritage Centre**
  ☎ 01698 251000

For **Shotts Heritage Centre**
see Days Out (places to visit)

- **Shotts Heritage Centre**
  ☎ 01501 821556

- **Shotts Leisure Centre**
  Benhar Road
  Shotts
  ML7
  ☎ 01698 823333

Shotts Leisure Centre is a community based indoor leisure centre offering a great range of activities. The centre has ample parking and an outdoor playground for children. There is something for everyone here, swim in the leisure pool complete with water cannons or make use of the small pool for younger children. Enrol the children – or even yourself – in our popular 'Learn to Swim' programme.

The leisure centre is open from Monday to Sunday from 9.00am–10.30pm. Come along and see what the centre has to offer.

- **Summerlee Heritage Park**
  ☎ 01236 431261

For **Summerlee Heritage Park**
see Days Out (places to visit)

- **The Time Capsule**
  ☎ 01236 449576

For **The Time Capsule**
see Days Out (places to visit)

- **Tryst Sports Centre**
  Tryst Road
  Cumbernauld
  G67
  ☎ 01236 728138

The **Tryst Sports Centre** is located in the heart of Cumbernauld, just off the A80 and is easily accessible by foot or by car, with ample car parking available. The centre boasts a 25m pool, plus a learners pool and teaching pool, all of which allow the Tryst to offer a comprehensive swimming programme.

The 'Learn to Swim' scheme with it's carefully constructed lesson structure can accommodate swimmers of all ages, levels and abilities. Commencing with parent and baby groups through to structured swimming lessons this gives the opportunity for progression into the club environment of the Cumbernauld Swimming Club.

The Tryst also offers crèche facilities and can cater for children's birthday parties. The sports centre is open Monday to Sunday from 9.00am–10.30pm.

Wishaw is one of the most comprehensive sporting complexes in central Scotland, offering an excellent range of indoor and outdoor facilities to suit both the serious competitor and the leisure seeker. The complex includes a 25 metre pool offering a wide range of activities such as aqua aerobics. There is also a teaching pool and a baby pool complete with water jets, water slides and bubble bursts. There is also a crèche within the facility which runs from Monday to Friday from 10.00am–12.00pm.

The centre is open from Monday to Sunday from 7.30am–11.00pm.

- **Wishaw Sports Centre**
  Alexander Street
  Wishaw
  ML2
  ☎ 01698 355821

Community Arts Activities

- **Jumping Beans Dance Group**
  ☎ 01236 607417

The Jumping Beans Dance Group caters for children aged between 5 and 7 years. The group studies creative dance by exploring dance themes and ideas. Technique in contemporary/jazz will also be taught. All groups are performance based and will have opportunities to work with other teachers, dancers and organisations such as Scottish Ballet, as part of their annual programme. The Jumping Beans Dance Groups meet weekly for rehearsals in venues throughout North Lanarkshire.

For more information on this class please contact the Arts Development Officer (Dance) on 01236 607417.

- **Music and Movement Classes for Younger Children**
  ☎ 01236 607417

Younger children will love this class which teaches movement in time to music. A great start for dancing boys and girls. These classes are for children from 3 to 4 years and cost £1.50 per week for a 45 minute session.

For more information on this class please contact the Arts Development Officer (Dance) on 01236 607417.

- **North Lanarkshire Children's Theatre**
  ☎ 01236 607416

North Lanarkshire Council run drama groups for children from the age of 3 up to the age of 13. It is open to all young people who are interested in drama and would enjoy being involved in performing a piece of theatre.

We offer a nursery drama class for children aged 3 to 4 years and a children's theatre group for children aged 5 to 8 years. The groups meet weekly in venues throughout North Lanarkshire.

For more information on this class please contact the Arts Development Officer (Drama) on 01236 607416.

Museums Regular Events

- **The Big Egg Event**
  ☎ 01236 431261 to confirm dates

A yearly event which takes place every Easter at Summerlee Heritage Park. In addition to our display of Easter animals there will be lots of fun and games, including quizzes, competitions, face painting, pony and cart rides and lots more. A fun day out for all the family. Call Summerlee on 01236 431261 to confirm dates.

- **Spring Fling**
  ☎ 01236 431261 to confirm dates

A real family day out for the May Bank Holiday Weekend. Two days of fun and games as the summer takes off at Summerlee! Great activities for children, as well as traction engines on parade, steam machinery and all the regular attractions. Not forgetting the huge indoor exhibition hall. Call Summerlee on 01236 431261 to confirm dates.

- **Grand Steam and Model Fair**
  ☎ 01236 431261 to confirm dates

Come along to Summerlee to celebrate steam! See steam engines of all shapes and sizes. The event has something for every child from storytelling to face painting. A great day out for adults and children alike. Call Summerlee on 01236 431261 to confirm dates.

- **Grand Summerlee Summer Funday**
  ☎ 01236 431261 to confirm dates

All the fun of the fair! Pipes and drums, grand parade hosts of entertainments and a full programme of fun and games for the children. An event not to be missed. Call Summerlee on 01236 431261 to confirm dates.

- **Summerlee's Christmas Show**
  ☎ 01236 431261 to confirm dates

Every year the Ironworks Gallery is transformed into a magical wonderland for the younger child. With a different theme each year the show welcomes all children but is especially suitable for nursery and early primary school children. Please book to avoid overcrowding. Call Summerlee on 01236 431261 to confirm dates.

Play Services Regular Events

- **Mobile Play Services**

The department offers a mobile play service which operates every year between May and August. Groups in North Lanarkshire can hire out a mobile playground (Towdabout for ages 3–10 yrs and Tadpull for ages 1–5 yrs) or skate park equipment staffed by a playworker for summer events. To check availability call Play Services on 0141 304 1894.

- **Summer Funtimes**

The Department of Community Services run summer funtimes across North Lanarkshire annually. They take place on weekdays during the school summer holidays at various locations throughout North Lanarkshire. Call Play Services on 0141 304 1894 to check when they will be in your area.

- **Playday**

Playday takes place on the first Wednesday in August at Strathclyde Country Park, Motherwell. Come along and join in with all the organised play events from face painting to craft activities and joining in our fun and games.

SPORTS REGULAR EVENTS

- **Gym Joey Classes**

These classes run at Airdrie Leisure Centre and Wishaw Sports Centre and cater for children under the age of six. Classes run every Tuesday at Airdrie Leisure Centre from 1.30pm–2.15pm and on Mondays, Tuesdays and Wednesdays at Wishaw Sports Centre from 10.00am–10.45am and 11.00am–11.45am. Places are limited, please call 01698 355821 for more information or to book a place.

- **Parent and Child Swim Classes**

These classes run at selected swimming pools throughout the Authority and cater for children under the age of 5 yrs. Places are limited, please call the Swim Development Officer on 01236 437756 for more information or to book a place.

Playschemes, Parties and Pools!

South Lanarkshire Leisure manage leisure facilities on behalf of South Lanarkshire Council and offer a varied programme of essential learning and fun activities for the under 6's, they include:

- **Playschemes and Mobile Play Service**
- **Birthday Parties**
- **Swimming Lessons**
- **Ice Skating Lessons**
- **Creche facilities**
- **Soft Play facilities**
- **Football and other sports skills programmes**

The activities are available at leisure facilities throughout the South Lanarkshire local areas of East Kilbride/Strathaven, Hamilton, Cambuslang/Rutherglen and Clydesdale.

For more information, see the listings in this guide or contact the main centres for each area:

East Kilbride/Strathaven: Dollan Aqua Centre 01355 260000
Hamilton: Blantyre Leisure Centre 01698 727800
Cambuslang/Rutherglen: Rutherglen Swimming Pool 0141 647 4530
Clydesdale: Carluke Leisure Centre 01555 751384

For information on Playschemes/Mobile Play Service contact Play Services on 01698 476112/476195

South Lanarkshire
Leisure

Delivering Services on behalf of South Lanarkshire Council

SOUTH LANARKSHIRE LEISURE

Please find in the following section listings of community and leisure facilities in South Lanarkshire

There are listings in Libraries, Sport and Leisure Facilities, Children's Activities, Birthday Parties, Crèches, Parks and Country Parks

LIBRARIES

- **Blantyre Library**
  Calder Street
  Blantyre
  ☎ 01698 823808

  Opening Times:
  Mon, Tues & Thurs 9.15am–7.30pm
  Wed & Sat 9.15am–5.00pm
  Fri 9.30am–7.30pm

- **Bothwell Library**
  Donald Institute
  Main Street
  Bothwell
  ☎ 01698 853150

  Opening Times:
  Mon, Wed & Sat 9.15am–1.00pm & 2.00pm–5.00pm
  Tues & Thurs 1.15pm–7.30pm
  Fri 9.30am–1.00pm & 2.00pm–5.00pm

- **Burnbank Library**
  76 Burnbank Centre
  Hamilton
  ☎ 01698 285730

  Opening Times:
  Mon, Wed & Sat 9.15am–1.00pm & 2.00pm–5.00pm
  Tues & Thurs 1.15pm–7.30pm
  Fri 9.30am–1.00pm & 2.00pm–5.00pm

- **Calderwood Library**
  Alison Lea
  East Kilbride
  ☎ 01355 224170

  Opening Times:
  Mon, Wed & Sat 9.15am–1.00pm & 2.00pm–5.00pm
  Tues & Thurs 1.15pm–7.30pm
  Fri 9.30am–1.00pm & 2.00pm–5.00pm

- **Cambuslang Library**
  6 Glasgow Road
  Cambuslang
  ☎ 0141 641 3909

  Opening Times:
  Mon, Tues & Thurs 9.15am–7.30pm
  Wed & Sat 9.15am–5.00pm
  Fri 9.30am–7.30pm

- **Carluke Library**
  Carnwarth Road
  Carluke
  ☎ 01555 772134

Opening Times:
Mon, Tues & Thurs 9.15am–7.30pm
Wed & Sat 9.15am–5.00pm
Fri 9.30am–7.30pm

- **Cathkin Library**
  21 Lovat Place
  Cathkin
  ☎ 0141 634 1249

Opening Times:
Mon, Tues & Thurs 9.15am–7.30pm
Wed & Sat 9.15am–5.00pm
Fri 9.30am–5.00pm

- **East Kilbride Central Library**
  Olympia
  East Kilbride
  ☎ 01355 220046

Opening Times:
Mon, Tues & Thurs 9.15am–7.30pm
Wed & Sat 9.15am–5.00pm
Fri 9.30am–7.30pm

- **Fairhill Library**
  Neilsland Road
  Hamilton
  ☎ 01698 282054

Opening Times:
Mon, Tues & Thurs 9.15am–7.30pm
Wed & Sat 9.15am–5.00pm
Fri 9.30am–5.00pm
(Fairhill closes Wed 1.00pm–2.00pm)

- **Forth Library**
  Forth Primary School
  Main Street, Forth
  ☎ 01555 811594

Opening Times:
Mon & Fri 1.30pm–7.30pm
(closed 5.00pm–5.30pm)
Tues & Thurs 9.15am–5.00pm
(closed 1.00pm–1.45pm)
Wed 9.30am–1.00pm
Sat – closed

- **Greenhills Library**
  Greenhills Shopping Centre
  East Kilbride
  ☎ 01355 242951

Opening Times:
Mon, Tues & Thurs 9.15am–7.30pm
Wed & Sat 9.15am–5.00pm
Fri 9.30am–7.30pm

- **Hamilton Central Library**
  4 Auchingramont
  Hamilton
  ☎ 01698 452411

Opening Times:
Mon, Tues & Thurs 9.15am–7.30pm
Wed & Sat 9.15am–5.00pm
Fri 9.30am–7.30pm

- **Hillhouse Library**
  Hillhouse Road
  Hamilton
  ☎ 01698 710400

Opening Times:
Mon, Tues & Thurs 9.15am–7.30pm
Wed & Sat 9.15am–5.00pm
Fri 9.30am–5.00pm

- **Kingspark Library**
  275 Castlemilk Road
  Glasgow
  ☎ 0141 632 3739

Opening Times:
Mon, Wed & Sat 9.15am–1.00pm & 2.00pm–5.00pm
Tues & Thurs 1.15pm–7.30pm
Fri 9.30am–1.00pm & 2.00pm–5.00pm

- **Lanark Library**
  16 Hope Street
  Lanark
  ☎ 01555 661144

Opening Times:
Mon, Tues & Thurs 9.15am–7.30pm
Wed & Sat 9.15am–5.00pm
Fri 9.30am–7.30pm

- **Larkhall Library**
  Muir Street
  Larkhall
  ☎ 01698 882867

Opening Times:
Mon, Tues & Thurs 9.15am–7.30pm
Wed & Sat 9.15am–5.00pm
Fri 9.30am–7.30pm

- **Lesmahagow Library**
  48 Abbeygreen
  Lesmahagow
  ☎ 01555 892606

Opening Times:
Mon, Tues & Thurs 9.15am–7.30pm
Wed & Sat 9.15am–5.00pm
Fri 9.30am–5.00pm

- **Rutherglen Library**
  163 Main Street
  Rutherglen
  ☎ 0141 613 5380

Opening Times:
Mon, Tues & Thurs 9.15am–7.30pm
Wed & Sat 9.15am–5.00pm
Fri 9.30am–7.30pm

St Leonard's Library St Leonard's Square East Kilbride ☎ 01355 241 573	Opening Times: Mon, Tues & Thurs 9.15am–7.30pm Wed & Sat 9.15am–5.00pm Fri 9.30am–7.30pm
Stonehouse Library 4/5 The Cross Stonehouse ☎ 01698 793984	Opening Times: Mon, Wed & Sat 9.15am–1.00pm & 2.00pm–5.00pm Tues & Thurs 1.15pm–7.30pm Fri 9.30am–1.00pm & 2.00pm–5.00pm
Strathaven Library Glasgow Road Strathaven ☎ 01357 521167	Opening Times: Mon, Tues & Thurs 9.15am–7.30pm Wed & Sat 9.15am–5.00pm Fri 9.30am–7.30pm
Uddingston Library 1 Main Street Uddingston ☎ 01698 813431	Opening Times: Mon, Tues & Thurs 9.15am–7.30pm Wed & Sat 9.15am–5.00pm Fri 9.30am–5.00pm
Westwood Library 121 Westwood Square East Kilbride ☎ 01355 224837	Opening Times: Mon, Wed & Sat 9.15am–1.00pm & 2.00pm–5.00pm Tues & Thurs 1.15pm–7.30pm Fri 9.30am–1.00pm & 2.00pm–5.00pm
Whitehill Library Margaret Road Hamilton ☎ 01698 283280	Opening Times: Mon, Wed & Sat 9.15am–1.00pm & 2.00pm–5.00pm Tues & Thurs 1.15pm–7.30pm Fri 9.30am–1.00pm & 2.00pm–5.00pm

MAIN SPORTS FACILITIES

- **Rutherglen Pool**
  44 Greenhill Road
  Rutherglen
  ☎ 0141 647 4530

Facilities:
25 metre pool, sauna/health suite, sunbed, baby-changing, changing rooms, showers, vending machines (hot/cold drinks and food), public telephone.
Mondays and Wednesdays adult and child swimming lessons and pre 5 swim classes.
Summer holidays – a variety of children's activities, games sessions and water safety.
Contact centre for further information, prices and booking.

- **Stonelaw Community Sports Centre**
  Calderwood Road
  Rutherglen
  ☎ 0141 647 6779 / 0141 647 4530

Facilities:
Dual use facility with main hall, 2 small halls, fitness suite, dance studio, outdoor football pitches (synthetic)

SOUTH – CLYDESDALE
SPORTS CENTRES & SWIMMING POOLS

- **Biggar Sports Centre**
  John's Loan
  Biggar
  ☎ 01899 221029

Facilities:
Dual use facility, Games Hall, changing rooms, showers, fitness gym
Children's activities during school holidays.

■ **Carluke Leisure Centre**
Carnwath Road
Carluke
☎ 01555 751384

Facilities:
Dual use facility, 25 metre pool, fitness gym, health suite (sauna/steam room/relaxation area and TV), tanning cabin, changing rooms, showers, hairdryers, two family change/group changing, theatre (full sound and lighting), games hall, gymnasium, dance studio, two committee/meeting rooms, 4 changing rooms, toilets, disabled toilets, first aid room, disabled change (shower and toilet), viewing area, vending machines (hot/cold drinks and food), public telephone, disabled parking and access.

Swimming lessons: various standards, parent and baby classes, contact centre for booking information.

Football classes boys and girls, Fit Kids classes, Olympic gymnastics.

Playschemes during school holidays. Contact centre for further information.

Birthday parties: various types of parties available – football, games pool, pirates etc. Contact centre for prices and booking.

■ **Coalburn Leisure Complex**
School Road
Coalburn
☎ 01555 820848

Facilities:
20 metre pool with spa, baby changing units, showers, fitness gym, sauna/health suite, sunbed, vending machines (hot/cold drinks and food), games hall, creche, meeting/training room, cafe area (50's Diner theme), beauty therapy, satellite TV, public telephone.

Children's Activities
Creche available Tuesday and Thursday 10.00am–12.00pm and 12.30pm–2.00pm (0-5 years)

Playschemes organised during school holidays. (5–12 years)

Parent and toddler coached swim classes (3 month–5 years)

Pool fun sessions during school holidays and every Sunday. (Children under 8 must be accompanied by an adult)

Pool Disco/Pool Fun nights (alternate Fridays) children under 8 must be accompanied by an adult.

Swimming lessons for 5–16 year olds and Pre School Swim Lessons 3–5 years.

Birthday parties available in the sports hall or a beach pool party.

Contact the centre for further information prices and booking details.

- **Forth Sports & Community Centre**
  Main Street
  Forth
  ☎ 01555 812058

Facilities:
Games Hall, fitness club, creche, community rooms, kitchen and function area

Creche open 10.00am–12.00pm Monday, Tuesday, Wednesday: Thursday 10.00am–1.00pm, Friday 10.00am–12.00pm, Wednesday evening 6.00pm–8.00pm.

Children's classes and activities - pre 5 football, Cool Kidz Club, trampolining, Recreation Club, Little Monkeys Club (bouncy castle, face painting etc) Junior Badminton, Dance Classes, gymnastics.

Birthday Parties available at weekends, a variety of different packages.

Contact centre for further information, prices and booking.

- **Lanark Pool**
  South Vennel
  Lanark
  ☎ 01555 666800

Facilities: 25 metre pool, changing rooms, showers, fitness gym, sauna/health suite, public telephone, sunbed.

Parent and baby swim lessons
Splash club water confidence
Pre 5 swim lessons
Playschemes during school holidays.
Fun sessions and themed nights.

Birthday parties: pool parties 1–1.5 hour's pool time 1 hour self-catering. 4–10 year olds maximum 35 kids, 1 adult to 5 kids under 8.

Contact centre for prices, further information and booking.

- **Leisuredome**
  Thornton Road
  Kirkmuirhill
  ☎ 01555 893093

Facilities:
Games Hall, changing rooms, showers, creche, fitness gym, cafeteria.

Creche open
Monday – Friday 10.00am–12.00pm,
Tuesday 2.00pm–4.00pm,
Thursday 1.00pm–3.00pm.

Childrens activities pre 5's soft play, gymnastics, football coaching, youth club.

Playschemes available during school holidays.

Birthday Parties available at weekends, a variety of packages available.

Contact the centre for further information, prices and booking.

South – East Kilbride
Sports Centres and Swimming Pools

■ **Dollan Aqua Centre**
Town Centre Park
Brouster Hill
East Kilbride
☎ 01355 260000

Facilities: - 50 metre pool (can be split into 2 separate pools), baby-changing, cafeteria, changing rooms, showers, committee/meeting room, crèche, floating floor, flume/tyre ride, health studio, high-tech fitness gym, jacuzzi, kiddies pool, public telephone, sauna/health suite, soft play area, sunbed.

Children's Activities.
Small Fry's Creche:
Available Monday – Friday 9.15am–1.45pm, Saturday 9.15am–11.45am.
Dolphin Domain Softplay:
Available Monday – Friday 2.00pm–5.00pm, Saturday 12.00pm–5.00pm,
Sunday 10.00am–5.00pm.

Swimming lessons available for pre school swimming 3–4 years and 4 years+ group swimming lessons.

Birthday Parties: These are available at weekends, various packages to choose from.

Contact the centre for further information and booking details.

■ **Duncanrig Sports Centre**
Alberta Avenue
Westwood
East Kilbride
☎ 01355 248922
(evenings and weekends)

Facilities:
Dual use facility with games hall, fitness gym, gymnasiums, grass rugby pitch, blaes running track, blaes hockey and football pitch, changing facilities.

Various classes suitable for children including judo and children's playschemes during school holidays.

Birthday parties available at weekends, various packages from football, bouncy castle and trampoline. Contact the centre for further information, prices and booking details.

- **East Kilbride Ice Rink**
  Olympia Centre
  East Kilbride
  ☎ 01355 244065

Facilities:
Skating rink (inc. curling) situated in the heart of the Olympia Shopping Mall. Foodcourts and shopping area.

Learn to Skate Courses from 5yrs+ Sunday evenings. Courses run throughout the year.

- **Greenhills Sports Centre**
  Stroud Road
  Greenhills
  East Kilbride
  ☎ 01355 221003

Facilities:
Badminton courts, basketball courts, five-a-side football, handball court, indoor hockey, main hall, indoor netball court, indoor tennis court, volleyball court, changing rooms, showers.

East Kilbride Gymnastic Club based at the centre covering general gymnastics and sports acrobatics.

Holiday Playschemes operate during school holidays and a weekly children's activity session during term time.

Pre school gymnastics classes available on a weekly basis.

For further information contact the centre for details and prices.

Facilities:
Athletics track, badminton courts, basketball courts, five-a-side football, blaes football pitch, gymnasium, handball court, health studio, main hall, netball court, shape-up suite, squash court, tennis court, volleyball court, committee/meeting room, general purpose room, crèche, first aid room, changing rooms, showers.

Children's Activities
Play Services: Playschemes organised during the summer, October and Easter holiday period for 5–12 years.

Sports Development Activities
Mini Movers 18 months–3 years
Pre School Gymnastics 3–5years
Trampoline Classes 5 years+
Junior Badminton 5 years+
Junior Judo 5 years+
Junior Football Skills 5 years+
Specific sports courses organised during school holidays 5 years+
Activities organised by John Wright Sports Centre.

Birthday parties open to all age groups (various packages)
Creche appointments every morning of the week Monday – Friday and a Tuesday/Wednesday afternoon. (Booking required)
Superkids Classes – fun sports circuits skipping, running, ball skills etc 5–8 years.

■ **John Wright Sports Centre**
Calderwood Road
Calderwood
East Kilbride
☎ 01355 237731

- **St Andrew's Sports Centre**
  Scholar's Gate
  Whitehills
  East Kilbride
  ☎ 01355 230020
  (Evenings and weekends)

Facilities:
Dual use centre with badminton courts, basketball court, five-a-side football, netball court, volleyball court, gymnasium, synthetic football pitch, committee/meeting room, changing rooms, showers.

Various Clubs are available suitable for children: Dance Classes, Aikido, Tae Kwon Do.

Birthday parties available on Sundays, various packages available from football, bouncy castle and trampoline. Contact centre for information, prices and booking details.

- **Stewartfield Community Centre**
  3 MacNeish Way
  East Kilbride
  ☎ 01355 227888

Facilities:
Sports/community centre with badminton courts, five-a-side, netball court, volleyball court, committee/meeting room, kitchen and bar facilities. Changing rooms and showers.

Various childrens classes; Tae Kwon Do, Judo, Pre School Gymnastics, Drama Club, Dance Classes and Football Skills.

The centre is available for evening functions (weddings, dances, ceilidh and children's birthday parties). Various packages available, contact centre for information prices and booking.

Facilities:
Dual use facility, 20 metre pool with pool hoist, baby-changing, vending machines, changing rooms, family changing rooms, showers, disabled change and toilet, committee/meeting room, crèche, sauna/health suite, high-tech fitness gym, jacuzzi, sunbed.

Tourist Information telephone point. Car parking with disabled spaces.

Swimming lessons available for 4–16 year olds. Pre school and water confidence swim classes aimed at 3–5 year olds. (Booking essential)

Fun pool sessions with the Aqua Run and Pool Discos on Fridays. Inflatable fun sessions at weekends.

Pre school gymnastics for under 5's, courses held throughout the year.

Judo classes for 5 year olds+ available weekly.

Sports Coaching sessions available during school holidays covering Judo, Soccer Skills, Trampolining, Basketball and Swimming lessons.

Creche available Mon – Fri, 10.15am–11.45am. The creche is supervised by qualified staff.

Birthday parties are available in a variety of packages from football, bouncy castle, trampoline and pool party.

Contact centre for further information, prices and booking.

■ **Strathaven Leisure Centre**
Bowling Green Road
off Townhead Street
Strathaven
East Kilbride
☎ 01357 522820

North – Hamilton
Sports Centres and Swimming Pools

- **Blantyre Leisure Centre**
  Glasgow Road
  Blantyre
  ☎ 01698 727800

Facilities:
25 metre pool (with pool hoist), teaching pool, four court activity hall, hi-tech gym, spinfit studio, aerobics studio, sauna/health suite, free-weights gym, squash court, soft play area, sunbeds and tan stand, beauty therapy workshop, committee/meeting room, cafeteria, baby changing, changing rooms, shower, crèche, public telephone, public lifts, photo kiosk, car parking. flume, tyre ride, jacuzzi, kiddies pool, health studio, sauna/health suite, high-tech fitness gym, soft play area, sunbed, cafeteria, committee/meeting room, baby-changing, changing rooms, showers, crèche, public telephone.

Gymnastic Club 6 years+ children work towards BAGA awards.

Gym Tots 2–4 year olds qualified coaching in a fun and safe environment.

Trampolining Club 5–9 years trampolining sessions where children work towards certificate gradings.

Fit Kidz 5–12 years. Qualified coaches encourage children in fitness and exercise techniques.

Parent and Tot swim sessions designed to give children water confidence.

Creche Monday – Friday 9.30am–1.00pm. Maximum time 2 hours. 2–5 years old

Contact the centre for further information.

- **Eddlewood Sportsbarn**
  Devonhill Avenue
  Hamilton
  ☎ 01698 422991

Facilities:
Sport/function hall, 6-station gymnasium, and shower/changing room changing facilities for disabled.

■ **Hamilton Palace Sports Grounds**
Motehill
Hamilton
☎ 01698 424101 or 01698 459447

Facilities:
One of the largest outdoor facilities in Scotland with numerous floodlit synthetic courts suitable for 5's, 7's and basketball, netball and hockey. Tennis courts. Grass full sized pitches for football and rugby. Bowling with pavilion. Modern changing pavilions with showers and vending facilities.

■ **Hamilton Water Palace**
35 Almada Street
Hamilton
☎ 01698 459950

Facilities:
25 metre pool (floating floor), leisure pool (comprising of flume, tyre slide, lazy river, bubble beds, bubble pool, water curtain, geysers, children's play pool and outdoor pool), health suite (comprising of sauna, steam room, jacuzzi and relaxation area with satellite television), sunbeds, Body Workshop (beauty therapy, aromatherapy and reflexology), fitness suite, cafeteria, changing rooms (including group, disabled and family changing), baby changing, showers, first aid room, spectator gallery, car parking (including disabled spaces) and public telephones.

■ **Hareleeshill Sportsbarn**
Donaldson Road
Larkhall
☎ 01698 887917

Facilities:
Sports/function hall, 11-station multi-gym, sunbed, showers/changing room, and kitchen facilities changing facilities for disabled.

■ **Jock Stein Sportsbarn**
Hillhouse Road
Hamilton
☎ 01698 828488

Facilities:
Basketball and badminton courts, changing rooms, showers, blaes football pitch, main hall, and public telephone

- **Larkhall Leisure Centre**
  Broomhill Road
  Larkhall
  ☎ 01698 881742

Facilities:
25 metre pool (floating floor), badminton courts, fitness gym, lesser hall, main hall, soft play area, squash court, baby-changing, changing rooms, showers, disabled toilets, public telephone.
Swimming lessons, Tae Kwon Do, Judo available at various times weekly.
Birthday parties available in the Pirate Bay and Ballpit, Bouncy Castle.
Contact the centre for further information, prices and booking.

The Glasgow Guide for Parents and Carers

2005 edition

NOTE TO ADVERTISERS

If you were not listed in ***The Glasgow Guide for Parents and Carers*** 2004 (2nd) edition, don't worry. Have your business or service listed in ***The Glasgow Guide for Parents and Carers*** 2005 (3rd) edition. Fill in your details below and return by the 30th September 2004 to:

Glasgow Under 6's Ltd
48 Flenders Avenue
Clarkston
Glasgow, G76 7XZ
Tel/Fax 0141 616 3661
E: glasgowunder6s@fsmail.net

Name of Business & Contact Name . . . .

Address . . . .

. . . .

Postcode . . . . Tel/Fax No. . . . .

Email . . . . www . . . .

PLEASE TICK BELOW

Free Listing ❑

Request advertising details ❑

NOTE TO READERS

We would like to hear your comments and suggestions for our 2005 edition. These should be sent to **Glasgow Under 6's Ltd** at the address above.

Days Out (places to visit)

Please find included in the following section listings of Days Out (places to visit) for all ages

- **Country Parks**
- **Farm Parks**
- **Historic Scotland Sites**
- **National Trust for Scotland Sites**
- **Wildlife Parks**
- **Zoos**

And many more...

For more Places to Visit *see* Community & Leisure (local authority)

Please find in the following section a selection of listings for Days Out (places to visit) in and around Glasgow for all the family.

In addition to some local attractions we have also included others further afield.

Many of the entries in this section have the facility to cater for children's birthday parties, but please check directly with the venue itself.

Information on The National Trust for Scotland was kindly supplied to Glasgow Under 6's by The National Trust for Scotland Headquarters at Greenbank House, Flenders Road, Clarkston.

For listings in Sports & Leisure Facilities, Libraries, Museums, Community Art and Parks & Country Parks *see* COMMUNITY & LEISURE *(LOCAL AUTHORITY)*

For Children's Birthday Parties *see* BIRTHDAY PARTIES (*CHILDREN'S ENTERTAINERS, CHILDREN'S BOWLING & ENTERTAINMENT CENTRES, BOUNCY CASTLES & INFLATABLES, CHILDRENS ACTIVITY & ADVENTURE CENTRES) AND* RESTAURANTS *(COFFEE & FAMILY EATING OUT)*

Almond Valley is open every day of the year (except December 25 & 26 and January 1 & 2) from 10.00am–5.00pm

There is an admission charge and children must be accompanied by an adult

There is an additional charge for trailer or train rides that operate every weekend between Easter and September and daily during most of July and August

Group discounts rates are available to those booking in advance

A wide range of special demonstrations and resources are available to visiting school groups: please contact directly for further details

We also run memorable birthday parties

Almond Valley is only 30 miles from Glasgow and 15 miles from Edinburgh

No matter what the season there is always something happening at Almond Valley and regardless of the weather there are always discoveries to be made and activities to be enjoyed by every member of the family

- **Almond Valley Heritage Trust**
  Museum, Farm & Discovery Centre
  Millfield
  Livingston Village
  Livingston
  West Lothian
  EH54 7AR
  ☎ 01506 414957

For **The Apollo** *see* BIRTHDAY PARTIES (CHILDRENS ACTIVITY & ADVENTURE CENTRES)

- **The Apollo**
  ☎ 01294 471777

The **Aquatec** is host to a wide range of leisure activities and includes a leisure pool and ice rink. The leisure pool is packed with fun and includes flumes, river rapids and a baby pool where you can watch the children at play! The ice rink has a range of unique features from the fibre optic light tunnel, ice trails, trees and a log fire. It's fun for all the family. The centre also includes a soft play area designed for our younger customers, aiding them to develop their imaginations. Enjoy the chutes, clamber space, colour areas and puzzles, all in the safest surroundings. The centre is open Monday to Sunday from 10.00am–10.30pm.

- **Aquatec**
  Menteith Road
  Motherwell
  ML11AZ
  ☎ 01698 276464

- **Argyll Wildlife Park**
  Dalehenna
  Inveraray
  Argyll
  PA32 8XT
  ☎ 01499 302264

Opening Times:
7 days, 10.00am–5.00pm, Easter to October
55 acres of ground including nature walks, where the animals come to meet you
Admission charge, discounts for parties
Café and small gift shop
Baby changing & disabled facilities

- **Auchingarrich Wildlife Centre**
  Comrie
  Perthshire
  PH6 2JS
  ☎ 01764 679469
  Email: auchingarrich@wilton.sol.co.uk

Opening Times:
Mid-March to Mid-November
Huge play barn with real tractors, sand-pit and swings
Fishing – Rod hire & tuition available
Woodland walks, picnic tables and barbecues, toilets and facilities for the disabled,
Free parking & coaches welcome
Also bring your child to the hatchery and they can handle our small animals and watch our chicks hatching

- **Blair Drummond Safari and Adventure Park**
  Near Stirling
  Scotland
  FK9 4UR
  ☎ 01786 841456

Opening Times:
20 March to 4 October, 7 days
10.00am–5.30pm
Attractions included within the Safari Park are a Pets Farm, Children's Play Area with Pirate Ship, a Sea Lion Show, Penguins, or take a boat trip round Chimp Island, picnic benches are available around the grassy areas and there are DIY barbecues available throughout the park in the picnic areas
There are also rides, slides, a bouncy castle, face painting and other attractions
Restaurant facilities and gift shop
Baby changing and disabled facilities

Open Easter to end of October every weekend and daily throughout July and August.

Bo'ness is on the south shore of the River Forth, 8 miles west of the Forth Road Bridge. From the east leave the M9 at J3 and follow A904 to Bo'ness.
From the west leave the M9 at J5 and follow the signs to Bo'ness on the A904.
In Bo'ness follow our brown tourist signs

- **Bo'ness & Kinneil Railway**
  ☎ 01506 822298
  www.srps.org.uk

Why not take your children to visit **Burngreen Recreation Park** in Kilsyth. Instead of jumping on the beds they can jump on trampolines or cycle round the enclosed bicycle park (bicycles and helmets are available for hire). There is also putting, tennis, table tennis and a football pitch. Within the park there is free parking, picnic areas and toilet facilities. Burngreen Recreation Park is a great place for kids and adults alike.

- **Burngreen Recreation Park**
  Burngreen
  Kilsyth
  G65

Opening Times:
Mon – Thu, Sat 10.00am–5.00pm,
Fri & Sun 11.00am–5.00pm
Closed 25 & 26 December, 1 & 2 January.
A ten minute walk from Pollokshaws West Rail Station, or 15 minute walk from Shawlands Rail Station.

- **The Burrell Collection**
  Pollok Country Park
  2060 Pollokshaws Road
  Glasgow
  G41 1AT
  ☎ 0141 287 2550
  🖹 0141 287 2597

Facilities: 18 hole golf course, one of the finest municipal courses in central Scotland. Changing rooms, showers and public telephone.
Children's play area, gardens, small zoo, conservatory, visitor centre, woodland walks, picnic areas, car parking.
A variety of events are organised throughout the year contact the Ranger Service for more information.

- **Calderglen Country Park**
  Strathaven Road
  East Kilbride
  ☎ 01355 236644

■ **Clydebuilt**
Scottish Maritime Museum at Braehead
☎ 0141 886 1013

Opening Times:
Mon, Thurs & Sat 10.00am–6.00pm
Fri – closed
Sun & Bank Holidays 11.00am–5.00pm
Admission prices:
Adult £3.50, Child £1.75, Concession £1.75, Family (2 adults + 2 children) £8.00

The museum is home to M.V. 'Kyles', the oldest Clydebuilt vessel still afloat in the UK. She is now moored only minutres from where she was built by Fullerton's of Paisley.

■ **Culzean Castle & Country Park**
(The National Trust for Scotland)
Maybole
South Ayrshire
KA19 8LE
For functions, events and Eisenhower Apartment
☎ 01655 884455
www.culzeancastle.net

For group/school bookings, ranger service and Country Park information ☎ 01655 884400
Opening Times:
Castle 1 April – 31 October, daily 10.30am–5.00pm (last entry 4.00pm)
Visitor Centre 1 April – 31 October, daily 9.00am–5.30pm
1 Nov – 31 March Sat & Sun, 11.00am–4.00pm
Other visitor facilities 1 April – 31 October, daily 10.30am–5.00pm
Country Park all year 9.30am – sunset
12m S of Ayr, on A719, 4m W of Maybole, off A77. 4m from National Cycle Route 7. Bus passes main entrance

■ **The David Livingstone Centre**
(The National Trust for Scotland)
165 Station Road
Blantyre
Just off M74, junction 5
☎ 01698 823140

Opening Times:
1 April – 24 December, Mon – Sat 10.00am–5.00pm,Sun 12.30pm–5.00pm
Scotland's most famous explorer and missionary was born in this historic tenement home in 1813.

Today his birthplace commemorates his life and work with exhibits including fascinating personal belongings and scientific equipment, shop, café and adventure playground.

- **Dean Castle Country Park**
  Dean Road
  Kilmarnock
  KA3 1XB
  ☎ 01563 554733

Opening Times:
April to end October the castle is open 7 days 12.00pm–5.00pm.
In winter the castle is open weekends only 12.00pm–4.00pm
Visitor centre and Country Park open all year 11.00am–5.00pm
Disabled parking and toilets
Cafe facilities

- **Deep Sea World**
  North Queensferry
  Fife
  KY11 1JR
  ☎ 01383 411880

Opening Times:
Open all year Peak 10.00am–6.00pm,
Off Peak 11.00am–5.00pm
Disabled facilities include toilets, free wheelchair hire & ramps leading to main walkway
Baby changing facilities
Lagoon café & gift shop

- **Drumpellier Country Park**
  Townhead Road
  Coatbridge
  ML5 1RX
  ☎ 01236 422257

Drumpellier Country Park is situated within North Lanarkshire, to the west of Coatbridge and east of Glasgow. Formerly a private estate, the land was given over as a public park in 1919. It was designated as a Country Park in 1984. The Country Park offers a wide range of activities including the visitors centre, café and Countryside Rangers service. There is also a road train, angling, boating, nature trail, golf course and driving range, pets corner, birdwatching hide and play areas.

The park is open from dawn to dusk all year round. The visitors centre operates seasonal opening hours and is open during April and May from 11.00am–4.00pm, June to August from 10.30am–7.45pm and September to March from 12.00pm–4.00pm and admission is free!

EDINBURGH BUTTERFLY & INSECT WORLD

- **Edinburgh Butterfly & Insect World**
  Dobbies Garden World
  Melville Nursery
  Lasswade
  Midlothian
  EH18 1AZ
  ☎ 0131 663 4932
  www.edinburgh-butterfly-world.co.uk

Open all year
9.30am–5.30pm seven days
10.00am–5.00pm in winter
Closed 25 & 26 December and 1 January
Full disabled access and facilities
Free-flying exotic butterflies in a large indoor rainforest. Walk through this tropical paradise and observe hundreds of stunning butterflies as they fly around you, feeding from flowers and laying eggs. Iguanas roam free through the jungle flora, and a hummingbird can be spotted darting in and out of the flowers looking for nectar.

The 'Bugs and Beasties' exhibition includes tarantulas, stick insects, leaf-cutting ants, scorpions and frogs. There are twice daily 'Meet the Beasties' handling sessions, and a unique Scottish Honey Bee display with regular activities.

The Reptile Room displays lizards, chameleons and giant pythons.

In the dark of the nocturnal zone the bugs and beasties can be seen going about their night time activities. The Leaf Cutter Ants nest is in here, along with scorpions that glow in the dark!

Located just off the Edinburgh City Bypass, (A720), facilities include Scotland's largest garden centre, restaurant, play and picnic areas and free parking. Full disabled access.

- **Edinburgh Castle**
  In the centre of Edinburgh
  ☎ 0131 225 9846

Opening Times:
All year 7 days a week
April to September 9.30am–6.00pm,
October – March 9.30am–5.00pm
Last ticket sold 45 minutes before closing
Closed Christmas Day and Boxing Day
Shop and castle café

- **Edinburgh Zoo**
  Corstorphine Road
  Edinburgh
  EH12 6TS
  ☎ 0131 334 9171

Opening Times:
Open 9.00am every day of the year, including Christmas Day, and closing at;
6.00pm (April – September)
5.00pm (October and March) and
4.30pm (November – February)
Scotland's largest and most exciting wildlife attraction. Discover over 1,000 animals from all over the world including many endangered species like the tigers, red pandas and rhinos, as well as the ever-popular penguins, giraffes and chimpanzees. Take the hilltop safari for a fun ride to the top of the hill and don't miss the penguin parade every day at 2.15pm (April – October). For children, we offer pushchair hire, highchairs and special kiddies menus in all our cafeterias, as well as new play areas and lots of fun activities like Animal Antics and Close Encounters. Please call 0131 314 0336 for details of our children's birthday parties.

- **The Falkirk Wheel**
  Lime Road
  Tamfourhill
  Falkirk
  FK1 4RS
  ☎ 08700 500208

The world's first and only rotating boatlift is open all year

For information on boat trip times, charges and events call the booking line on 08700 500208. Advance bookings are recommended as daily availability cannot be guaranteed
How to get there from Glasgow: From the M80/A80 follow signs for Falkirk and follow the brown and white tourist signs for The Falkirk Wheel

■ **Fossil Grove**
Victoria Park
Glasgow
G14 1BN
☎ 0141 287 2000

Opening Times:
Open daily 12noon–5pm April – September, closed October – March

■ **Gallery of Modern Art**
Queen Street
Glasgow
G1 3AZ
☎ 0141 229 1996
🖹 0141 204 5316

Opening Times:
Mon – Thu, Sat 10.00am–5.00pm,
Fri & Sun 11.00am–5.00pm
Closed 25 & 26 December, 1 & 2 January.
Located in the city centre close to Queen Street, Argyle Street and Central Rail Stations, and Buchanan Street and St Enoch's Underground Stations.

■ **Geilston Garden**
(The National Trust for Scotland)
Off the A814 at West End of Cardross
8m North of Glasgow
☎ 01389 849187

Opening Times:
Daily 1 April – 31 October 9.30am–5.00pm daily
House not open
A delightful garden, typical of the small country estates on the banks of the Clyde, purchased by merchants and industrialists in the 18th and 19th centuries.

Enjoy the attractive walled garden and follow the burn as it winds through the wooded glen

■ **Glasgow Science Centre**
50 Pacific Quay
Glasgow
G51 1EA
☎ 0141 420 5000

Opening Times:
The Mall 10.00am–6.00pm daily,
The Imax 11.00am–6.00pm daily
The Tower contact directly for opening times
Closed 25 & 26 December and 1 January
Café brasserie, coffee bar & shop
Baby changing & disabled facilities
A loop system is available in the theatre for the hard of hearing Under 3's are free
Burthday party facilities available

Visit the Scottish Power Space Theatre, one of the finest planetariums in Europe, situated within The Mall

- **Gorgie City Farm**
  51 Gorgie Road
  Edinburgh
  EH11 2LA
  ☎ 0131 337 4202

Opening Times:
7 days, 9.00am–4.30pm, March – October
9.30am–4.00pm, November – February
Admission is free
Visit the farm and meet all the animals, cows, goats, pigs, sheep, hens and ducks
Visit the Pet Lodge and see all our smaller animals
There is a play park and picnic benches
Café and parking facilities
Baby changing and disabled facilities

- **Gogglebox (Soft Play)**
  ☎ 01436 670909

For **Gogglebox** *see* BIRTHDAY PARTIES (CHILDREN'S ACTIVITY & ADVENTURE CENTRES)

- **Greenbank Garden**
  (The National Trust for Scotland)
  Flenders Road
  Off Mearns Road
  Clarkston
  ☎ 0141 616 5126

Off M77 and A726, 6m south of Glasgow City Centre
A unique walled garden with plants and designs of special interest to suburban gardeners. Fountains, woodland walk and special area for disabled visitors.
Gardening demonstrations and social events throughout the year.
Shop, tearoom and plant sales.
Opening Times:
Garden all year, daily 9.30am – sunset
Shop & Tearoom, 1 November – 31 March
Sat & Sun 2.00pm–4.00pm,
1 April – 31 October daily 11.00am–5.00pm
House 1 April – 31 October every Sun
2.00pm – 4.00pm

- **Heads of Ayr Park**
  Dunure Road
  Ayr
  KA7 4LD
  ☎ 01292 441210

Opening Times: April – October daily
10.00am–5.00pm
Admission charge, group rates available
Disabled & baby changing facilities
Café & gift shop
Enjoy our giant trampoline and quad bikes, indoor & outdoor play areas, climbing wall, combine castle, summer sledging, activity tower and then visit our exotic animals

- **The Hill House**
  (The National Trust for Scotland)
  Upper Colquhoun Street
  Helensburgh
  Off B832, between A82 and A814 23m North-West of Glasgow
  ☎ 01436 673900

Opening Times: 1 April – 31 October, daily
1.30pm–5.30pm.
Groups should be pre-booked
Weekday morning visits available for pre-booked groups
The finest of Charles Rennie Mackintosh's domestic creations, this inspiring house was commissioned in 1902 by publisher Walter Blackie, and still looks startlingly modern. Mackintosh and his wife Margaret also designed the interior fittings and decorative schemes. Exciting exhibition of new designers' work;

Shops with exclusive craft products;
Macallan 'Taste of Scotland' tearoom

- **Holmwood House**
  (The National Trust for Scotland)
  61–3 Netherlee Road
  Cathcart
  Glasgow
  ☎ 0141 637 2129

Sign posted from Clarkston Road, B767, 4m south of Glasgow City Centre
Opening Times:
1 April – 31 October, daily 12.00pm–5.00pm
Morning visits available for pre-booked groups
Possibly the finest domestic design by Alexander 'Greek' Thomson, Glasgow's greatest Victorian architect, this villa was built in 1857–8 for a local mill owner.

Inside, visitors can see restoration work on Thomson's rich neo-classical ornamentation and decoration.

Attractive riverside grounds, audio tour, exhibition and study rooms.

- **Hutcheson's Hall**
  (The National Trust for Scotland)
  158 Ingram Street
  Near South-East corner of George Square, Glasgow
  ☎ 0141 552 8391

Opening Times:
Gallery, shop and function hall
20 January – 24 December, Mon – Sat
10.00am–5.00pm
Hall on view subject to functions in progress
One of the most elegant buildings in the City Centre, the Hall was designed in 1802–5 by David Hamilton. Major reconstruction in 1876 resulted in today's elegant interior. Exciting multi-media exhibition, Glasgow Style, and work for sale by young designers from this vibrant city

- **The Inveraray Maritime Museum / West of Scotland Maritime Experience**
  The Pier
  Front Street
  Inveraray
  PA32 8UY
  ☎ 01499 302213

Opening Times:
7 days, April – September 10.00am–6.00pm,
October – March 10.00am–5.00pm
School Parties welcome
Gift shop, admission prices, 10% discount available for parties

- **James Hamilton Heritage Park**
  Stewartfield Way
  East Kilbride
  ☎ 01355 276611

Facilities:
Adventure playground, bird hide and sanctuary, boating pond, bumper boats, fun canoes, pedalos, rowing boats, watersports, picnic area, cafeteria, changing rooms, showers, baby-changing, public telephone.

- **Kelburn Castle & Country Centre**
  Fairlie
  By Largs
  Ayrshire
  KA29 0BE
  ☎ 01475 568685
  www.kelburncountrycentre.com

Opening Times:
Castle 10.00am–6.00pm, daily,
26 June – 5 September
Centre 10.00am–6.00pm, daily
3 April – 31 October
In winter only grounds and riding school open 11.00am – dusk
A78 between Largs and Fairlie

The Natural Place to go
The family home of the Earls of Glasgow, **Kelburn Castle and Country Centre** has long been an inspiration for adults and a paradise for children. Explore the Secret Forest, brave the Adventure Courses, saddle up at the Riding and Trekking Centre, learn about Falconry, join a Pottery Workshop, or a Countryside Ranger-led activity, experience the unique Kelburn Glen and soak up the history of the Earls of Glasgow, still living in the castle after 800 years. There is a Soft Play Area for young children, a Pets Corner, licensed cafe and gift shop.

- **Kelvingrove Art Gallery and Museum**
  Kelvingrove
  Glasgow
  G3 8AG
  ☎ 0141 287 2699
  🖷 0141 287 2690

Opening Times:
Mon – Thu, Sat 10.00am–5.00pm,
Fri & Sun 11.00am–5.00pm
Closed 25 & 26 December, 1 & 2 January.
Conveniently located near Kelvin Hall Underground Station. A 15 minute walk from Partick Rail Station. Information on public bus services call Traveline 0870 608 2608.

New Century Project
Kelvingrove Art Gallery and Museum has won the largest Heritage Lottery grant ever awarded in Scotland, £12.8m. The completion of the £25 million New Century Project will take Kelvingrove from its early 20th century beginnings, into the 21st century with new emphasis on education and interactive displays, bringing history and art to life.

The refurbished venue will feature 35% more display space and ground level access into the building for the first time by opening up the current lower ground floor to the public. There will be better access around the building for disabled people and greater freedom to display more of the city's wide-ranging collections.

To carry out the necessary building and display works the museum will have to close in summer 2003 for over two years, re-opening early in 2006. However, favourites from the collections, by artists such as Rembrandt, Van Gogh and the Glasgow Boys, will be displayed at the McLellan Galleries during the closure period.

- **Kittochside**
  The Museum of Country Life
  (The National Trust for Scotland)
  Stewartfield Way
  East Kilbride
  Glasgow
  G76 9HR
  ☎ 01355 224181

Opening Times:
All year, daily 10.00am–5.00pm
Closed 25 & 26 December, and 1 & 2 January
Created in partnership with the National Museums of Scotland, this living museum illustrated changes in Scottish farming over the last 300 years. The farm will be worked using techniques and equipment of the 1950s, and special events will illustrate life in the countryside. Café & shop

Between A726 and A749; from M74, turn off at junction 5; from M77, turn off at junction 3

- **Loudoun Castle Family Theme Park**
  Galston
  Ayrshire
  KA4 8PE
  ☎ 01563 822296
  Email:
  loundouncastle@btinternet.com
  www.loudouncastle.co.uk

Opening Times:
Easter to September 10.00am–5.00pm daily (subject to change)

Set in over 500 acres of majestic Ayrshire countryside, **Loudoun Castle** is Scotland's biggest and safest family theme park. Relax and picnic in the Park then try a whole host of new rides, to suit all ages, for 2004 including; 'Dougal McDougal's' Mini-Tractor and Pony rides, new 'live' entertainment featuring 'Rory', and the famous 'Lion of 'Loudoun' and his friends, new and exciting Rare Breeds, Birds of Prey and Bouncy Castles. Add to that mouthwatering food outlets throughout the park and you can see how it can be a 'grrreat' day out at Loudoun. It will certainly give their mouths 'something to shout about!'

Visit the website or give us a call for opening details and prices

Opening Times:
Mon – Thu, Sat 10.00am–4.00pm,
Fri & Sun 11.00am–4.00pm
Information on public bus services.
Call Traveline 0870 608 2608

General Information
The **Martyrs' Public School**, in the Townhead area of Glasgow, was opened in 1897. Charles Rennie Mackintosh was closely involved in the design of Martyrs' School and this is perhaps the first building where we are able to recognise his distinctive architectural personality. Martyrs' School is home to Glasgow's Open Museum, which aims to take Glasgow Museums' exhibits into the community.

- **Martyrs' School/Open Museum**
  Parson Street
  Glasgow
  G4 0PX
  ☎ 0141 552 2356

For **Mega Mania Play Space** *see* BIRTHDAY PARTIES (CHILDREN'S ACTIVITY & ADVENTURE CENTRES)

- **Mega Mania Play Space**
  ☎ 01563 570424

For **Megazone** *see* BIRTHDAY PARTIES (BOWLING & ENTERTAINMENT CENTRES)

- **Megazone (laser games)**
  ☎ 01324 634828

Opening Times:
Mon – Thu, Sat 10.00am–5.00pm,
Fri & Sun 11.00am–5.00pm
Closed 25 & 26 December, 1 & 2 January.
A five minute walk from Cowcaddens Underground, or a ten minute walk from Charing Cross or Queen Street stations.

- **McLellan Galleries**
  270 Sauchiehall Street
  Glasgow
  G2 3EH
  ☎ 0141 331 1854
  🖹 0141 332 9957

- **Motherwell Heritage Centre**
  High Road
  Motherwell
  ML1 3HU
  ☎ 01698 251000

Discover the heritage of the area's past in the Technopolis multimedia experience. Or search out your family tree in the local history room. Then take in the sweeping panorama of the Clyde Valley from the centre's fifth floor viewing platform. The heritage centre is a fully hands on interactive display on the area's past. It leads the visitor from the coming of the Romans, through the agricultural period to the iron and steel industries.
Admission is free!
Opening hours are as follows:
10.00am–5.00pm (Thurs 7.00pm), Wed – Sat and Sun from 12.00pm–5.00pm.
Closed on Mon and Tues
The heritage centre offers a wide programme of activites throughout the year for children from traditional games, craft sessions and heritage workshops. Activities are either free of charge or carry only a modest charge for materials. Come along and join the fun!

- **Museum of Transport**
  Kelvin Hall
  1 Bunhouse Road
  Glasgow
  G3 8DP
  ☎ 0141 287 2720
  🖷 0141 287 2692

Opening Times:
Mon – Thu, Sat 10.00am–5.00pm,
Fri & Sun 11.00am–5.00pm
Closed 25 & 26 December, 1 & 2 January.
Conveniently located near Kelvin Hall Underground station. A 15 minute walk from Partick rail station.

- **New Lanark World Heritage Village**
  New Lanark Mills
  Lanark
  ML11 9DB
  ☎ 01555 661345
  www.newlanark.org

Visit **New Lanark World Heritage Village** with its award-winning Visitor Centre, open 11.00am–5.00pm daily throughout the year. There are exhibitions and attractions for the whole family including the exciting *New Millennium Experience* dark ride and *Annie McLeod's Story* audio-visual show. Younger visitors will enjoy exploring the *Interactive Gallery* of light, sound and colour, and dressing-up in the 1820s *Historic Classroom*

Set in the hills to the south-east of Cumbernauld, **Palacerigg Country Park** is well sign posted from the town centre road network. It is less than half an hours drive from Glasgow. Established in the 1970's, Palacerigg has been developed around the objectives of wildlife conservation, environmental education and countryside recreation.

The Country Park covers 700 acres and hosts an extensive Scottish and European wildlife collection, exhibition centre, play area and nature trails. There is also a gift shop and tearoom. Palacerigg is home to wild populations of roe dear and owls. Visitors can watch red deer, reindeer and ancient White Park Cattle.

The park is open during the summer months from Monday to Sunday from 10.00am–6.00pm and during the winter months from Monday to Sunday from 10.00am–4.30pm.

■ **Palacerigg Country Park**
Palacerigg
Cumbernauld
G67 3HU
☎ 01236 720047

Opening Times:
Mon – Thu, Sat 10.00am–5.00pm,
Fri & Sun 11.00am–5.00pm
Closed 25 & 26 December, 1 & 2 January.
A fifteen minute walk from High Street and Argyle Street Rail Stations or St Enoch's Underground.

■ **People's Palace**
Glasgow Green
Glasgow
G40 1AT
☎ 0141 554 0223
🖹 0141 550 0892

Opening Times:
Mid-March until end of October School week
Have a fun day out for all the family
Pirate ship, cups & saucers, motor bikes & cars, remote controlled trucks, bumper cars, snack bar, magic roundabout, water blasters, bumper boats, kiddies rides and much more...

■ **Pitlochry Children's Amusement Park**
Armoury Road
Pitlochry
Perthshire
PH16 5AP
☎ 01796 472 876

- **Pollok House**
  Pollok Country Park
  2060 Pollokshaws Road
  Glasgow
  G43 1AT
  ☎ 0141 616 6410
  🖹 0141 552 4744

Opening Times:
House, shop & restaurant
All year, daily 10.00am–5.00pm
Closed 25 & 26 December, 1 & 2 January.
Gardens, Country Park and Burrell Collection all year, daily
Between April and October an entrance charge of £5 (£3.75 children and concessions) applies.
Entrance is free from November to March.
A ten minute walk from Pollokshaws West rail station or a 15 minute walk from Shawlands Rail Station.

- **Pride o' the Clyde Waterbus**
  ☎ 07711 250969
  www.clydewaterbusservices.co.uk

Enjoy a day out for a sail on the **Pride o' the Clyde waterbus** for a trip along Glasgow's river Clyde sailing between Breahead shopping centre and Glasgow city centre. Departure points are at Jamaica Street on Broomielaw or at Breahead shopping centre adjacent to the Clydebuilt Maritime Centre. Please call for departure times

- **Provand's Lordship**
  3 Castle Street
  Glasgow
  G4 0RB
  ☎ 0141 552 8819
  🖹 0141 552 4744

Opening Times:
Mon – Thu, Sat 10.00am–5 00pm,
Fri & Sun 11.00am–5.00pm
Closed 25 & 26 December, 1 & 2 January.
A ten minute walk from High Street Rail Station.

- **Scotland Street School Museum**
  225 Scotland Street
  Glasgow
  G5 8QB
  ☎ 0141 287 0500
  🖹 0141 287 0515

Opening Times:
Mon – Thurs 10.00am–5.00pm,
Fri – Sun 11.00am–5.00pm
Closed 25 & 26 December, 1 & 2 January
Conveniently located opposite Shields Road Underground Station

Opening Times:
Mon – Sat 10.00am–5.00pm
Sun 11.00am–5.00pm
(subject to events)

Scottish Football Museum & Hampden Stadium Tour

See over 2500 exhibits in 14 galleries! It's a day out that you will always remember, spent at the spiritual home of football – Hampden Park.

The Scottish Football Museum will reveal the sights, sounds and stories of the world's favourite game, in the country that took football to the world.The exhibits are relics of Scottish History and the story is told with the help of men and women who made football what it is today. Spend a day enjoying Scotland's football heritage, remembering the legends that insipred champions.

You can also add a Stadium Tour to your visit. See the Stadium as the players do on Matchday – visit the underground roadway, team changing rooms, players warm-up area. Walk down the tunnel and hear the famous Hampden Roar, follow in the footsteps of legends by climbing the stairs to the Cup Presentation Area.

You can also relax in the Museum café and purchase gifts and souvenirs from the shop.

- **Scottish Football Museum**
  Hampden Park
  Glasgow
  G42 9BA
  ☎ 0141 616 6139
  www.scottishfootballmuseum.org.uk

Shotts Heritage Centre is a small community based heritage facility within Shotts Library. The heritage centre tells the story of Shotts and includes displays on mining, the iron industry and the social and cultural life of the community.

The centre is open Monday to Friday from 9.30am–7.00pm (early close at 12.00pm on Wednesday) and from 9.30am–5.00pm on Saturday. Admission to the centre is free!

- **Shotts Heritage Centre**
  Benhar Road
  Shotts
  ☎ 01501 821556

- **St Mungo Museum of Religious Life and Art**
  2 Castle Street
  Glasgow
  G4 0RH
  ☎ 0141 553 2557
  🖹 0141 552 4744

Opening Times:
Mon – Thu, Sat 10.00am–5.00pm,
Fri & Sun 11.00am–5.00pm
Closed 25 & 26 December, 1 & 2 January.
A ten minute walk from High Street Rail Station.

- **Stirling Castle**
  At the head of Stirling's historic old town, off the M9
  ☎ 01786 450000

Opening Times:
Open all year 7 days a week
April – September 9.30am–6.00pm
October – March 9.30am–5.00pm
Last ticket sold 45 minutes before closing
Car and coach parking
Specialist bookshop, a gift shop and a café are available

- **Strathaven Park**
  Glasgow Road
  Strathaven
  ☎ 01355 521995

Facilities:
Boating pond, bowling rink, children's play area, putting green, outdoor tennis court, grass soccer pitches, band stand, miniature railway, paddling pool, Barrie shelter (Community hall and group facility inc. kitchen, function hall), sports pavilion (function hall, kitchen, changing facilities), football changing pavilions.

- **Strathclyde Country Park**
  366 Hamilton Road
  Motherwell
  ML1 3ED
  ☎ 01698 266155

Strathclyde Country Park is established as one of the leading Scottish centres for outdoor recreation. Thousands of visitors come every year to enjoy a huge range of activities available. The park lies in 1100 acres of countryside in the valley of the River Clyde.

M & D's, Scotland's first theme park, is located within the country park.

The park features a visitors centre, caravan and camping site, footpaths and nature trails and wildlife refuges. There are also a series of guided walks throughout the year led by members of the North Lanarkshire Council Countryside Rangers service. Other facilities include playgrounds, sandy beaches and refreshment kiosks.

The park is open from January to December from dawn till dusk. Strathclyde Country Park has something for everyone.

Summerlee Heritage Park's 22 acres form one of Scotland's foremost heritage visitor attractions. There is a great programme of events run at the Heritage Park all year round from Easter's 'Big Egg' event to the Grand Steam and Model Fair at the end of August.

Summerlee operates the only electric tramway in Scotland offering rides on board an Edwardian open top tram. Tickets cost just 75p for an adult and 40p for a child and are valid for the whole day of issue so you can ride as many times as you want! There is also a huge undercover exhibitions hall with working machinery. See how the miners lived in the 'miners row' cottages and go down the recreated addit mine.

A superb new children's playpark opened in 2003, with all sorts of safe fun for tots to teens.

Summerlee is open seven days a week from 10.00am–5.00pm during April to October and from 10.00am–4.00pm from November to March.

Summerlee is an attraction not to be missed, and admission is free!

- **Summerlee Heritage Park**
  Heritage Way
  Coatbridge
  ML5 1QD
  ☎ 01236 431261

- **The Tall Ship**
  Stobcross Road
  Glasgow
  G3
  ☎ 0141 222 2513
  www.thetallship.com

Ahoy Maties!

Get down to **The Tall Ship** at Glasgow Harbour and enjoy a great family day out for less than £10! The S.V. Glenlee is a fun and educational visitor attraction, which appeals to children and adults alike, and is one of only 5 remaining sailing ships built on the Clyde. There is an excellent programme of events running throughout the year, with everything from Halloween parties and craft workshops to movie days and treasure trails. The Tall Ship has something to suit everyone and activities run throughout each school holiday and most seasonal weekends.

The Tall Ship is also a great venue to hold your child's birthday party. The 'new improved' package offers additional extras to the basic hire of the space on board the Glenlee, including loot bags, invitations and refreshments. The ship makes an unusual venue and makes sure your party will be remembered for years to come. Get really into the swing of it by asking your guests to dress up as pirates and mermaids!

For more information, please call 0141 222 2513 or check the website at www.thetallship.com.
The Tall Ship is open seven days a week from 10.00am – 5.00pm May – October, and 10.00am – 4.00pm November – April.
For birthday parties at The Tall Ship *see* BIRTHDAY PARTIES (CHILDREN'S ACTIVITY & ADVENTURE CENTRES)

- **The Tenement House**
  (The National Trust for Scotland)
  145 Buccleugh Street
  Garnethill (third left off Rose Street or Cambridge Street NW of Sauchiehall Street, pedestrian shopping area),
  Glasgow
  ☎ 0141 333 0183

Opening Times:
1 March – 31 October, daily
1.00pm–5.00pm
A typical Victorian tenement flat of 1892, this was the home of a shorthand typist for over 50 years, and little has changed since the early 20th century. It retains many original fittings, including the splendid kitchen range, and fascinating family items. Exhibition on tenement life.

- **The Time Capsule**
  Buchanan Street
  Coatbridge
  ML5 1ET
  ☎ 01236 449576

A unique combination of theme water and adventure. Swim through dinosaur infested waters, ride the river rapids or skate in snow storms across a frozen loch. Swing across the icicle chamber and down the monster tango slide.

There are weekly events held for children of all ages including the Ice Kool Kiddies Club, held on Sunday mornings from 10.00am–12.00pm. The club is suitable for children from tots to 11 years and mums and dads are welcome too. Come along and take part in the competitions and win prizes. It's fun and games for all the family!

Come and visit the adventure zone, a multilevel play area for children from 3 to 11 years. Play in the icicle chamber, on the giant slide and in the time tunnel.

The Time Capsule is open daily from 10.00am–10.00pm. It's the biggest fun in a million years!

- **Viewpark Gardens**
  Old Edinburgh Road
  Viewpark
  Uddingston
  G71
  ☎ 01698 818269

This horticultural centre incorporates several types of gardens and glasshouse displays. Features include Japanese and Highland plant displays where visitors can view collections such as conifers, heathers, acers and azaleas. There are also various water features such as ponds, channels and miniature waterfalls that attract various wildlife.

Viewpark Gardens also hosts the annual Summer Flower Festival, which is an annual family event attracting over 17,500 visitors last year. Watch out for next years date and give your family a treat.

The Gardens have seasonal opening hours as follows: summer months Mon to Sun, 10.00am–4.00pm (except Fri 3.00pm and Sat 5.00pm); winter months Mon to Fri, 10.00am–4.00pm (except Fri 3.00pm, closed Sat and Sun).

- **Weaver's Cottage**
  (The National Trust for Scotland)
  Shuttle Street at the Cross, Kilbarchan,
  M8 junction 28a, A737, follow signs for
  Kilbarchan, 12m South-West of Glasgow
  ☎ 01505 705588

Opening Times:
1 April – 30 September, daily
1.00pm–5.00pm
Morning visits available for pre-booked groups
This typical handloom weaver's cottage, built in 1723, houses the last of the 800 looms that once worked in this village. On most days the clack, clack of a weaver at work brings the cottage to life again, and visitors can try weaving, pirn winding and spinning. Plant and herbs used to make natural are a feature of the attractive cottage garden.

Domestic & Pet Services

Please find in the following section listings of:

- **Au Pair & Nanny Services**
- **Pet Services / Pet Shops**

Au Pair & Nanny Services

Please find in the following section listings of Au Pair and Nanny Services in and around the Glasgow area.

- **Au Pair Exchange**
  7 Charlotte Street
  Perth
  PH1 5LW
  ☎ 01738 444789

The **Au Pair Exchange** is located in Perth – 90% of the Scottish population is within 90 minutes travelling distance – making us ideally situated to service all of Scotland.

We aim to match families with the au pair that best suits the families' needs. To do this we liase with our well established partner agents throughout Europe to identify suitable au pairs, (who actually want to be in Scotland!)

We are only a phone call away should you or your au pair need any help or advice and we encourage direct contact in person where possible. Many au pairs regularly call in for coffee and a chat, to use our students' internet lounge or just meet up with their friends, (we also run English courses).

With over 10 years experience in organising au pair placements, we feel that we offer a reliable friendly service to our families that has helped create long term friendships and many happy memories between our families and their au pairs.

- **Eviecare**
  ☎ 0141 636 1668

Nanny and nursery nurse agency

- **The Glasgow Nanny Agency**
  ☎ 01505 874 141

Childcare specialists
Covering Glasgow & West Coast Areas

- **Mini Mums Ltd**
  ☎ 0141 647 8429

Family and home care / baby sitting service available

A sitter service available in North Lanarkshire

Select Au-Pairs is run by Nancy Ingram who, as a mother of two, has used a variety of childcare options over the last 16 years, including Nannies, Mother's Helps, Au Pairs and family. She has found Au-Pairs to be the best solution for her family and also found she was regularly approached by other families to source Au-Pairs. As a result she set up **Select Au-Pairs** with a view to providing a service which is friendly, approachable, efficient and professional – caring about both the families' and Au-Pairs' welfare.

Select Au-Pairs has professional relationships with several European agencies, which Nancy screens and selects on the basis that she herself would be confident of their services. She understands the importance of the right match and seeks to provide a more personalized service.

Select Au-Pairs is a member of IAPA – International Au-Pair Association. IAPA's main goal is to protect the rights of all au-pairs and host families and at the same time establish internationally approved guidelines for au-pair exchange programmes.

- **North Lanarkshire Sitter Service**
  ☎ 01698 250025
- **Select Au-Pairs**
  ☎ 0141 884 8361

PET SERVICES / PET SHOPS

Please find in the following section listings of Pet Services in and around the Glasgow area.

- **Canine Care Services**
  Dog Walking Service
  ☎ 0141 589 4819

- **Creature Comforts**
  25 Eaglesham Road
  Clarkston
  Glasgow
  G76 7DH
  ☎ 0141 644 5030
  www.creaturecomfortsglasgow.com

- **Creature Comforts**
  3 Mugdock Road
  Milngavie
  Glasgow
  G62 8PD
  ☎ 0141 956 1999
  www.creaturecomfortsglasgow.com

- **Pet and Home Comforts**
  Pet Sitting & Home-Care Services for Cats
  ☎ 0141 423 3025

Opening Times
Mon – Sat 9.00am–5.30pm
Sun 12.00pm–4.00pm

Opening Times
Mon – Sat 9.00am–5.30pm

Creature Comforts, established in 1997, stock an extensive variety of quality pets, ranging from hamsters and rabbits to hand-reared parrots and fish. We also stock a large selection of top brand cages, accessories, foods and bedding to suit all your pets requirements. With our Clarkston and Milngavie branches, it enables us to provide a first class free home delivery service covering Glasgow and its surrounding areas. Our small animal, bird and reptile holiday boarding facility has proven to be extremely popular, particularly during peak school holiday periods. For free friendly advice on any of these services, why not come and visit us.

EDUCATION

This section of the guide is split into the following categories:

- **After School Care**
- **Independent Schools & Nurseries**
- **Local Authority Primary Schools**
- **Nursery Schools (Private & Partnership)**
- **Scottish Childminding Association**

After School Care

Please find in the following section listings of After School Care Clubs and Services in and around the Glasgow area.

Many Primary Schools offer After School Care Services so please check directly with your child's school or contact your local council, contact telephone numbers are available at the beginning of each local authority Primary School section of the guide.

Most clubs operate Mon – Fri during term time and many offer a play scheme during school holidays, bank/public holidays and in-service days.

Some provide pre-school care as well as after school care.

Most clubs provide a drop off and pick up service but please check directly with the club itself.

- **Auchinairn After School Care**
  (within Community Education Centre)
  Auchinairn Road
  Bishopbriggs
  Glasgow
  G64 1NG
  ☎ 0141 772 9122

Opening Times:
Mon – Fri 8.00am–9.00 am &
3.00pm–6.00pm (term time)
Mon – Fri 8.00am–6.00pm (holiday play scheme)
A pickup service is available from all local Primary Schools.

- **Barlanark Out of School Care** (within Barlanark Community Education Centre)
  33 Burnmouth Road
  Barlanark
  Glasgow
  G33 4RZ
  ☎ 0141 771 7690

Opening Times:
Mon – Fri 8.00am–9.00am &
3.00pm–6.00pm (term time)
Mon – Fri 8.00am–6.00pm (holiday play scheme)
A pickup service is available from the following Primary Schools: Barlanark Primary, Sandaig Primary & St Jude's Primary
East Muir Primary (special needs school) will provide their transport to Barlanark Out of School Care

- **Braidbar After School Care**
  (within Braidbar Primary School)
  Kyle Drive
  Giffnock
  Glasgow
  G46 6ES
  ☎ 0141 633 0900

Opening Times:
Mon – Fri 8.00am–9.00am &
2.45pm–6.00pm (term time)
Holiday Play Scheme (not available)
A pickup service is not available.

- **Cadder Out of School Service**
  (within Cadder Primary School)
  60 Herma Street
  Glasgow
  G23 5AR
  ☎ 0141 946 6569

Opening Times:
Mon – Fri 3.00pm–6.00pm
Mon – Fri 8.15am–6.00pm (holiday play scheme)
Infant Time is also available with this Out of School Service from: 11.00am–6.00pm
A pickup service is available from the following Primary Schools: Cadder Primary, Wyndford Primary, Maryhill Primary, St Agnes's Primary, Parkview Primary St Mary's Primary & St Gregory's

■ **Cambuslang Out of School Care Project**
14 Vicars Walk
Cambuslang
Glasgow
G72 8JS
☎ 0141 641 0911

Opening Times:
Mon – Fri 8.00am–9.00am & 3.15pm–6.15pm (term time)
Mon – Fri 8.00am–6.00pm (holiday play scheme)
A pickup service is available from the following Primary Schools: James Aiton Primary, St Charles' Primary, Hallside Primary, St Cadoc's Primary, Cairns Primary, West Coats Primary & St Bride's Primary

■ **Childcare Greater Easterhouse**
Westwood Business Centre
69 Aberdalgie Road
Easterhouse
Glasgow
G34
☎ 0140 781 9212

Office Hours 9.00am–4.30pm
Local forum for childcare provision in Greater Easterhouse

■ **Childcare In The Community**
Whitehill Sports Barn
Margaret Road
Hamilton
☎ 01698 458909

Opening Times:
Mon – Fri 3.00pm–6.00pm (term time)
Mon – Fri 8.30am–6.00pm (holiday play scheme)
A pickup service is available from the following Primary Schools: Beckford Primary & St Paul's Primary

■ **Craigholme Before & After School Care**

For **Craigholme Before & After School Care** *see* EDUCATION (INDEPENDENT SCHOOLS & NURSERIES)

■ **Cumbernauld Childminders Association**
☎ 01236 614288

Office Hours 9.00am–5.00pm
This is a support group for childminders and offers a parents advice service.

- **Dennistoun After School Care**
  (within Dennistoun Central Church)
  Armadale Street
  Glasgow
  G31 2UU
  ☎ 0141 556 7135

Opening Times:
Mon – Fri 2.30pm–6.00pm (term time)
Mon – Fri 8.00am–6.00pm (holiday play scheme)
🚌 A pickup service is available from the following Primary Schools: Alexandra Parade Primary, St Dennis's Primary & Golfhill Primary

- **Devonview Out of School Care**
  Devonview Nursery
  Devonview Street
  Airdrie
  ML5 9DH
  ☎ 01236 760742

Opening Times:
Mon – Fri 2.30pm–6.00pm (term time)
Mon – Fri 8.30am–5.30pm (holiday play scheme)
🚌 A pickup service is available from the following Primary Schools: Alexander Primary & Rochsolloch Primary

- **Duntocher Out of School Care**
  Duntocher Public Hall
  New Street
  Clydebank
  Dunbartonshire
  G81 6DF
  ☎ 01389 891441

Opening Times:
Mon – Fri 8.00am–9.00am & 2.45pm–5.45pm (term time)
Mon – Fri 8.00am–5.45pm (holiday play scheme)
🚌 A pickup service is available from the following Primary Schools: St Mary's Primary
(This particular Out of School Care Club is closed for two weeks during the Glasgow Fair Fortnight and for two weeks at Christmas) Check directly with the club for dates.

- **Firtrees Nursery Out of School Care**
  Dalzell Drive
  Motherwell
  ML3 9PQ
  ☎ 01698 232285

Opening Times:
Mon – Fri 8.00am–9.00am & 3.15pm–6.00pm (term time)
Mon – Fri 8.00am–6.00pm (holiday play scheme)
🚌 A pickup service is available from Knowetop Primary School

- **Glasgow Academy After School Club**
(Kidcare Ltd)
Colebrook Street
Glasgow
G12 8HE
☎ 0141 249 9935

Opening Times:
Mon – Fri 3.10pm–6.00pm (term time)
For Kidcare Ltd nurseries *see* EDUCATION (NURSERY SCHOOLS PRIVATE & PARTNERSHIP)
For Glasgow Academy School *see* EDUCATION (INDEPENDENT SCHOOLS & NURSERIES)

- **Greenhills Out of School Care**
(within St Vincent's Primary School)
Crosshouse Road
East Kilbride
Glasgow
G75 9DG
☎ 01355 241511

Opening Times:
Mon – Fri 8.00am– 9.00am, 3.00pm–5.45pm (term time)
Mon – Fri 8.00am–5.45pm (holiday play scheme)
🚍 A pickup service is available from the following Primary Schools: St Vincent's Primary, Crosshouse Primary, Greenhills Primary & Castlefield Primary (children are welcome from other local Primary Schools but a pickup service is not available).

- **Happy Days Too (After School Care)**
9 East Kilbride Road
Busby
G76 8JY
☎ 0141 644 5858

Opening Times:
Mon – Fri 8.00am– 9.00am, 3.00pm–6.00pm (term time)
Mon – Fri 8.00am–6.00pm (holiday play scheme)
🚍 A pickup service is available from the following Primary Schools: Carolside Primary, Carmunock Primary, Netherlee Primary, Eaglesham Primary & St Joseph's Primary.
For **Happy Days Too** *see* EDUCATION NURSERY SCHOOLS (PRIVATE & PARTNERSHIP)

- **Happy Days Too (Southfield House)(After School Care)**
Mearns Kirk
Glasgow
☎ 0141 639 9191

Opening Times:
Mon – Fri 8.00am– 9.00am, 3.00pm–6.00pm (term time)
Mon – Fri 8.00am–6.00pm (holiday play scheme)
🚍 A pickup service is available from the following Primary Schools: Mearns Primary & St Cadoc's Primary
For **Happy Days Too** *see* EDUCATION NURSERY SCHOOLS (PRIVATE & PARTNERSHIP)

■ **Ibrox Cessnock After School Care**
46 Hinshelwood Drive
Glasgow
G51 2XP
☎ 0141 427 7243

Opening Times:
Mon – Fri 3.00pm–6.00pm (term time)
Mon – Fri 8.30am–6.00pm (holiday play scheme)
🚌 A pickup service is available from the following Primary Schools: Ibrox Primary, St Saviours Primary & Bellahousten Primary

■ **Kelvinside Academy After School Care**

For **Kelvinside Academy After School Care** *see* EDUCATION (INDEPENDENT SCHOOLS & NURSERIES)

■ **Kinning Park Schools Out Service**
Kinning Park Complex
40 Cornwall Street
Glasgow
G41 1AH
☎ 0141 419 0449

Opening Times:
Mon – Fri 3.00pm–6.00pm (term time)
Mon – Fri 8.00am–6.00pm (holiday play scheme)
🚌 A pickup service is available from the following Primary Schools: Bellahouston Primary, Elderpark Primary, Ibrox Primary, Lorne St Primary & Mosspark Primary

■ **Kirkie Kids Out Of School Project**
(within Hillhead Primary School)
Newdyke Avenue
Kirkintilloch
Glasgow
G66 2DQ
☎ 0141 776 8344

Opening Times:
Mon – Fri 7.30am–9.00am,
3.00pm–6.00pm (term time)
Mon – Fri 8.00am–6.00pm (holiday play scheme)
🚌 A pickup service is available from the following Primary Schools: Harestanes Primary, Hillhead Primary, Oxgang Primary & St Flannan's Primary

■ **Kirtonholme Private Nursery**
(After School Care)
401 Kirtonholme Road
East Kilbride
G74 1RS
☎ 01355 222000

Opening Times:
Mon – Fri 8.00am–9.00am,
3.00pm–6.00pm (term time)
Mon – Fri 8.00am–6.00pm (holiday play scheme)
🚌 A pickup service is available from the following Primary Schools: Kirtonholme Primary, Mossneuk Primary, Mount Cameron Primary & St Kenneth's Primary

For **Kirtonholme Private Nursery** *see* EDUCATION NURSERY SCHOOLS (PRIVATE & PARTNERSHIP)

- **Langside College Glasgow**
Contact Clare Cairns on
☎ 0141 272 3770

For **Langside College Glasgow Summer Activity Program** *see* BIRTHDAY PARTIES (CHILDREN'S ACTIVITY & ADVENTURE CENTRES)

- **Little Gems Nursery & After School Care**
57 Stockiemuir Avenue
Bearsden
G61 3JJ
☎ 0141 931 5333

Opening Times:
Mon – Fri 8.00am–9.00am, 3.00pm–6.00pm (term time)
Mon – Fri 8.00am–6.00pm (holiday play scheme)
A pickup service is available from the following Primary Schools: Mosshead Primary & St Andrew's Primary

For **Little Gems Nursery & Baby Unit** *see* EDUCATION NURSERY SCHOOLS (PRIVATE & PARTNERSHIP)

- **Maryhill Out of School Service**
35 Avenuepark Street
Glasgow
G20 8TS
☎ 0141 946 8581

Opening Times:
Mon – Fri 3.00pm–6.00pm (term time)
Mon – Fri 9.00am–6.00pm (holiday play scheme)
A pickup service is available from the following Primary Schools: Dunard Street Primary, St Gregory's Primary, St Charles' Primary, St Mary's Primary, Wyndford Primary & Parkview Primary

- **Mearns After School Care Service Ltd**
Eastwood High School
Capelrig Road
Newton Mearns
Glasgow
G77
☎ 0141 639 7574

Opening Times:
Mon – Fri 8.00am–9.00am & 2.45pm–6.00pm (term time)
Mon – Fri 7.45am–6.00pm (holiday play scheme)
A pickup service is available from the following Primary Schools: Crookfur Primary & Mearns Primary

- **Mearns After School Care Service Ltd**
  (within Busby Primary School)
  Church Road
  Busby
  Glasgow
  ☎ 0141 644 4241

Opening Times:
Mon – Fri 8.00am–9.00am &
2.45pm–6.00pm (term time)
Mon – Fri 7.45am–6.00pm (holiday play scheme)
A pickup service is available from the following Primary Schools: Busby Primary and St Joseph's Primary

- **Mearns After School Care Service Ltd**
  (within Kirkhill Primary School)
  Kirkhill Road
  Newton Mearns
  Glasgow
  ☎ 0141 639 8636

Opening Times:
Mon – Fri 7.45am–9.00am &
3.15pm–6.00pm (term time)
A pickup service is available from the following Primary Schools: Kirkhill Primary

- **Mearns After School Care Service Ltd**
  (within St Cadoc's Primary School)
  Crookfur Road
  Newton Mearns
  Glasgow
  ☎ 0141 616 3769

Opening Times:
Mon – Fri 8.00am–9.00am &
3.30pm–6.00pm (term time)
Holiday play scheme not available
A pickup service is available from the following Primary Schools: St Cadoc's Primary

- **Mearns After School Care Service Ltd**
  (within St Thomas's Primary)
  Broadlie Road
  Neilston
  Glasgow
  ☎ Office 0141 638 5599

Opening Times:
Mon – Fri 7.45am–9.00am &
3.00pm–6.00pm (term time)
Holiday play scheme not available
A pickup service is available from the following Primary Schools: Neilston Primary & St Thomas's Primary

- **Mearns After School Care Service Ltd**
  (within Williamwood Church)
  4 Vardar Avenue
  Clarkston
  Glasgow
  ☎ 0141 638 2708

Opening Times:
Mon – Fri 2.45pm–6.00pm (term time)
Holiday play scheme not available
A pickup service is available from the following Primary Schools: Carolside Primary & St Joseph's Primary

- **Oakwood Out of School Care**
  Eastfield Resource Centre
  285 Cambuslang Road
  Rutherglen
  Glasgow
  ☎ 0141 646 0431

Opening Times: Mon – Fri 8.00am–9.00am & 3.00pm–6.00pm (term time)
Mon – Fri 8.00am–6.00pm (holiday play scheme)

🚌 A pickup service is available from the following Primary Schools: Burnside Primary, Calderwood Primary, St Columbskilles Primary & Westcoats Primary

For Oakwood House Nurseries *see* EDUCATION NURSERY SCHOOLS (PRIVATE & PARTNERSHIP)

- **One Plus**
  25 Ardoch Street
  Glasgow
  G22 5QG
  Office ☎ 0141 336 6772

One Plus Schools Out Service has 7 Units in various locations in North Glasgow.
Please contact Carol (Project Manager) or Suzanne (Child Care Coordinator) at the above office Tel No for further details.

- **One Plus Childcare in the Community Schools Out Service**
  4 Balado Road
  Easterhouse
  Glasgow
  G33
  ☎ 0141 781 1559

Opening Times:
Mon – Fri 3.00pm–6.00pm (term time)
Mon – Fri 8.30–6.00pm (holiday play scheme)
Runs from 4 locations in the Glasgow area:

St Benedict's Schools Out
(within St Benedict's Primary School)

🚌 A pickup service is available from the following Primary Schools: Provanhall Primary, St Benedict's Primary, Easthall Primary, Blairtummoch Primary & St John Ogilvie Primary

Commonhead Primary School

🚌 A pickup service is available from the following Primary Schools: St Collettes Commonhead Primary, Rogerfield Primary & Bishoploch Primary

Sunnyside Primary School

🚌 A pickup service is available from the following Primary Schools: Sunnyside Primary & Ruchazie Primary

St Roselima Primary School

- A pickup service is available from the following Primary Schools: St Rose of Lima Primary, St Philip's Primary & Garthamloch Primary

After School Care Facilities available throughout East Dunbartonshire & North Lanarkshire, pease contact for further details

Opening Times:
Mon – Fri 7.30am–9.00am & 3.00pm–5.45pm (term time)
Mon – Fri 8.00am–5.45pm (holiday play scheme)
Mon – Fri 12.00pm–5.45pm (Primary 1 children until September)

- A pickup service is available from the following Primary Schools: Heathery Knowe Primary, Lady of Lourdes Primary, Murray Primary & St Louise's Primary

- **Peace of Mind for Parents Out of School Care**
  ☎ 01236 721382

- **Playcareclub**
  (within Murray Primary School)
  Napier Hill
  East Kilbride
  Glasgow
  G75 0JP
  ☎ 01355 267670

- **Puffin Care Services**
(within McGill Primary School)
80 Meiklerig Crescent
Pollok
Glasgow
G53 5UF
☎ 0141 892 0840

Opening Times:
Mon – Fri 3.00pm–6.00pm (term time)
Mon – Fri 8.00am–6.00pm (holiday play scheme)
🚍 A pickup service is available from all primary schools in Greater Pollok

- **Shawlands Out of School Care**
(within Shawlands Primary School)
1284 Pollokshaws Road
Glasgow
G41 3QP
☎ 0141 632 2444

Opening Times:
Mon – Fri 8.00am–9.00am & 3.00pm–6.00pm (term time)
Mon – Fri 8.00am–6.00pm (holiday play scheme)
🚍 A pickup up service is available from the following Primary Schools: Shawlands Primary

- **Simshill After School Care**
(within Simshill Primary School)
148 Simshill Road
Glasgow
G44 5EP
☎ 0141 569 3141

Opening Times:
Mon – Fri 2.00pm–6.00pm (term time)
Mon – Fri 8.00am–6.00pm (holiday play scheme)
🚍 A pickup service is available from the following Primary Schools: Croftfoot Primary & Simshill Primary

- **Small World Day Nursery (After School Care)**
105 New City Road
Cowcaddens
☎ 0141 353 2626

Opening Times:
Mon – Fri 3.15pm–6.00pm (term time)
Mon – Fri 8.00am–6.00pm (holiday play scheme)
🚍 A pickup service is available from the following Primary Schools: Hillhead Primary, Oakgrove Primary, St Aloysius Primary & St Joseph's Primary

For Small World Day Nursery *see* EDUCATION NURSERY SCHOOLS (PRIVATE & PARTNERSHIP)

- **St Clare's Out of School Care**
  (within St Clare's Primary School)
  21 Peel Glen Road
  Drumchapel
  Glasgow
  G15 7XN
  ☎ 0141 944 1758

Opening Times:
Mon – Fri 3.00pm–5.45pm (term time)
Mon – Fri 8.30am–5.45pm (holiday play scheme)

- **Stonefield Out of School Care**
  75 Stonefield Road
  Blantyre
  G72 9SA
  ☎ 01698 825549

Opening Times:
Mon – Fri 3.00pm–6.00pm (term time)
Mon – Fri 8.00am–6.00pm (holiday play scheme)
A pickup service is available from all local Primary Schools
For Stonefield Private Day Nursery *see* EDUCATION NURSERY SCHOOLS (PRIVATE & PARTNERSHIP)

- **Summer Playscheme (Kidcare Ltd)**
  Allen Glen Building
  Central College of Commerce
  Cathedral Street
  ☎ 0141 564 1150

Opening Times:
Mon – Fri 8.00am–6.00pm
Age: 5 yrs to 12 yrs
C/o Kidcare Head office
☎ 0141 564 1150

- **Summerston After School Care**
  (within Caldercuilt Primary School)
  101 Invershiel Road
  Glasgow
  G23 5JG
  ☎ 0141 946 3343

Opening Times:
Mon – Fri 7.30am–9.00am & 2.30pm–6.00pm (term time)
Mon – Fri 8.00am–6.00pm (holiday play scheme)
A pickup service is available from the following Primary Schools: Caldercuilt Primary & St Blane's Primary.

- **Task Childcare Service After School Care**
  192 McNeil Street
  Glasgow
  ☎ 0141 429 1140

Opening Times:
Mon – Fri 3.00pm–6.00pm (term time)
Mon – Fri 8.00am–6.00pm (holiday play scheme)
A pickup service is available from the following Primary Schools: Blackfriars , St Francis' & St Johns
For Task Childcare Service *see* EDUCATION NURSERY SCHOOLS (PRIVATE & PARTNERSHIP)

■ **Technotots**
Transfer House
Scottish Enterprise Technology Park
Rankine Avenue
East Kilbride
☎ 01355 272255

Opening Times:
Mon – Fri 7.45am–9.00am,
3.00pm–6.00pm (term time)
Mon – Fri 7.45am–6.00pm (holiday play scheme)
For Technotots (Childcare) Ltd *see* EDUCATION NURSERY SCHOOLS (PRIVATE & PARTNERSHIP)

■ **Thornwood Out of School Service**
11 Thornwood Terrace
Glasgow
G11 7QZ
☎ 0141 334 0400

Opening Times:
Mon – Fri 3.00pm–6.00pm (term time)
Mon – Fri 8.30am–6.00pm (holiday play scheme)
A pickup service is available from St Paul's Primary & Whiteinch Primary

■ **Time Out Club**
Allander Road
Milngavie
Glasgow
G62 8PN
☎ 0141 563 9573

Opening Times:
Mon – Fri 2.45pm–6.00pm (term time)
Mon – Fri 8.30am–6.00pm (holiday play scheme)
Runs from 3 locations in the Glasgow area;
Castlehill Primary School (Bearsden)
A pickup service is available from the following Primary Schools: Castlehill Primary & St Andrew's Primary
St. Luke's Church (Milngavie)
A pickup service is available from the following Primary Schools: Craigdhu Primary, Clober Primary School
Milngavie Community Centre (Milngavie)
A pickup service is available from the following Primary Schools: Milngavie Primary & St. Joseph's Primary
A breakfast club is now available 8.00am–9.00am at Castlehill Primary School

Opening Times:
Mon – Fri 3.00pm–6.00pm (term time)
Mon – Fri 8.30am–6.00pm (holiday play scheme)

A pickup service is available from the following Primary Schools: Bankhead Primary, Toryglen Primary & St Brigid's Primary

- **Toryglen After-School Service**
  (within Geoff Shaw Community Centre)
  Kerrylamont Avenue
  Toryglen
  Glasgow
  G42
  ☎ 0141 613 3098

Independent Schools & Nurseries

Please find in the following section listings of Independent Schools and Nurseries in and around the Glasgow area.

- **Scottish Council of Independent Schools**
  21 Melville Street
  Edinburgh
  Edinburgh
  EH3 7PE
  ☎ 0131 220 2106
  www.scis.org.uk

The Scottish Council of Independent Schools, (SCIS), provides information and advice to parents who are seeking an independent school for their children. A free directory is available giving details of independent schools in Scotland. The information is also available on the web at www.scis.org.uk

Fiona Valpy, Information Officer for SCIS, says, *'Independent schools in Scotland have a long tradition of achievement in many different fields. From examination results to sports, from music and drama to technology, the schools aim to fulfil the potential of each individual pupil, helping them to do their very best across a range of subjects and interests. The opportunities offered to pupils are second to none.'*

For further details contact SCIS at 21 Melville Street, Edinburgh EH3 7PE; telephone 0131 220 2106; email information@scis.org.uk

For boys & girls 2½–9 yrs

Founded in 1929, **Belmont House School** is a leading independent school offering an excellent all-round education for girls and boys aged three to eighteen.

Combining a dynamic and forward-thinking approach to education, the fostering of traditional values and some of the smallest average class sizes in Scotland creates a friendly and caring environment, which allows each individual pupil to flourish and gain the skills necessary for success in today's society.

The all-round education provided by Belmont House School encourages all pupils to excel in academic subjects, the Arts and sports; and a diverse range of extra-curricular activities allows pupils to expand their interests and opportunities.

Belmont House School's Nursery is vital in laying the foundations for each child's education.

At this crucial stage in a child's development Belmont's Nursery pupils are encouraged to learn through an exciting and varied programme that captures their imagination.

Belmont's Nursery pupils are encouraged to work to their full potential and are introduced to the early stages of reading, writing and numerical skills. Pupils are also taught PE and Music.

The Nursery is an integral part of the School community and the children have contact with Junior School pupils and teachers, resulting in a smooth and happy transition to Junior One.

- **Atholl Prep School**
  (part of Glasgow Academy)
  Mutdock Road
  Milngavie
  ☎ 0141 956 3758

- **Belmont House School**
  Sandringham Avenue
  Newton Mearns
  Glasgow
  G77 5DU
  ☎ 0141 639 2922

BELMONT HOUSE SCHOOL

FOR GIRLS AND BOYS AGED 3 - 18

Where small class sizes allow each individual to flourish

Belmont House School
Sandringham Avenue
Newton Mearns
G77 5DU
T: 0141 639 2922
F: 0141 639 9860
W: www.belmontschool.co.uk
E: headmaster@belmontschool.co.uk

ENCOURAGING EXCELLENCE IN EACH INDIVIDUAL

For more information about Belmont House School, please contact the School Office on 0141 639 2922 or
e-mail: headmaster@belmontschool.co.uk

■ **Craigholme School Nursery**
62 St Andrew's Drive
Pollokshields
Glasgow
G41 5EZ
Admissions ☎ 0141 427 0375
email: admissions@craigholme.co.uk
www.craigholme.co.uk

Pre-school education has been a long-standing tradition at **Craigholme** and our new state of the art facility opened in August 2002. The Nursery takes girls and boys aged 3-5 and entry is by application via the Admissions Office.

Our facility offers 2 large playrooms; a music room, a physical room and large gardens and outside play area. In a caring environment and following the curriculum for under 5's, the children learn through play and exploration. Themed activities are designed to capture their imagination and stir their natural curiosity. Specialist teaching staff in PE, Music and French also support our learning programme.

Healthy snacks are provided morning and afternoon and before and after school care takes place at our Nursery and Infant school sites from 8.00am to 5.45pm. This service operates during term time and is run by experienced staff with appropriate activities for different age groups.

Craigholme enjoys partnership status with Glasgow City Council.

■ **Craigholme Nursery**
72 St Andrew's Drive
Pollokshields
Glasgow
G41 4HS
Admissions ☎ 0141 427 0375
email: admissions@craigholme.co.uk
www.craigholme.co.uk

At the forefront of independent education in Scotland, **Craigholme** believes passionately in the strengths, opportunities and sense of community provided by the all-girl environment.

Proud of our reputation for academic excellence, Craigholme is highly respected for its sporting achievements at district and national levels and is also recognised for its traditions in the creative arts.

We offer an outstanding, all-round education for girls aged 5-18, which is highly effective, empowering and inspiring.

- **Dairsie House School Ltd**
  54 Newlands Road
  Newlands
  Glasgow
  G43 2JG
  ☎ 0141 632 0736

- **East Park**
  1092 Maryhill Road
  Glasgow
  G20 9TD
  ☎ 0141 946 8315

  For boys & girls from 5–19yrs

- **Fernhill School**
  Fernbrae Avenue
  Burnside
  Rutherglen
  Glasgow
  G73 4SG
  ☎ 0141 634 2674

  From 5 yrs
  Primary – boys and girls
  Secondary – all girls

- **The Glasgow Academy**
  Colebrook Street
  Glasgow
  G12 8HE
  ☎ 0141 334 8558
  www.theglasgowacademy.org.uk

  For boys & girls age 2½–18 yrs
  For **Glasgow Academy After School Care** *see* EDUCATION (AFTER SCHOOL CARE)

For boys & girls 3–14 yrs

For boys & girls $3^1/_2$ – Junior 6

Hutchesons' Grammar School at Kingarth St

The 1876 main primary building and 1994 infant block at Kingarth St stand as the perfect symbol of the old and the new, the traditional and the modern.

With its three Primary One and three Primary Two classes, the infant block abounds freshness. An infant hall and infant library give a taste of school life lying ahead.

The older building offers an impressive Assembly Hall, home of the summer and Christmas shows. It plays host to junior parties and PE lessons.

Beyond are airy classrooms, art and craft rooms bursting with imagination and music rooms, offering pupils the chance to add another string to their bows.

The library invites children into a whole new world, adding daily discoveries in print to their stretching minds.

Children expand their horizons with the specialist help of staff from Art, Craft, Music and Physical Education departments.

There is as much to be learned outside the classroom as in it. The annual trip of P7 to the Island of Raasay's outdoor centre is a popular fixture.

- **Glasgow Steiner School**
  52 Lumsden Street
  Yorkhill
  Glasgow
  G3 8RH
  ☎ 0141 334 8855

- **The High School of Glasgow Junior**
  27 Ledcameroch Road
  Bearsden
  Glasgow
  G61 4AE
  ☎ 0141 942 0158

- **Hutchesons' Grammar Junior School**
  44 Kingarth Street
  Glasgow
  G42 7RN
  ☎ 0141 423 2700

When the work is finished in the computer suite, playing fields and classrooms, children learn how to use their talents constructively for others, organising tuck shops for charities.

Competition is nurtured through inter-house speaking, quizzes and games. If there is any energy left, it is directed to optional out-of-school activities like badminton, table-tennis, cycling proficiency classes or Scripture Union.

- **Hutchesons' Grammar Junior School**
  3 Lilybank Terrace
  Glasgow
  G12 8RX
  ☎ 0141 339 9127

Hutchesons' Grammar School at Lilybank Terrace

Situated in the West End of Glasgow, Hutchesons' Grammar School at Lilybank Terrace offers and excellent all-round education for primary-aged children in a stimulating, disciplined and secure setting.

The warmth of atmosphere of the converted Victorian townhouses and church added to the fine traditions and standards of Hutchesons' when the new primary opened its doors in 2001.

The site provides a safe and attractive environment for children.

One of our prime aims for the primary 1–7 pupils is happiness. We believe happy children, nurtured in an environment of self-respect and respect for others, develop confidence in themselves and in their learning.

Our curriculum is based on the 5–14 National Guidelines. Classrooms are bright and well-stocked with all the learning tools.

Apart from the expected emphasis on 'the three Rs,' Music, Art and French are high on the agenda.

We firmly believe in giving children every opportunity to participate in as many experiences as possible...a belief backed up by a range of clubs and extra-curricular activity.

With our Kingarth St primary, we share the goal of preparing children for the adventure and diversity of life in secondary school at Beaton Rd by giving them the best platform from which to take the wonderful great leap into secondary school.

Hutchesons' Lilybank Terrace Nursery
When you entrust your three year old to our care in Lilybank Terrace Nursery, co-located with one of our two Primary Schools, your child is at the centre of everyone's care and concern.

The well being, safety and security of children are paramount and are a pre-requisite for their progression and development.

Facilities provided for the children include three bright, stimulating playrooms and a safe, supervised and secure outdoor play area.

All children are given every opportunity to explore and learn through play, while the four year olds have more structured activities to prepare them for school.

Ballet, PE and Music are taught by specialist teachers.

- **Hutchesons' Nursery**
  3 Lilybank Terrace
  Glasgow
  G12 8RX
  ☎ 0141 339 9127

Kelvinside Academy is a leading independent school in the West of Scotland catering for boys and girls aged 3–18. The school comprises 3 stages: Junior Start (3-4 year olds), Junior School and Senior School.

An experienced teacher and a team of Nursery Nurses lead Junior Start, with some 35 boys and girls in total. The accommodation is light, spacious, colourful and well resourced offering a stimulating pre-school experience.

Boys and girls from Junior Start are given priority places in Junior 1 where there are two

- **Kelvinside Academy**
  33 Kirklee Road
  Glasgow
  G12 0SW
  ☎ 0141 357 3376

classes of 20. Small classes are a feature of Kelvinside Academy as a whole and being an all-through school, the children in the early years benefit from the extensive facilities and specialised teaching (eg French from Junior 1).

Pre 4s attend 5 half day sessions per week, with some whole day places available. For both Junior Start and Junior School supervised after school care is available until 5.30 pm.

Our partnership with Glasgow City Council allows parents a rebate for some or most of the cost of pre-school education.

For a Prospectus contact the School at 33 Kirklee Road, Glasgow G12 OSW, by telephone on 0141 357 3376, by E-mail registrar@kelvinsideacademy.gla.sch.uk, or visit our web site, www.kelvinsideacademy.gla.sch.uk.

For boys & girls 3–18 yrs

- **St Aloysius College**
  45 Hill Street
  Garnethill
  Glasgow
  G3 6RJ
  ☎ 0141 332 3190

THE GLASGOW GUIDE FOR PARENTS AND CARERS

2005 edition

NOTE TO ADVERTISERS

If you were not listed in ***The Glasgow Guide for Parents and Carers*** 2004 (2nd) edition, don't worry. Have your business or service listed in ***The Glasgow Guide for Parents and Carers*** 2005 (3rd) edition. Fill in your details below and return by the 30th September 2004 to:

Glasgow Under 6's Ltd
48 Flenders Avenue
Clarkston
Glasgow, G76 7XZ
Tel/Fax 0141 616 3661
E: glasgowunder6s@fsmail.net

Name of Business & Contact Name . . . .

Address . . . .

. . . .

Postcode . . . . Tel/Fax No. . . . .

Email . . . . www . . . .

PLEASE TICK BELOW

Free Listing ❑

Request advertising details ❑

NOTE TO READERS

We would like to hear your comments and suggestions for our 2005 edition. These should be sent to **Glasgow Under 6's Ltd** at the address above.

Local Authority Primary Schools

- East Dunbartonshire Council

Please find in the following section listings of all the local authority Primary Schools, Nurseries within Primary Schools and Nursery Classes in East Dunbartonshire.

- **East Dunbartonshire Council Headquarters**
  Tom Johnston House
  Civic Way
  Kirkintilloch
  Glasgow
  G66 4TJ
  ☎ 0141 578 8000

- **Childcare Information Service**
  ☎ 0141 578 8687

- **Childcare Information Service Helpline**
  ☎ 0141 570 0091

- **Childcare Information Website**
  www.childcarelink.gov.uk/
  eastdunbartonshire

- **Early Years Office**
  ☎ 0141 578 8731

- **Auchinairn Primary School**
Beech Road
Bishopbriggs
G64 1NE
☎ 0141 772 3753

- **Auchinairn Nursery Class**
Beech Road
Bishopbriggs
G64 1NE
☎ 0141 772 3753

- **Baldernock Primary School**
Balmore
Torrance
G64 4AS
☎ 01360 620317

- **Baljaffray Primary School**
Grampian Way
Bearsden
G61 4RA
☎ 0141 942 3638

- **Baljaffray Nursery Class**
Grampian Way
Bearsden
G61 4RA
☎ 0141 943 1738

- **Balmuildy Primary School**
Stirling Drive
Bishopbriggs
G64 3AJ
☎ 0141 772 3824

- **Bearsden Primary School**
Roman Road
Bearsden
G61 2SY
☎ 0141 942 2378

- **Castlehill Primary School**
Rosslyn Road
Bearsden
G61 4DL
☎ 0141 942 6830

- **Clober Primary School**
Kirk Street
Milngavie
G62 7PN
☎ 0141 956 3874

- **Clober Nursery Class**
Kirk Street
Milngavie
G62 7PN
☎ 0141 955 1477

- **Colquhoun Park Primary School**
Canniesburn Road
Bearsden
G61 1HD
☎ 0141 942 7552

- **Colquhoun Park Nursery Class**
Canniesburn Road
Bearsden
G61 1HD
☎ 0141 942 7552

- **Craighu Primary School**
Prestonfield
Milngavie
G62 7PZ
☎ 0141 956 5720

- **Craighead Primary School**
Milton Of Campsie
G66 8DL
☎ 01360 311570

- **Craighead Nursery Class**
  Milton of Campsie
  G66 8DL
  ☎ 01360 312276

- **Gartconner Primary School**
  Gartshore Road
  Kirkintilloch
  G66 3TH
  ☎ 0141 775 0170

- **Gartconner Nursery Class**
  Gartshore Road
  Kirkintilloch
  G66 3TH
  ☎ 0141 775 0170

- **Harestanes Primary School**
  Mauchline Court
  Kikintilloch
  G66 2SA
  ☎ 0141 776 7245

- **Hillhead Primary School**
  Newdyke Avenue
  Kirkintilloch
  G66 2DQ
  ☎ 0141 578 1200

- **Hillhead Nursery Class**
  Newdyke Avenue
  Kirkintilloch
  G66 2DQ
  ☎ 0141 578 1200

- **Holy Family Primary School**
  Boghead Road
  Kirkintilloch
  G66 4AT
  ☎ 0141 776 2585

- **Holy Family Nursery Class**
  Boghead Road
  Kirkintilloch
  G66 4AT
  ☎ 0141 776 2585

- **Killermont Primary School**
  1 Aviemore Gardens
  Bearsden
  G61 2BL
  ☎ 0141 942 0359

- **Killermont Nursery Class**
  1 Aviemore Gardens
  Bearsden
  G61 2BL
  ☎ 0141 942 0359

- **Lennoxtown Nursery Class**
  School Lane
  Lennoxtown
  G65 7LX
  ☎ 01360 313285

- **Lairdsland Primary School**
  Kerr Street
  Kirkintilloch
  G66 1JZ
  ☎ 0141 776 1595

- **Lennoxtown Primary School**
  School Lane
  Lennoxtown
  G66 7LX
  ☎ 01360 312352

- **Lenzie Primary School**
  Kirkintilloch Road
  Lenzie
  G66 4LF
  ☎ 0141 776 1361

- **Lenzie Nursery Class**
Kirkintilloch Road
Lenzie
G66 4LF
☎ 0141 776 1361

- **Lenzie Moss Primary School**
Moss Road
Lenzie
G66 4HW
☎ 0141 776 4120

- **Meadowburn Primary School**
Bishopbriggs
G64 3LL
☎ 0141 772 4543

- **Meadowburn Nursery Class**
Lendale Lane
Bishopbriggs
G64 3LL
☎ 0141 772 4543

- **Millersneuk Primary School**
Lindsaybeg Road
Lenzie
G66 5HZ
☎ 0141 775 0720

- **Milngavie Primary School**
Hillhead Street
Milngavie
G62 8AG
☎ 0141 956 1564

- **Milngavie Nursery Class**
Hillhead Street
Milngavie
G62 8AG
☎ 0141 956 1564

- **Mosshead Primary School**
Stockiemuir Avenue
Bearsden
G61 3LZ
☎ 0141 942 7366

- **Oxgang Primary School**
Lammermoor Road
Kirkintilloch
G66 2AB
☎ 0141 776 2894

- **St Agatha's Primary School**
Gartshore Road
Kirkintilloch
G66 3TH
☎ 0141 776 1598

- **St Andrew's Primary School**
Duntocher Road
Bearsden
G61 4QL
☎ 0141942 5988

- **St Flannan's Primary School**
Newdyke Road
Kirkintilloch
G66 2JW
☎ 0141 776 2850

- **St Helen's Primary School**
Wester Cleddens Road
Bishopbriggs
G64 1EH
☎ 0141 772 7019

- **St Joseph's Primary School**
North Campbell Avenue
Milngavie
G62 7AA
☎ 0141 956 1600

- **St Machan's Primary School**
  St Machan's Way
  Lennoxtown
  G66 7HG
  ☎ 01360-311586

- **St Mathew's Primary School**
  Park Road
  Bishopbriggs
  G64 2NP
  ☎ 0141 772 2535

- **Torrance Primary School**
  West Road
  Torrance
  G64 4DE
  ☎ 01360 622275

- **Torrance Nursery Class**
  West Road
  Torrance
  G64 4DE
  ☎ 01360 620807

- **Twechar Primary School**
  Main Street
  Twechar
  G65 9TA
  ☎ 01236 822280

- **Twechar Nursery Class**
  Main Street
  Twechar
  G65 9TA
  ☎ 01236 822280

- **Wester Cleddens Primary School**
  Wester Cleddens Road
  Bishopbriggs
  G64 2NQ
  ☎ 0141 772 4148

- **Westerton Primary School**
  Crarae Avenue
  Bearsden
  G61 1HY
  ☎ 0141 942 5124

- **Woodhill Primary School**
  Kirriemuir Road
  Bishopbriggs
  G64 1DL
  ☎ 0141 772 1762

- **Woodhill Nursery Class**
  Kirriemuir Road
  Bishopbriggs
  G64 1DL
  ☎ 0141 772 7621

■ EAST RENFREWSHIRE COUNCIL

Please find in the following section listings of local authority Primary Schools, Nurseries within Primary Schools and Nursery Classes in East Renfrewshire

■ **East Renfrewshire Council Headquarters**
Eastwood Park
Rouken Glen Road
Giffnock
East Renfrewshire
G46 6UG
☎ 0141 577 3000

■ **Childcare Information Service Helpline**
☎ 0141 577 3990

■ **Childcare Information Website**
www.childcarelink.gov.uk/eastrenfrewshire

■ **Early Years Office**
☎ 0141 577 3990

- **Arthurlie Nursery School**
  Burnbank Drive
  Barrhead
  East Renfrewshire
  G78 2ER
  ☎ 0141 881 5117

- **Auchenback Primary School**
  Auburn Drive
  Barrhead
  East Renfrewshire
  G78 2EU
  ☎ 0141 881 1703

- **Barrhead Community Nursery**
  c/o St John's Primary School
  Commercial Road
  Barrhead
  East Renfrewshire
  G78 1TA
  ☎ 0141 881 2279

- **Braidbar Primary School**
  Kyle Drive
  Giffnock
  East Renfrewshire
  G46 6JL
  ☎ 0141 633 2046

- **Busby Primary School**
  Church Road
  Clarkston
  East Renfrewshire
  G76 8EB
  ☎ 0141 644 1866

- **Busby Nursery School**
  (within Busby Primary School)
  Church Road
  Clarkston
  East Renfrewshire
  ☎ 0141 644 1866

- **Calderwood Lodge Primary School**
  28 Calderwood Road
  Glasgow
  G43 2RU
  ☎ 0141 637 5654

- **Calderwood Lodge Nursery School**
  (within Calderwood Primary School)
  28 Calderwood Road
  Glasgow
  G43 2RU
  ☎ 0141 637 5654

- **Carlibar Primary School**
  Main Street
  Barrhead
  East Renfrewshire
  G78 1SW
  ☎ 0141 881 1254

- **Carlibar Nursery School**
  (within Carlibar Primary School)
  Main Street
  Barrhead
  East Renfrewshire
  G78 1SW
  ☎ 0141 881 1254

- **Carolside Primary School**
  Ashfield Road
  Clarkston
  East Renfrewshire
  G76 7TX
  ☎ 0141 644 1668

- **Carolside Nursery School**
  (within Carolside Primary School)
  Ashfield Road
  Clarkston
  East Renfrewshire
  G76 7TX
  ☎ 0141 644 0815

- **Crookfur Primary School**
  Capelrig Road
  Newton Mearns
  East Renfrewshire
  G77 6LF
  ☎ 0141 639 6448

- **Cross Arthurlie Primary School**
  Fern Drive
  Barrhead
  East Renfrewshire
  G78 1JF
  ☎ 0141 881 2920

- **Eaglesham Primary School**
  Strathaven Road
  Eaglesham
  East Renfrewshire
  G76 0LF
  ☎ 01355 302336

- **Eaglesham Nursery School**
  (within Eaglesham Primary School)
  Strathaven Road
  Eaglesham
  East Renfrewshire
  G76 0LF
  ☎ 01355 302336

- **Giffnock Primary School**
  Academy Road
  Giffnock
  East Renfrewshire
  G46 7JL
  ☎ 0141 638 3641

- **Giffnock Nursery School**
  (within Giffnock Primary School)
  Academy Road
  Giffnock
  East Renfrewshire
  G46 7JL
  ☎ 0141 638 3641

- **Glen Family Centre**
  Woodfarm Road
  Thornliebank
  East Renfrewshire
  G46 7JL
  ☎ 0141 585 3838

- **Glenwood Nursery School**
  Woodfarm Road
  Thornliebank
  East Renfrewshire
  G46 7JJ
  ☎ 0141 638 9185

- **Hazeldene Nursery School**
  9 Rosemount Avenue
  Newton Mearns
  East Renfrewshire
  G77
  ☎ 0141 616 3327

- **The Isobel Mair School**
  (special needs)
  Drumby Crescent
  Clarkston
  East Renfrewshire
  G76 7HN
  ☎ 0141 577 4546/7

- **Kirkhill Primary School**
  Kirkhill Road
  Newton Mearns
  East Renfrewshire
  G77 5RJ
  ☎ 0141 639 3601

- **Madras Nursery School**
  High Street
  Neilston
  East Renfrewshire
  G78 3HJ
  ☎ 0141 880 5593

- **Mearns Primary School**
  Hunter Drive
  Newton Mearns
  East Renfrewshire
  G77 6PR
  ☎ 0141 560 3810

- **Mearns Nursery School**
  (within Mearns Primary School)
  Hunter Drive
  Newton Mearns
  East Renfrewshire
  G77 6PR
  ☎ 0141 560 3810

- **Neilston Primary School**
  43 High Street
  Neilston
  East Renfrewshire
  G78 7HJ
  ☎ 0141 881 5500

- **Netherlee Primary School**
  Clarkston Road
  Netherlee
  East Renfrewshire
  G44 3SF
  ☎ 0141 637 5892

- **Netherlee Nursery School**
  (within Netherlee Primary School)
  Clarkston
  Netherlee
  East Renfrewshire
  G44 3SF
  ☎ 0141 637 5892

- **Our Lady of the Mission Primary**
  Robslee Road
  Thornliebank
  East Renfrewshire
  G46 7DD
  ☎ 0141 620 1914

- **Robslee Primary School**
  Woodfarm Road
  Thornliebank
  East Renfrewshire
  G46 7DD
  ☎ 0141 638 5179

- **Springhill Primary School**
  Springhill Road
  Barrhead
  East Renfrewshire
  G78 2SE
  ☎ 0141 881 2442

- **St Cadoc's Primary School**
  Crookfur Road
  Newton Mearns
  East Renfrewshire
  G77 6ND
  ☎ 0141 639 7163

- **St John's Primary School**
  Commercial Road
  Barrhead
  East Renfrewshire
  G78 1TA
  ☎ 0141 881 4085

- **St Joseph's Primary School**
  Oliphant Crescent
  Busby
  East Renfrewshire
  G76 8PT
  ☎ 0141 644 1909

- **St Mark's Primary School**
  Roebank Drive
  Barrhead
  East Renfrewshire
  G78 2JA
  ☎ 0141 881 3662

- **St Thomas's Primary School**
  Broadlie Road
  Neilston
  East Renfrewshire
  G78 3ET
  ☎ 0141 881 1256

- **Thornliebank Primary School**
  Main Street
  Thornliebank
  East Renfrewshire
  G46 7RW
  ☎ 0141 638 3738

- **Thornliebank Nursery School**
  (within Thornliebank Primary School)
  Main Street
  Thornliebank
  East Renfrewshire
  G46 7RW
  ☎ 0141 638 3738

- **Uplawmoor Primary School**
  Tannoch Road
  Uplawmoor
  East Renfrewshire
  G78 4AD
  ☎ 01505 850246

■ GLASGOW CITY COUNCIL

Please find in the following section listings of local authority Primary Schools, Nurseries within Primary Schools and Nursery Classes in Glasgow City.

■ **Glasgow City Council Headquarters**
City Chambers
Glasgow
G2 1DU
☎ 0141 287 2000

■ **Childcare Information Service**
☎ 0141 287 8307

■ **Childcare Information Website**
www.childcarelink.gov.uk/glasgowcity

■ **Early Years Office**
☎ 0141 287 6863

Nursery Schools

- **Acredyke Nursery School**
  (within Knockburn Primary)
  1 Ferness Oval
  G21 3SQ
  ☎ 0141 558 6770

- **Adelphi Nursery School**
  40 Waddell Court
  G5 0QA
  ☎ 0141 429 1474

- **Anderson Street Nursery**
  20 Anderson Street
  G11 6AZ
  ☎ 0141 339 2388

- **Arderncraig Nursery School**
  25 Ardencraig Drive
  G45 0HS
  ☎ 0141 631 1550

- **Ardnahoe Nursery School**
  18 Ardnahoe Place
  G45 0HS
  ☎ 0141 647 8934

- **Arnwood Nursery School**
  72 Dougrie Road
  G45 9NW
  ☎ 0141 634 2809

- **Belhaven Nursery School**
  54 Kelvinside Avenue
  G20 6PY
  ☎ 0141 946 3169

- **Bellrock Crescent Nursery School**
  21 Bellrock Crescent
  G33 3HJ
  ☎ 0141 774 8036

- **Bonnybroom Nursery School**
  233 Petershill Drive
  G21 4QU
  ☎ 0141 557 2550

- **Broomloan Nursery School**
  (c/o St Gerard's Secondary)
  80 Vicarfield Street
  G51 2DF
  ☎ 0141 445 1762

- **Buchlyvie Nursery School**
  45 Aberdalgie Road
  G34 9LT
  ☎ 0141 771 1056

- **Caldercuilt Nursery School**
  101 Invershiel Road
  G23 5JG
  ☎ 0141 946 7450

- **Chesters Nursery School**
  129 Drummore Road
  G15 7NH
  ☎ 0141 944 1831

- **Cloan Nursery School**
  45 Cloan Avenue
  G15 6DE
  ☎ 0141 944 2191

- **Cloverbank Nursery School**
  193 Moraine Avenue
  G15 6LG
  ☎ 0141 944 8678

- **Craigbank Nursery School**
  26 Glenlora Drive
  G53 6BH
  ☎ 0141 881 9720

- **Craigton Nursery School**
  13 Montrave Street
  G52 2TS
  ☎ 0141 882 7604

- **Cranstonhill Nursery School**
  3 Little Street
  G3 8DQ
  ☎ 0141 248 4899

- **Deanpark Nursery School**
  10 Deanston Drive
  G41 3AE
  ☎ 0141 649 8949

- **Dowanhill Nursery School**
  30 Havelock Street
  G11 5JE
  ☎ 0141 334 8741

- **Easthall Nursery School**
  (c/o Easthall Primary)
  33 Ware Road
  G34 9AR
  ☎ 0141 771 4348

- **Eastwood Nursery School**
  Bonnyrigg Drive
  G43 1HW
  ☎ 0141 632 9773

- **Elba Lane Nursery**
  1346 Gallowgate
  G31 4DJ
  ☎ 0141 554 2174

- **Elmcroft Nursery School**
  40 Croftcroighn Road
  G33 3SE
  ☎ 0141 774 9311

- **Fortrose Nursery School**
  74 Peel Street
  G11 5LR
  ☎ 0141 339 1808

- **Garscube Nursery School**
  Manresa Place
  G4 9NB
  ☎ 0141 332 3170

- **Govanhill Nursery**
  335 Allison Street
  G42 8HH
  ☎ 0141 424 1063

- **Halgreen Nursery School**
  51 Halgreen Avenue
  G15 8AL
  ☎ 0141 944 2060

- **Helenslea Nursery School**
  36 Methven Street
  G31 4RB
  ☎ 0141 551 0504

- **Hilltop Nursery School**
  (c/o King's Park Primary)
  44 Kingbridge Drive
  G44 4JS
  ☎ 0141 649 1786

- **Kelso Nursery School**
  (c/o St Brendan's Primary)
  170 Hawick Street
  G13 4HG
  ☎ 0141 952 2502

- **Kennedy Street Nursery School**
(c/o St Mungo's Primary)
45 Parson Street
G4 0PX
☎ 0141 552 2484

- **Keppoch Nursery School**
73 Mansion Street
G22 5NT
☎ 0141 336 7750

- **Kincardine Nursery School**
60 Kincardine Square
G33 5BU
☎ 0141 774 5677

- **Kinning Park Nursery**
540 Scotland Street
G41 1BZ
☎ 0141 429 6835

- **Lamlash Nursery School**
5 Lamlash Crescent
G33 3LH
☎ 0141 774 3541

- **Langa Street Nursery School**
83 Langa Street
G20 0SQ
☎ 0141 946 3721

- **Langside Nursery School**
(c/o Battlefield Primary)
Carmichael Place
G42 9UE
☎ 0141 649 5668

- **Linthaugh Nursery School**
533 Crookston Road
G53 7TX
☎ 0141 882 7105

- **Lochview Nursery School**
145 Lochend Road
G34 0LW
☎ 0141 773 1842

- **London Road Nursery School**
1147 London Road
G40 3RF
☎ 0141 554 0578

- **Lyoncross Nursery School**
Lyoncross Road
G53 5UR
☎ 0141 882 2172

- **Machrie Nursery School**
33 Machrie Road
G45 0AG
☎ 0141 631 2255

- **Maryhill Park Nursery School**
Kilmun Street
G20 0EL
☎ 0141 946 7752

- **Mile-End Nursery School**
(c/o St Anne's Primary)
35 David Street
G40 2UN
☎ 0141 554 1675

- **Newark Drive Nursery School**
10 Newark Drive
G41 4QE
☎ 0141 423 0585

- **Newhurst Nursery School**
49 Wellhouse Crescent
G33 4LA
☎ 0141 773 2911

- **Nithsdale Road Nursery School**
  264 Nithsdale Road
  G41 5LB
  ☎ 0141 427 1896

- **Novar Nursery School**
  5 Lauderdale Gardens
  G12 9UA
  ☎ 0141 339 2938

- **Oatlands Nursery School**
  347 Caledonia Road
  G5 0JY
  ☎ 0141 429 0053

- **Penilee Nursery School**
  23 Inkerman Road
  G52 2RW
  ☎ 0141 882 7605

- **Pikeman Nursery School**
  21 Archerhill Road
  G13 3NJ
  ☎ 0141 954 2971

- **Prospecthill Nursery School**
  124 Prospecthill Road
  G42 9LH
  ☎ 0141 632 6682

- **Queen Mary Street Nursery School**
  20 Queen Mary Street
  G40 3BB
  ☎ 0141 554 7658

- **Renfrew Street Nursery School**
  256 Renfrew Street
  G3 6TT
  ☎ 0141 332 3236

- **Rosshall Nursery School**
  Cronberry Quadrant
  G52 3NU
  ☎ 0141 882 3605

- **Rowena Nursery School**
  36 Knightscliffe Avenue
  G13 2TE
  ☎ 0141 959 4183

- **Royston Nursery**
  (c/o St Roch's Secondary)
  40 Royston Road
  G21 2NF
  ☎ 0141 552 1045

- **Sandaig Nursery School**
  Uig Place
  G33 4TB
  ☎ 0141 771 1898

- **Scaraway Nursery School**
  24 Shapinsay Street
  G22 7JN
  ☎ 0141 772 1604

- **Shawbridge Nursery School**
  132 Shawbridge Street
  G43 1NP
  ☎ 0141 649 6464

- **Sighthill Nursery School**
  61 Fountainwell Road
  G21 1RG
  ☎ 0141 557 0903

- **Springburn Nursery School**
  48 Gourlay Street
  G21 1AE
  ☎ 0141 558 5279

- **Strathclyde Nursery School**
  106 Allan Street
  G40 4TD
  ☎ 0141 554 0587

- **Thornlaw Nursery School**
  34 Kilmuir Road
  Arden
  G46 8BQ
  ☎ 0141 638 9712

- **Wellfield Nursery School**
  308 Edgefauld Road
  G21 4YT
  ☎ 0141 558 5128

- **Westercommon Nursery School**
  (c/o Westercommon Primary)
  198 Auckland Street
  G22 5QN
  ☎ 0141 336 6594

- **Westercraigs Nursery School**
  (c/o) Golfhill Primary)
  13 Circus Drive
  G31 2JR
  ☎ 554 3180

- **Westerhouse Nursery School**
  55 Dubton Street
  G34 0NF
  ☎ 0141 773 0055

- **Whiteinch Nursery School**
  Glendore Street
  G14 9RW
  ☎ 0141 959 3823

- **Willows Nursery School**
  (c/o Willowbank Primary)
  Willowbank Crescent
  G3 6NB
  ☎ 0141 332 3582

- **Woodacre Nursery School**
  30 Willowford Road
  G53 7LP
  ☎ 0141 881 9043

- **Woodside Nursery School**
  445 St George's Road
  G3 6JX
  ☎ 0141 332 7661

- **Wyndford Nursery School**
  33 Latherton Drive
  G20 8JR
  ☎ 0141 945 1366

Nursery Classes

- **Anderston Nursery Class**
  (c/o Anderston Primary)
  3 Port Street
  G3 8HY
  ☎ 0141 221 3429

- **Bellahouston Nursery Class**
  70 Clifford Street
  G51 1QB
  ☎ 0141 427 6411

- **Carmyle Nursery Class**
  (c/o Carmyle Primary)
  Hillcrest Road
  G32 8AG
  ☎ 0141 641 2269

- **Dunard Nursery Class**
  (c/o Dunard Primary)
  65 Dunard Street
  G20 6RL
  ☎ 0141 946 2808

- **Elmvale Nursery Class**
  (c/o) Elmvale Primary)
  712 Hawthorn Street
  G22 6ED
  ☎ 0141 558 5238

- **Glasgow Gaelic Nursery Class**
  (c/o Glasgow Gaelic Primary)
  44 Ashley Street
  G3 6DS
  ☎ 0141 353 2321

- **Greenfield Nursery Class**
  (c/o Greenfield Primary)
  290 Nimmo Drive
  G51 3SZ
  ☎ 0141 445 3522

- **Haghill Nursery Class**
  (c/o Haghill Primary)
  16 Marwick Street
  G31 3NE
  ☎ 0141 554 3086

- **Holmlea Nursery Class**
  (c/o Holmlea Primary)
  325 Holmlea Road
  G44 4BY
  ☎ 0141 637 3989

- **Littlehill Nursery Class**
  (c/o Littlehill Primary)
  84 Craighead Avenue
  G33 1LH
  ☎ 0141 770 8374

- **Pollokshields Nursery Class**
  (c/o Pollokshields Primary)
  241 Albert Drive
  G41 2NA
  ☎ 0141 423 7330

- **Provanhill Nursery Class**
  (c/o Provanhill Primary)
  32 Balcurvie Road
  G34 9QL
  ☎ 0141 771 3694

- **Quarrybrae Nursery Class**
  (c/o Quarrybrae Primary)
  139 Crail Street
  G31 5RB
  ☎ 0141 554 3259

- **Thornwood Nursery Class**
(c/o Thornwood Primary)
11 Thornwood Terrace
G11 7QZ
☎ 0141 339 7445

- **St Angela's Nursery Class**
(c/o St Angela's Primary)
227 Glenmoriston Road
G53 7HT
☎ 0141 638 9646

- **St Bridget's Nursery Class**
(c/o St Bridget's Primary)
Camp Road
G69 6DF
☎ 0141 771 1294

- **St Fillan's Nursery Class**
(c/o St Fillan's Primary)
20 Crompton Avenue
G44 5AF
☎ 0141 633 0566

- **St Mark's Nursery Class**
(c/o St Mark's Primary)
170 Muiryfauld Drive
G31 5LF
☎ 0141 778 4114

- **St Timothy's Nursery Class**
(c/o St Timothy's Primary)
41 Inveresh Street
G32 6SL
☎ 0141 774 7821

- **Victoria Nursery Class**
(c/o Victoria Primary)
67 Batson Street
G42 7HD
☎ 0141 423 2759

Children's Centres/ Day Nurseries/Family Centres

- **Barlanark Family Learning Centre**
  125 Barlanark Road
  G33 4PL
  ☎ 0141 771 4833

- **Bridgeton Day Nursery**
  106 Orr Street
  G40 2QF
  ☎ 0141 554 3719

- **Broompark Day Nursery**
  7 Broompark Circus
  G31 2JF
  ☎ 0141 554 0272

- **Budhill Family Learning and Community Education Centre**
  Hallhill Road
  G32 0PR
  ☎ 0141 774 4722

- **Burnbrae Children's Centre**
  Burnbrae Annexe
  2 Priesthill Road
  G53 6PR
  ☎ 0141 881 6971

- **Castlemilk Day Nursery**
  8 Barlia Street
  G45 0NT
  ☎ 0141 631 1834

- **Castlemilk Family Learning Centre**
  128 Tormusk Road
  G45 0HE
  ☎ 0141 634 3154

- **Clutha Street Day Nursery**
  3 Clutha Street
  G51 1BL
  ☎ 0141 427 2301

- **Cowcaddens Day Nursery**
  12 Manresa Place
  G4 9SZ
  ☎ 0141 332 3218

- **Craigielea Day Nursery**
  2 Craigpark
  G31 2NA
  ☎ 0141 554 4000

- **Drumchapel Day Nursery**
  60 Kinfauns Drive
  G15 7TS
  ☎ 0141 944 7095

- **Drumchapel Opportunities Nursery**
  (c/o Drumry Primary)
  3 Abbotshall Avenue
  G15 8PR
  ☎ 0141 944 1650

- **The Jimmy Dunachie Family Learning Centre**
  (c/o Thornlaw Community Annexe)
  34b Kilmuir Road
  Arden
  G46 8BQ
  ☎ 0141 638 6397

- **Elderpark Day Nursery**
  20 Arklet Road
  G51 3XR
  ☎ 0141 445 1298

- **Fasque Family Centre**
9 Ladyloan Place
G15 8HU
☎ 0141 944 0566

- **Gathamlock Family Centre**
60 Kincardine Square
G33 5BU
☎ 0141 774 7684

- **Hamiltonhill Family Learning Centre**
115 Ellesmere Street
G22 5QT
☎ 0141 332 2797

- **Holmlea Day Nursery**
77 Holmlea Road
G44 4AQ
☎ 0141 632 4340

- **Laurieston Day Nursery**
99 Norfolk Street
G5 9LZ
☎ 0141 429 2480

- **Milton Community Nursery**
190 Liddesdale Road
G22 7QS
☎ 0141 772 4490

- **Molendinar Family Learning Centre**
45 Craighead Avenue
G33 1LH
☎ 0141 770 7692

- **Onslow Drive Day Nursery**
6 Onslow Drive
G31 2LX
☎ 0141 554 3061

- **Parkhead Community Nursery**
Unit 1 60 Crail Street
G31 5AL
☎ 0141 554 0440

- **Parkhead Pre-School Assessment Centre**
1346 Gallowgate
G31 4DJ
☎ 0141 551 9591

- **Pollok Children's Centre**
8 Netherplace Crescent
G53 5AA
☎ 0141 882 7773

- **Pollokshaws Day Nursery**
55 Greenview Street
G43 1SN
☎ 0141 649 2515

- **St Clare's Day Nursery**
(c/o Blairtummock Primary)
89 Baldinnie Road
G34 9EP
☎ 0141 771 2301

- **Sandyford Day Nursery**
(c/o St Patrick's Primary)
10 Perth Street
G3 8UQ
☎ 0141 221 5502

- **Sandy Road Day Nursery**
22 Sandy Road
G11 6HE
☎ 0141 334 1581

- **Thirlstane Day Nursery**
(c/o Yoker Primary)
56 Craggan Drive
G14 0SE
☎ 0141 959 4043

Primary Schools

- **Albert Primary School**
  10 Barclay Street
  G21 4UH
  ☎ 0141 558 5430

- **Alexandra Parade Primary School**
  136 Armadale Street
  G31 2TL
  ☎ 0141 554 3742

- **Anderston Primary School**
  3 Port Street
  G3 8HY
  ☎ 0141 221 1263

- **Annette Street Primary School**
  27 Annette Street
  G42 8YB
  ☎ 0141 423 0192

- **Arden Primary School**
  75 Kyleakin Road
  Arden
  G46 8DQ
  ☎ 0141 638 5656

- **Balornock Primary School**
  422 Broomfield Road
  G21 3UT
  ☎ 0141 558 5224

- **Bankhead Primary School**
  66 Caldwell Avenue
  G13 3AS
  ☎ 0141 959 3531

- **Barlanark Primary School**
  343 Hallhill Road
  G33 4RY
  ☎ 0141 771 3111

- **Barmulloch Primary School**
  60 Berryburn Road
  G21 3DA
  ☎ 0141 558 6711

- **Barrowfield Primary**
  126 Barrowfield Street
  G40 3SL
  ☎ 0141 556 7800

- **Battlefield Primary School**
  44 Carmichael Place
  G42 9SY
  ☎ 0141 632 2162

- **Bellahouston Primary School**
  425 Paisley Road West
  G51 1PZ
  ☎ 0141 427 2157

- **Bishoploch Primary School**
  2 Auchengill Place
  G34 0EY
  ☎ 0141 771 5016

- **Blackfriars Primary School**
  310 Cumberland Street
  G5 0SS
  ☎ 0141 429 2444

- **Blairdardie Primary School**
  78 Kearn Avenue
  G15 6HL
  ☎ 0141 944 1462

- **Blairtummock Primary School**
89 Baldinnie Road
G34 9EP
☎ 0141 771 3343

- **Bonnyholm Primary School**
24 Bonnyholm Avenue
G53 5RF
☎ 0141 810 4789

- **Braeside Primary School**
43 Machrie Drive
G45 0AL
☎ 0141 634 5122

- **Broadholm Primary School**
88 Linkwood Drive
G15 7SN
☎ 0141 944 3077

- **Broomhill Primary School**
57 Edgehill Road
G11 7HZ
☎ 0141 334 5171

- **Burnbrae Primary School**
179 Muirshiel Crescent
G53 6PW
☎ 0141 881 2496

- **Cadder Primary School**
60 Herma Street
G23 5AR
☎ 0141 946 3063

- **Caldercuilt Primary School**
101 Invershiel Road
G23 5JG
☎ 0141 945 0633

- **Caledonia Primary School**
Calderwood Drive
G69 7DJ
☎ 0141 771 8214

- **Cardonald Primary School**
1 Angus Oval
G52 3HD
☎ 0141 883 9668

- **Carmunnock Primary School**
158 Waterside Road
G76 9AJ
☎ 0141 644 4164

- **Carmyle Primary School**
Hillcrest Road
G32 8AG
☎ 0141 641 2269

- **Carntyne Primary School**
38 Liberton Street
G33 2HF
☎ 0141 770 4305

- **Carnwadrick Primary School**
29 Capelrig Street
G46 8PH
☎ 0141 638 0217

- **Castleton Primary School**
70 Dougrie Road
G45 9NW
☎ 0141 634 6913

- **Chirnsyde Primary School**
288 Ashgill Road
G22 7SB
☎ 0141 336 8672

- **Copeland Primary School**
  3 Burndyke Court
  G51 2BG
  ☎ 0141 445 1767

- **Craigton Primary School**
  9 Morven Street
  G52 1AL
  ☎ 0141 882 2856

- **Croftfoot Primary School**
  114 Crofthill Road
  G44 5QQ
  ☎ 0141 637 4007

- **Cuthbertson Primary School**
  35 Cuthbertson Street
  G42 7RJ
  ☎ 0141 423 0452

- **Dalmarnock Primary School**
  35 Albany Street
  G40 3EE
  ☎ 0141 554 3558

- **Darnley Primary School**
  169 Glen Moriston Road
  G53 7HT
  ☎ 0141 638 8009

- **Dowanhill Primary School**
  30 Havelock Street
  G11 5JE
  ☎ 0141 339 0778

- **Drumoyne Primary School**
  200 Shieldhall Road
  G51 4EH
  ☎ 0141 445 1766

- **Drumry Primary School**
  3 Abbotshill Avenue
  G15 8PR
  ☎ 0141 944 2559

- **Dunard Primary School**
  65 Dunard Street
  G20 6RL
  ☎ 0141 946 1417

- **Eastbank Primary School**
  80 Gartocher Road
  G32 0HA
  ☎ 0141 778 6659

- **Easthall Primary School**
  33 Ware Road
  G34 9AR
  ☎ 0141 771 4646

- **Elder Park Primary School**
  20 St Kenneth Drive
  G51 4QD
  ☎ 0141 445 1074

- **Elmvale Primary School**
  712 Hawthorn Street
  G22 6ED
  ☎ 0141 558 5238

- **Garnetbank Primary School**
  231 Renfrew Street
  G3 6TX
  ☎ 0141 332 5158

- **Garrowhill Primary School**
  Springhall Road
  G69 6PP
  ☎ 0141 771 1235

- **Garscadden Primary School**
  15–19 Hulford Avenue
  G13 4AY
  ☎ 0141 959 2292

- **Garthamlock Primary School**
  3 Guildford Street
  G33 5BH
  ☎ 0141 774 2544

- **Glasgow Gaelic Primary School**
  Bunsgoil Ghaidhlig Ghlaschu
  44 Ashley Street
  G3 6DS
  ☎ 0141 353 2321

- **Glendale Primary School**
  120 McCulloch Street
  G41 1NX
  ☎ 0141 429 6973

- **Golfhill Primary School**
  13 Circus Drive
  G31 2JR
  ☎ 0141 554 0041

- **Gowanbank Primary School**
  20 Overtown Avenue
  G53 6JB
  ☎ 0141 881 2424

- **Greenfield Primary School**
  29 Nimmo Drive
  G51 3SZ
  ☎ 0141 445 1774

- **Haghill Primary School**
  16 Marwick Street
  G31 3NG
  ☎ 0141 554 3780

- **Hawthorn Primary School**
  (c/o St Teresa's Primary)
  97 Scone Street
  G21 1JF
  ☎ 0141 336 7624

- **Hillhead Primary School**
  21 Cecil Street
  G12 8RL
  ☎ 0141 339 9175

- **Hillington Primary School**
  227 Hartlaw Crescent
  G52 2JL
  ☎ 0141 882 2144

- **Hill's Trust Primary School**
  29 Nethan Street
  G51 3LX
  ☎ 0141 445 4365

- **Holmlea Primary School**
  352 Holmlea Road
  G44 4BY
  ☎ 0141 637 3989

- **Househillmuir Primary School**
  271 Househillmuir Road
  G53 6NL
  ☎ 0141 881 5016

- **Hyndland Primary School**
  44 Fortrose Street
  G11 5LP
  ☎ 0141 339 7207

- **Ibrox Primary School**
  46 Hinshelwood Drive
  G51 2XP
  ☎ 0141 427 0922

- **Kelvindale Primary School**
  11 Dorchester Place
  G12 0BP
  ☎ 0141 334 5005

- **Kelvinhaugh Primary School**
  20 Sandyford Street
  G3 8QJ
  ☎ 0141 339 0559

- **King's Park Primary School**
  44 Kingbridge Drive
  G44 4JS
  ☎ 0141 632 2193

- **Knightswood Primary School**
  60 Knightswood Road
  G13 2XD
  ☎ 0141 959 3284

- **Knockburn Primary School**
  1 Ferness Oval
  G21 3SQ
  ☎ 0141 558 6635

- **Lamlash Primary School**
  21 Lamlash Crescent
  G33 3LH
  ☎ 0141 774 3511

- **Langfaulds Primary School**
  56 Ledmore Drive
  G15 7AQ
  ☎ 0141 944 0340

- **Langside Primary School**
  223 Tantallon Road
  G41 3JW
  0141 632 0874

- **Leithland Primary School**
  188 Leithland Road
  G53 5AT
  ☎ 0141 882 2031

- **Littlehill Primary School**
  84 Craighead Avenue
  G33 1LH
  ☎ 0141 770 8374

- **Lochgoin Primary School**
  12 Lochgoin Avenue
  G15 8RA
  ☎ 0141 944 3082

- **London Road Primary School**
  1147 London Road
  G40 3RF
  ☎ 0141 554 3011

- **Lorne Street Primary School**
  28 Lorne Street
  G51 1DP
  ☎ 0141 427 1315

- **McGill Primary School**
  80 Meiklerig Crescent
  G53 5UF
  ☎ 0141 882 6592

- **Maryhill Primary School**
  2 Viewmount Drive
  G20 0LW
  ☎ 0141 946 1409

- **Merrylee Primary School**
  68 Ashmore Road
  G44 3DD
  ☎ 0141 637 8569

- **Milncroft Primary School**
15 Skerryvore Road
G33 3LT
☎ 0141 774 2821

- **Miltonbank Primary School**
11 Skerray Street
G22 7PT
☎ 0141 772 8877

- **Mosspark Primary School**
20 Mosspark Square
G52 1LZ
☎ 0141 882 3602

- **Mount Florida Primary School**
1127 Cathcart Road
G42 9HF
☎ 0141 632 4455

- **Mount Vernon Primary School**
Penryn Gardens
G32 9NY
☎ 0141 778 9616

- **Netherton Primary School**
16 Blaeloch Drive
G45 9QN
☎ 0141 634 6472

- **Nitshill Primary School**
8 Willowford Road
G53 7LP
☎ 0141 881 2877

- **Oakgrove Primary School**
20 St Peter's Street
G4 9PW
☎ 0141 332 6210

- **Parkview Primary School**
19 Rothes Drive
G23 5PZ
☎ 0141 946 4622

- **Pinewood Primary School**
140 Drummore Road
G15 7NJ
☎ 0141 944 2971

- **Pollokshields Primary School**
241 Albert Drive
G41 2NA
☎ 0141 423 1363

- **Provanhall Primary School**
32 Balcurvie Road
G34 9QL
☎ 0141 771 2910

- **Quarrybrae Primary School**
139 Crail Street
G31 5RB
☎ 0141 554 3419

- **Rogerfield Primary School**
20 Corsehill Street
G34 0PW
☎ 0141 771 3116

- **Royston Primary School**
102 Royston Road
G21 2NU
☎ 0141 552 2872

- **Ruchazie Primary School**
15 Drumlochy Road
G33 3RB
☎ 0141 774 4900

- **Ruchill Primary School**
  29 Brassey Street
  G20 9HW
  ☎ 0141 946 1408

- **Sandaig Primary School**
  31 Burnmouth Road
  G33 4SA
  ☎ 0141 773 1744

- **Sandwood Primary School**
  120 Sandwood Road
  G52 2QY
  ☎ 0141 883 8367

- **Saracen Primary School**
  Stonyhurst Street
  G22 5NP
  ☎ 0141 336 8392

- **Scotstoun Primary School**
  21 Duncan Avenue
  G14 9HN
  ☎ 0141 959 3247

- **Shawlands Primary School**
  1284 Pollokshaws Road
  G41 3QP
  ☎ 0141 632 1840

- **Sighthill Primary School**
  8 Fountainwell Place
  G21 1QH
  ☎ 0141 558 7843

- **Simshill Primary School**
  148 Simshill Road
  G44 5EP
  ☎ 0141 637 0472

- **Sir John Maxwell Primary School**
  Christian Street
  G43 1RH
  ☎ 0141 632 1336

- **Springfield Primary School**
  106 Allan Street
  G40 4TD
  ☎ 0141 556 2790

- **St James' Primary School**
  88 Green Street
  G40 2TG
  ☎ 0141 554 3272

- **Stonedyke Primary School**
  37 Cloan Avenue
  G15 6DD
  ☎ 0141 944 2156

- **Summerhill Primary School**
  55 Summerhill Road
  G15 7JR
  ☎ 0141 944 2551

- **Sunnyside Primary School**
  1 Powrie Street
  G33 5LA
  ☎ 0141 774 5777

- **Swinton Primary School**
  2 Rhindmuir Road
  G69 6AZ
  ☎ 0141 771 1776

- **Temple Primary School**
  Spencer Street
  G13 1EA
  ☎ 0141 954 8806

- **Thorntree Primary School**
  55 Cobinshaw Street
  G32 6XL
  ☎ 0141 774 4966

- **Thornwood Primary School**
  11 Thornwood Terrace
  G11 7QZ
  ☎ 0141 334 4271

- **Tinto Primary School**
  22 Tinto Road
  G43 2BA
  ☎ 0141 637 1303

- **Tormusk Primary School**
  128 Tormusk Rd
  G45 0HE
  ☎ 0141 634 6482

- **Toryglen Primary School**
  6 Drumreoch Place
  G42 0ER
  ☎ 0141 647 4396

- **Victoria Primary School**
  67 Batson Street
  G42 7HD
  ☎ 0141 423 2759

- **Wellhouse Primary School**
  4 Balado Road
  G33 4EZ
  ☎ 0141 771 2447

- **Wellshot Primary School**
  285 Wellshot Road
  G32 7QD
  ☎ 0141 778 1091

- **Westercommon Primary School**
  231 Ellesmere Street
  G22 5QN
  ☎ 0141 336 6116

- **Whiteinch Primary School**
  56 Medwyn Street
  G14 9RP
  ☎ 0141 959 3271

- **Willowbank Primary School**
  Willowbank Crescent
  G3 6NB
  ☎ 0141 332 6281

- **Windlaw Primary School**
  29 Dunagoil Road
  G45 9UR
  ☎ 0141 634 6452

- **Wyndford Primary School**
  116 Glenfinnan Drive
  G20 8HL
  ☎ 0141 946 6222

- **Yoker Primary School**
  56 Craggan Drive
  G14 0ES
  ☎ 0141 954 2522

- **Corpus Christi Primary School**
  179 Pikeman Road
  G13 3BH
  ☎ 0141 954 5380

- **Holy Cross Primary School**
  316 Calder Street
  G42 7NH
  ☎ 0141 423 2538

- **Lourdes Primary School**
  21 Montrave Street
  G52 2TS
  ☎ 0141 882 2305

- **Notre Dame Primary School**
  66 Victoria Crescent Road
  G12 9JL
  ☎ 0141 334 2762

- **Ogilvie Primary School**
  48 Newhills Road
  G33 4HJ
  ☎ 0141 771 2900

- **Our Lady of the Annuniciation Primary School**
  80 Friarton Road
  G43 2PR
  ☎ 0141 637 7457

- **Our Lady of the Assumption Primary School**
  439 Bilsland Drive
  G20 9JN
  ☎ 0141 946 2644

- **Our Lady of the Rosary Primary School**
  50 Tarfside Gardens
  G52 3AA
  ☎ 0141 883 2010

- **Sacred Heart Primary School**
  31 Reid Street
  G40 4AR
  ☎ 0141 554 5949

- **St Agnes' Primary School**
  5 Tresta Road
  G23 5LB
  ☎ 0141 946 1458

- **St Albert's Primary School**
  36 Maxwell Drive
  G41 5DU
  ☎ 0141 429 1983

- **St Aloysius' Primary School**
  12 Carron Crescent
  G22 6BS
  ☎ 0141 558 8468

- **St Ambrose's Primary School**
  6 Mingulay Place
  G22 7DX
  ☎ 0141 772 1775

- **St Angela's Primary School**
  227 Glen Moriston Road
  G53 7HT
  ☎ 0141 638 9646

- **St Anne's Primary School**
  35 David Street
  G40 2UN
  ☎ 0141 554 2734

- **St Anthony's Primary School**
  30 Elder Street
  G51 3LT
  ☎ 0141 445 3828

- **St Augustine's Primary School**
  256 Liddesdale Road
  G22 7QR
  ☎ 0141 772 1921

- **St Bartholomew's Primary School**
  5 Cavin Road
  G45 9TX
  ☎ 0141 634 7114

- **St Benedict's Primary School**
745 Westerhouse Road
G34 9RP
☎ 0141 771 3224

- **St Bernard's Primary School**
14–16 Dove Street
G53 7BP
☎ 0141 881 2457

- **St Blane's Primary School**
23 Arrochar Drive
G23 5QB
☎ 0141 945 1276

- **St Brendan's Primary School**
170 Hawick Street
G13 4HG
☎ 0141 952 4449

- **St Bride's Primary School**
83 Craigie Street
G42 8NB
☎ 0141 423 7733

- **St Brigid's Primary School**
Camp Road
G69 6DF
☎ 0141 771 1294

- **St Brigid's Primary School**
4 Glenmore Avenue
G42 0EH
☎ 0141 647 3952

- **St Catherine's Primary School**
274 Rye Road
G21 3JR
☎ 0141 558 8582

- **St Charles's Primary School**
13 Kelvinside Gardens
G20 6BG
☎ 0141 946 1391

- **St Clare's Primary School**
(Drumchapel)
21 Peel Glen Road
G15 7XN
☎ 0141 944 2554

- **St Clare's Primary School**
(Easterhouse)
22 Drumlanrig Avenue
G34 0JD
☎ 0141 771 2911

- **St Colette's Primary School**
15 Dungeonhill Road
G34 0AT
☎ 0141 773 0928

- **St Conval's Primary School**
140 Shawhill Road
G43 1SY
☎ 0141 632 0745

- **St Cuthbert's Primary School**
198 Auckland Street
G22 5NT
☎ 0141 336 8374

- **St Denis' Primary School**
129 Roslea Drive
G31 2RZ
☎ 0141 554 2020

- **St Dominic's Primary School**
25 Ardencraig Drive
G45 0HS
☎ 0141 634 3113

- **St Edmund's Primary School**
  160 Damshot Crescent
  G53 5EE
  ☎ 0141 810 4792

- **St Elizabeth Seton Primary School**
  23 Toward Road
  G33 3NW
  ☎ 0141 774 3849

- **St Fillan's Primary School**
  20 Crompton Avenue
  G44 5AF
  ☎ 0141 633 0566

- **St Francis' Primary School**
  430 Old Rutherglen Road
  G5 0PA
  ☎ 0141 429 3687

- **St Francis of Assisi Primary School**
  Crown Street
  G69 7XB
  ☎ 0141 773 2052

- **St George's Primary School**
  101 Muirdykes Road
  G52 2QJ
  ☎ 0141 883 9671

- **St Gilbert's Primary School**
  305 Forge Street
  G21 8AH
  ☎ 0141 770 7889

- **St Gregory's Primary School**
  186 Wyndford Road
  G20 8HF
  ☎ 0141 946 6255

- **St Jerome's Primary School**
  45 Drumoyne Road
  G51 4AX
  ☎ 0141 445 1368

- **St Joachim's Primary School**
  Montrose Avenue
  G32 8BZ
  ☎ 0141 641 6840

- **St John's Primary School**
  99 Norfolk Street
  G5 9LQ
  ☎ 0141 429 6017

- **St Joseph's Primary School**
  39 Raglan Street
  G4 9QX
  ☎ 0141 332 7836

- **St Jude's Primary School**
  29 Garvel Road
  G33 4PR
  ☎ 0141 771 2055

- **St Julie's Primary School**
  100 Croftfoot Road
  G45 9HW
  ☎ 0141 634 6559

- **St Louise's Primary School**
  69 Kyleakin Road
  G46 8DE
  ☎ 0141 638 0783

- **St Margaret Mary's Primary School**
  40 Downcraig Road
  G45 9PG
  ☎ 0141 634 1652

- **St Mark's Primary School**
170 Muiryfauld Drive
G31 5LF
☎ 01471 778 4114

- **St Marnock's Primary School**
Langton Crescent
G53 5LW
☎ 0141 882 1915

- **St Martha's Primary School**
85 Menzies Road
G21 3NG
☎ 0141 558 6193

- **St Martin's Primary School**
223 Ardencraig Road
G45 0JS
☎ 0141 634 1348

- **St Mary's Primary School**
Kilmun Street
G20 0EL
☎ 0141 946 6766

- **St Michael's Primary School**
865 Springfield Road
G31 4HZ
☎ 0141 554 3105

- **St Mirin's Primary School**
260 Carmunnock Road
G44 5AP
☎ 0141 637 7455

- **St Modan's Primary School**
109 Bellrock Crescent
G33 3HF
☎ 0141 774 4085

- **St Mungo's Primary School**
45 Parson Street
G4 0PX
☎ 0141 552 3120

- **St Ninian's Primary School**
2150 Great Western Road
G13 2AB
☎ 0141 959 3242

- **St Patrick's Primary School**
10 Perth Street
G3 8UQ
☎ 0141 221 2921

- **St Paul's Primary School** (Shettleston)
85 Anworth Street
G32 7RR
☎ 0141 778 6227

- **St Paul's Primary School** (Whiteinch)
17 Primrose Street
G14 0TF
☎ 0141 959 3263

- **St Peter's Primary School**
58 Chancelor Street
G11 5QN
☎ 0141 339 1989

- **St Philip's Primary School**
157 Drumlochy Road
G33 3RD
☎ 0141 774 4545

- **St Philomena's Primary School**
21 Robroyston Road
G33 1EA
☎ 0141 770 4134

- **St Pius' Primary School**
  32 Ryedale Place
  G15 7HU
  ☎ 0141 944 3400

- **St Robert's Primary School**
  60 Priesthill Crescent
  G53 6PT
  ☎ 0141 881 1816

- **St Roch's Primary School**
  267 Royston Road
  G21 2BS
  ☎ 0141 552 0010

- **St Rose of Lima Primary School**
  291 Mossvale Road
  G33 5QS
  ☎ 0141 774 7209

- **St Saviour's Primary School**
  41 Dunsmuir Street
  G51 2DN
  ☎ 0141 445 1775

- **St Stephen's Primary School**
  22 Pinkston Drive
  G21 1NL
  ☎ 0141 558 9085

- **St Teresa's Primary School**
  97 Scone Street
  G21 1JF
  ☎ 0141 336 7634

- **St Thomas' Primary School**
  8 Smithycroft Road
  G33 2QJ
  ☎ 0141 770 4360

- **St Timothy's Primary School**
  41 Inveresk Street
  G32 6SL
  ☎ 0141 774 7821

- **St Vincent's Primary School**
  40 Crebar Street
  G46 8EQ
  ☎ 0141 638 8927

■ North Lanarkshire Council

Please find in the following section listings of local authority Primary Schools, Nurseries within Primary Schools and Nursery Classes in North Lanarkshire

■ **North Lanarkshire Council Headquarters**
PO Box 14
14 Civic Centre
Motherwell
ML1 1TW
Lanarkshire
☎ 01698 302222

■ **Childcare Information Service**
☎ 01236 812 281

■ **Childcare Information Website**
www.childcarelink.gov.uk/northlanarkshire

■ **Early Years Office – Motherwell**
☎ 01236 428943

■ **Early Years Office – Monklands**
☎ 01236 428036

■ **Early Years Office – Cumbernauld**
☎ 01236 429238

- **Abronhill Primary School**
  Medlar Road
  Abronhill
  Cumbernauld
  G67 3BJ
  ☎ 01236 723649

- **Abronhill Nursery School**
  2/8 Hornbeam Road
  Abronhill
  Cumbernauld
  G67 3NQ
  ☎ 01236 722171

- **Ailsa Nursery Centre**
  The Loaning
  Motherwell
  ML1 3NQ
  ☎ 01698 276229

- **Aitkenhead Primary School**
  Lincoln Avenue
  Uddingston
  G71 5QZ
  ☎ 01698 818123

- **Albert Primary School**
  31 North Biggar Road
  Airdrie
  ML6 6EJ
  ☎ 01236 763349

- **Alexander Peden Primary School & Nursery**
  West Main Street
  Harthill
  ML7 5TU
  ☎ 01501 752185

- **Alexandria Primary School**
  Broomknoll Street
  Airdrie
  ML6 9EX
  ☎ 01236 767622

- **Allanton Primary School**
  Dura Road
  Allanton
  ML7 5AB
  ☎ 01501 821864

- **Auchinloch Primary School**
  Forth Avenue
  Auchinloch
  Kirkintilloch
  G66 5DU
  ☎ 0141 776 3223

- **Baird Memorial Primary School**
  Glenacre Road
  N.Carbrain
  Cumbernauld
  G67
  ☎ 01236 612670

- **Balmalloch Primary School**
  Kingsway
  Kilsyth
  G65 9UJ
  ☎ 01236 823960

- **Banton Primary School**
  Lammerknowes Road
  Banton
  Kilsyth
  G65 0QT
  ☎ 01236 822249

- **Bargeddie Primary School**
Coatbridge Road
Bargeddie
Glasgow
G69 7PH
☎ 0141 771 1848

- **Bellshill Nursery Centre**
David Anderson Centre
Deans Street
Bellshill
ML4 1PD
☎ 01698 849526

- **Belvidere Primary School & Nursery**
Belvidere Road
Bellshill
ML4 2DZ
☎ 01698 747772

- **Berryhill Primary School & Nursery**
Hillcrest Avenue
Wishaw
ML2 7RB
☎ 01698 375888

- **Burnhead Primary School**
Cedar Drive
Viewpark
Uddingston
G71 5LE
☎ 01698 813128

- **Calder Primary School**
Draffen Street
Motherwell
ML1 1NJ
☎ 01698 264436

- **Calderbank Primary School**
Main Street
Calderbank
Airdrie
ML6 9SG
☎ 01236 763642

- **Calderhead Nursery School**
Kirk Road
Shotts
ML7 5ET
☎ 01501 822509

- **Cambusnethan Nursery Centre**
Greenfield Drive
Cambusnethan
Wishaw
ML2
☎ 01698 381144

- **Cambusnethan Primary School**
Kirk Road
Cambusnethan
Wishaw
ML2 8LJ
☎ 01698 385888

- **Carbrain Primary School**
Millcroft Road
Carbrain
Cumbernauld
G67 2LD
☎ 01236 722707

- **Carnbroe Primary School**
Kirkton Crescent
Coatbridge
ML5 4TP
☎ 01236 434518

- **Castlehill Primary School & Nursery**
  Birkshaw Brae
  Wishaw
  ML2 OND
  ☎ 01698 357497

- **Cathedral Primary School**
  Park Street
  Motherwell
  ML1 1PT
  ☎ 01698 262692

- **Cedar Road Nursery School**
  196 Cedar Road
  Abronhill
  Cumbernauld
  G67 3AS
  ☎ 01236 733604

- **Chapelgreen Primary School**
  Mill Road
  Queenzieburn
  Kilsyth
  G65 9EF
  ☎ 01236 822242

- **Chapelhall Primary School & Nursery**
  Gibb Street
  Chapelhall
  Airdrie
  ML6 8UG
  ☎ 01236 762515

- **Chapelside Primary School**
  Chapel Street
  Airdrie
  ML6 6LH
  ☎ 01236 765764

- **Christ The King Primary School**
  Melrose Avenue
  Holytown
  Motherwell
  ML1 4SG
  ☎ 01698 733815

- **Chryston Primary School**
  Lindsaybeg Road
  Chryston
  G69 9DW
  ☎ 0141 779 2700

- **Clarkston Primary School**
  Forrest Street
  Airdrie
  ML6 7AE
  ☎ 01236 763274

- **Cleland Primary School**
  26 Main Street
  Cleland
  Motherwell
  ML1 5QN
  ☎ 01698 860354

- **Coatholm Nursery School**
  Wallace Street
  Whifflet
  Coatbridge
  ML5 4DA
  ☎ 01236 423684

- **Coltness Primary School & Nursery**
  Coltness Road
  Coltness
  Wishaw
  ML2 7EY
  ☎ 01698 384434

- **Condorrat Primary School**
  Morar Drive
  Condorrat
  Cumbernauld
  G67 4LA
  ☎ 01236 720970

- **Corpus Primary School & Nursery**
  Crowwood Crescent
  Calderbank
  Airdrie
  ML6 9TA
  ☎ 01236 763985

- **Craigneuk Nursery Centre**
  641 Glasgow Road
  Wishaw
  ML2 7SR
  ☎ 01698 373942

- **Croy Nursery School**
  Macsparran Road
  Croy
  G65 9HN
  ☎ 01236 823901

- **Cumbernauld Primary School**
  Glasgow Road
  Cumbernauld
  G67 2RZ
  ☎ 01236 723542

- **Devonview Nursery Centre**
  Devonview Street
  Airdrie
  ML5 9DH
  ☎ 01236 765815

- **Drumpark Primary School & Nursery**
  Bargeddie
  Coatbridge
  G69 7TW
  ☎ 01236 423955
  Fax 01236 423879

- **Dunbeth Nursery Centre**
  Kildonan Street
  Coatbridge
  ML5 3LS
  ☎ 01236 425717

- **Dunrobin Primary School**
  Petersburn Road
  Airdrie
  ML6 8BH
  ☎ 01236 763084

- **Dykehead Primary School**
  Easter Road
  Shotts
  ML7 4AS
  ☎ 01501 821772

- **Eastfield Primary School**
  23 Cairntoul Court
  Cumbernauld
  G68 9JT
  ☎ 01236 725501

- **Firpark Primary School & Nursery**
  Firpark Street
  Motherwell
  ML1 2PR
  ☎ 01698 251313

- **Forgewood Annexe Nursery Centre**
  c/o Braidhurst High School
  Dalriada Crescent
  Motherwell ML1 3XF
  ☎ 01698 259652

- **Forgewood Nursery Centre**
  Fife Drive
  Motherwell
  ML1 3UP
  ☎ 01698 252045

- **Gartcosh Primary School**
  Lochend Road
  Gartcosh
  G69 8AB
  ☎ 01236 872314

- **Gartsherrie Primary School**
  Gartsherrie Road
  Coatbridge
  ML5 2EU
  ☎ 01236 423272

- **Glenboig Primary School**
  Whitelaw Avenue
  Glenboig
  Coatbridge
  ML5 2PX
  ☎ 01236 872444

- **Glencairn Primary School & Nursery**
  Glencairn Street
  Motherwell
  ML1 1TT
  ☎ 01698 300281

- **Glencryan Primary School & Nursery**
  Greenfaulds
  Cumbernauld
  G67 2XJ
  ☎ 01236 724125

- **Glengowan Primary School & Nursery**
  Drumfin Avenue
  Caldercruix
  Airdrie ML6 7QP
  ☎ 01236 842308

- **Glenmanor Primary School & Nursery**
  Glenmanor Avenue
  Moodiesburn
  G69 0JA
  ☎ 01236 872641

- **Golfhill Primary School**
  Ballochney Street
  Burnfoot
  Airdrie
  ML6 0LT
  ☎ 01236 606401

- **Greengairs Primary School**
  Greengairs Road
  Greengairs
  Airdrie
  ML6 7TE
  ☎ 01236 830587

- **Greenhill Primary School**
  Coltswood Road
  Coatbridge
  ML5 2DB
  ☎ 01236 421350

- **Holy Cross Primary School**
  Constarry Road
  Croy
  Kilsyth
  G65 9JG
  ☎ 01236 822099

- **Holy Family Primary School**
  Hope Street
  Mossend
  Bellshill
  ML4 1QA
  ☎ 01698 747108

■ **Holytown Primary School & Nursery**
Willow Grove
Holytown
Motherwell
ML1 4SB
☎ 01698 732672

■ **Hozier Nursery School**
Cedar Drive
Viewpark
Uddingston
G71 5LE
☎ 01698 814810

■ **Jigsaw Nursery Centre**
Elmira Road
Muirhead
Glasgow
G69 9EJ
☎ 0141 779 4516

■ **Keir Hardie Memorial Primary School**
Brannock Road
Newarthill
Motherwell
ML1 5DU
☎ 01698 732259

■ **Kildrum Nursery Centre**
Afton Road
Cumbernauld
G67 2ET
☎ 01236 782310

■ **Kildrum Primary School**
Afton Road
Kildrum
Cumbernauld
G67 2ET
☎ 01236 724232

■ **Kilsyth Primary School**
Shuttle Street
Kilsyth
G65 0BL
☎ 01236 823133

■ **Kirk O'Shotts Primary School**
School Road
Salsburgh
Shotts
ML7 4NS
☎ 01698 870245

■ **Kirkshaws Primary School & Nursery**
Old Monkland Road
Coatbridge
ML5 5EJ
☎ 01236 424731

■ **Knowetop Primary School**
Knowetop Avenue
Motherwell ML1 2AG
☎ 01698 262610

■ **Ladywell Primary School**
240 Ladywell Road
Motherwell
ML1 3EU
☎ 01698 262597

■ **Lammermoor Primary School & Nursery**
Rowan Street
Coltness
Wishaw
ML2 7EG
☎ 01698 385266

■ **Langloan Primary School**
Bank Street
Coatbridge ML5 1EG
☎ 01236 423851

- **Lawmuir Primary School**
  Footfield Road
  Orbiston
  Bellshill
  ML4 2BY
  ☎ 01698 747130

- **Logans Primary School**
  Logans Road
  Motherwell
  ML1 3PH
  ☎ 01698 263708

- **Mavisbank Primary School & Nursery**
  Mitchell Street
  Airdrie
  ML6 OEB
  ☎ 01236 752725

- **Morningside Primary School**
  School Road
  Morningside
  Wishaw
  ML2 9QW
  ☎ 01698 384102

- **Mossend Primary School & Nursery**
  Calder Road
  Bellshill
  ML4 2RH
  ☎ 01698 747315

- **Muir Street Primary School**
  Parkneuk Street
  Motherwell
  ML1 1BY
  ☎ 01698 262681

- **Muirhouse Primary School & Nursery**
  66 Barons Road
  Motherwell ML1 2NB
  ☎ 01698 262337

- **Netherton Primary School**
  Netherton Road
  Wishaw
  ML2 ODD
  ☎ 01698 372055

- **New Monkland Primary School**
  Raebog Road
  Glenmavis
  Airdrie
  ML6 ONW
  ☎ 01236 762634

- **New Stevenston Primary School & Nursery**
  Clydesdale Street
  New Steveston
  Motherwell
  ML1 4JG
  ☎ 01698 732579

- **Newarthill Nursery Centre**
  c/o St Teresas Primary
  85a Loanhead Road
  Newarthill
  ML1 5AY
  ☎ 01698 833971

- **Newarthill Primary School**
  High Street
  Newarthill
  Motherwell
  ML1 5GU
  ☎ 01698 860476

- **Newmains Nursery Centre**
  The Annexe
  School Road
  Newmains
  Wishaw
  ML2 9BE
  ☎ 01698 383432

■ **Newmains Primary School & Nursery**
School Road
Wishaw
ML2 9BE
☎ 01698 384093

■ **Noble Primary School & Nursery**
Shirrel Avenue
Bellshill
ML4 1JR
☎ 01698 748372

■ **Old Monkland Primary School & Nursery**
Sharp Avenue
Coatbridge
ML5 5TJ
☎ 01236 424732

■ **Orbiston Nursery Centre**
Liberty Road
Orbiston
Bellshill
ML4 2EU
☎ 01698 746153

■ **Our Lady & St Francis Primary School & Nursery**
Newarthill Road
Carfin
Motherwell
ML1 5AL
☎ 01698 263967

■ **Our Lady & St Joseph's Primary School & Nursery**
South Medrox Street
Glenboig
Coatbridge
ML 2RU
☎ 01236 874507

■ **Petersburn Primary School**
Petersburn Road
Airdrie
ML6 8DX
☎ 01236 765763

■ **Plains Primary School**
Meadowhead Road
Plains
Airdrie
ML6 7JF
☎ 01236 842339

■ **Ravenswood Primary School**
Tiree Road
Cumbernauld
G67 1NR
☎ 01236 734875

■ **Redburn Primary School & Nursery**
Mossknowe Building
Kildrum Ring Road
Cumbernauld
G72 2EC
☎ 01236 736904

■ **Richard Stewart Nursery Centre & Gaelic Unit**
Chapelside Centre
Waddell Street
Airdrie
ML6 6LH
☎ 01236 767359

■ **Rochsolloch Primary School & Nursery**
Kippen Street
Airdrie
ML6 9AX
☎ 01236 763643

- **Sacred Heart Primary School**
  Liberty Road
  Orbiston
  Bellshill
  ML4 2ES
  ☎ 01698 747134

- **Shawhead Nursery Centre**
  c/o St Bernards Primary
  Berwick Place
  Shawhead
  Coatbridge
  ML5 4NQ
  ☎ 01236 436257

- **Shawhead Primary School**
  Neidpath Avenue
  Coatbridge
  ML5 4NG
  ☎ 01236 421747

- **Shotts Nursery Centre**
  Shotts Kirk Road
  Shotts
  ML7 4ER
  ☎ 01501 822831

- **Sikeside Primary School & Nursery**
  Sikeside Street
  Coatbridge
  ML5 4QH
  ☎ 01236 428082

- **St Aidan's Primary School**
  Coltness Road
  Wishaw
  ML2 7EY
  ☎ 01698 381510

- **St Aloysius' Primary School**
  Main Street
  Chapelhall
  Airdrie
  ML6 8SF
  ☎ 01236 763200

- **St Andrew's Primary School & Nursery**
  Laggan Road
  Burnfoot
  Airdrie
  ML6 0LL
  ☎ 01236 762622

- **St Augustine's Primary School**
  Henderson Street
  Coatbridge
  ML5 1BL
  ☎ 01236 424461

- **St Barbara's Primary School**
  Elmira Road
  Muirhead
  G69 9ER
  ☎ 0141 779 2611

- **St Bartholomews's Primary School**
  Deveron Street
  Townhead
  Coatbridge
  ML5 2JB
  ☎ 01236 424356

- **St Bernadette's Primary School**
  Vickers Street
  Motherwell
  ML1 3RE
  ☎ 01698 264350
  Fax 01236 264350

- **St Bernard's Primary School**
  Berwick Place
  Shawhead
  Coatbridge
  ML5 4NQ
  ☎ 01236 422017

- **St Brendan's Primary School**
  45 Barons Road
  Motherwell
  ML1 2NB
  ☎ 01698 265877

- **St Brigid's Primary School**
  Newton Drive
  Newmains
  Wishaw
  ML2 9DE
  ☎ 01698 384967

- **St Columba's Primary School & Nursery**
  Old Edinburgh Road
  Uddingston
  G71 6HF
  ☎ 01698 813804

- **St Davids's Primary School & Nursery**
  Meadowhead Road
  Plains
  Airdrie
  ML6 7JF
  ☎ 01236 764623

- **St Dominic's Primary School & Nursery**
  Petersburn Road
  Airdrie
  ML6 8BX
  ☎ 01236 769663

- **St Edward's Primary School & Nursery**
  South Biggar Road
  Airdrie
  ML6 9LZ
  ☎ 01236 763748

- **St Francis of Assisi Primary School**
  Westfield Drive
  Westfield
  Cumbernauld
  G68 9HJ
  ☎ 01236 722236

- **St Gabriel's Primary School**
  Juniper Road
  Viewpark
  Uddingston
  G71 5AX
  ☎ 01698 813776

- **St Gerard's Primary School & Nursery**
  Kelvin Road
  Bellshill
  ML4 1LN
  ☎ 01698 745555

- **St Helen's Primary School & Nursery**
  Lomond Drive
  Condorrat
  Cumbernauld
  G67 4JL
  ☎ 01236 720070

- **St Ignatius' Primary School**
  Graham Street
  Wishaw
  ML2 8HR
  ☎ 01698 372899

- **St James' Primary School**
  Marshall Street
  Woodside
  Coatbridge
  ML5 5JN
  ☎ 01236 421864

- **St Joseph's Primary School**
  Cardowan Road
  Stepps
  G33 6AA
  ☎ 0141 779 2689

- **St Kevin's Primary School**
  Langmuir Road
  Bargeddie
  Glasgow
  G69 7RS
  ☎ 0141 771 4066

- **St Lucy's Primary School**
  Oak Road
  Abronhill
  Cumbernauld
  G67 3LQ
  ☎ 01236 720556

- **St Margaret of Scotland Primary School & Nursery**
  Broomlands Road
  S.Carbrain
  Cumbernauld
  G67 4PT
  ☎ 01236 726200

- **St Mary's Primary School & Nursery**
  Chapel Street
  Cleland
  Motherwell
  ML1 5QX
  ☎ 01698 860359

- **St Mary's Primary School**
  Glen Road
  Caldercruix
  Airdrie
  ML6 7PZ
  ☎ 01236 842247

- **St Mary's Primary School**
  Dundyvan Road
  Whifflet
  Coatbridge
  ML5 4BA
  ☎ 01236 433757

- **St Mary's Primary School & Nursery**
  Liddell Road
  Cumbernauld
  G67 1JB
  ☎ 01236 724206

- **St Matthew's Primary School**
  Pentland Road
  Wishawhill
  Wishaw
  ML2 7QF
  ☎ 01698 373556

- **St Michael's Primary School & Nursery**
  Burnbrae Avenue
  Moodiesburn
  G69 0ER
  ☎ 01236 872132

- **St Monica's Primary School**
  Craigend Drive
  Kirkwood
  Coatbridge
  ML5 5TJ
  ☎ 01236 424733

- **St Patricks Nursery School**
Blackbrae Avenue
Kilsyth
G65 0NA
☎ 01236 827751

- **St Patrick's Primary School & Nursery**
Kildonan Street
Coatbridge
ML5 3LG
☎ 01236 421869

- **St Patrick's Primary School**
Backbrae Avenue
Kilsyth
G65 0NA
☎ 01236 822052

- **St Patrick's Primary School**
Station Road
Shotts
ML7 4BJ
☎ 01501 821859

- **St Patrick's Primary School & Nursery**
Coronation Road East
Newarthill
Motherwell
ML1 4HX
☎ 01698 732539

- **St Serf's Primary School & Nursery**
Thrashbush Road
Thrashbush
Airdrie
ML6 6QU
☎ 01236 762781

- **St Stephen's Primary School**
Sikeside Street
Coatbridge
ML5 4QH
☎ 01236 428080

- **St Teresa's Primary School**
85a Loanhead Road
Newarthill
Motherwell
ML1 5AY
☎ 01698 732329

- **St Thomas' Primary School**
Caledonian Road
Wishaw
ML2 0HY
☎ 01698 376941

- **St Timothy's Primary School & Nursery**
Old Monkland Road
Coatbridge
ML5 5EA
☎ 01236 421835

- **Stane Primary School**
West Benhar Road
Shotts
ML7 5JJ
☎ 01501 752596

- **Stepps Nursery**
Cumbernauld Road
Stepps
Glasgow
G33
☎ 0141-779-3942

- **Stepps Primary School**
  School Road
  Stepps
  G33 6HN
  ☎ 0141 779 2163

- **Tannochside Primary School & Nursery**
  Douglas Street
  Tannochside
  Uddingston
  G71 5RH
  ☎ 01698 813252

- **Thrashbush Child & Family Centre**
  Kennyhill
  Airdrie
  ML6 6PE
  ☎ 01236 747807/8

- **Thornlie Primary School**
  Lomond Drive
  Wishaw
  ML2 0JR
  ☎ 01236 372503

- **Tollbrae Primary School**
  South Biggar Road
  Airdrie
  ML6 9LZ
  ☎ 01236 762900

- **Townhead Primary School & Nursery**
  Dochart Drive
  Coatbridge
  ML5 2PG
  ☎ 01236 421143

- **Victoria Primary School & Nursery**
  79 Aitchison Street
  Airdrie
  ML6 0DB
  ☎ 01236 763113

- **Westfield Primary School & Nursery**
  Westfield Drive
  Westfiled
  Cumbernauld
  G67 9HJ
  ☎ 01236 736457

- **Wishaw Nursery Centre**
  Greenside Road
  Greenhead
  Wishaw
  ML2 8DF
  ☎ 01698 292700

- **Whitelees Primary School**
  Whitelees Road
  Abronhill
  Cumbernauld
  G67 3NJ
  ☎ 01236 734509

- **Wishaw Academy Primary School**
  East Academy Street
  Wishaw
  ML2 8BG
  ☎ 01698 372309

- **Woodlands Primary School & Nursery**
  Melrose Road
  Cumbernauld
  G67 4BA
  ☎ 01236 720546

- SOUTH LANARKSHIRE COUNCIL

Please find in the following section listings of local authority Primary Schools, Nurseries within Primary Schools and Nursery Classes in South Lanarkshire

- **South Lanarkshire Council Headquarters**

Almanda Street
Hamilton
Lanarkshire
ML3 0AA
☎ 01698 454444

- **Childcare Information Service Helpline**

☎ 01698 527154

- **Childcare Information Website**

www.childcarelink.gov.uk/southlanarkshire

- **Early Years Service**

☎ 01698 454470

- **SPELL**
Support for Play and Early Learning in Lanarkshire

c/o The Advisory Service
Hope Street
Hamilton
ML3 6AF
☎ 01698 285636 / 285768
email Spell.org@btopenworld.com

Opening Times: Weekdays 9.30am–1.00pm
SPELL are a voluntary organisation providing free advise and information to all under five voluntary groups, parents and carers in the South Lanarkshire area.

- **Abington Primary School**
Carlisle Road
Abington
Biggar
ML12 6SD
☎ 01864 502 341

- **Auchengray Primary School**
Auchengray Road
Carnwarth
Lanark
ML11 8LN
☎ 01501 785245

- **Auchinraith Primary School**
Calder Street
Blantyre
G72 0AU
☎ 01698 823286

- **Auchinraith Primary School Nursery Class**
Calder Street
Blantyre
G72 0AU
☎ 01698 823286

- **Auldhouse Primary School**
Auldhouse
East Kilbride
G75 9DT
☎ 01355 263200

- **Ballerup Nursery Centre**
c/o Ballerup High School
Crosshouse Road
G75 9DG
☎ 01355 236737

■ **Bankhead Primary School**
Bankhead Road
Rutherglen
G73 2BQ
☎ 0141 647 6967

■ **Bankhead Primary School Nursery Class**
Bankhead Road
Rutherglen
G73 2BQ
☎ 0141 647 6967

■ **Beckford Primary School**
Auchinraith Avenue
Hamilton
ML3 0JQ
01698 423200

■ **Bent Primary School**
Boghead
Lesmahagow
ML11 0JD
☎ 01555 892281

■ **Biggar Primary School**
South Back Road
Biggar
ML12 6AG
☎ 01899 221177

■ **Biggar Primary School Nursery Class**
South Back Road
Biggar
ML12 6AG
☎ 01899 221177

■ **Blacklaw Primary School**
Glen Arroch
East Kilbride
G74 2BP
☎ 01355 232064

■ **Blackwood Primary School**
Carlisle Road
Lanark
ML11 9SB
☎ 01555 892438

■ **Blackwood Primary School Nursery Class**
Carlisle Road
Kirkmuirhill
Lanark
ML11 9SB
☎ 01555 892438

■ **Blantyre Nursery Centre**
Calder Street
Blantyre
G72 0AU
01698 829188

■ **Bothwell Primary School**
Blantyre Road
Bothwell
G71 8PJ
☎ 01698 852919

■ **Braehead Primary School**
Braehead
Lanark
ML11 8EY
☎ 01555 811252

■ **Braidwood Primary School**
Harestanes Road
Carluke
ML8 5NY
☎ 01555 770279

- **Burgh Primary School**
  41 King Street
  Rutherglen
  G73 1JY
  ☎ 0141 647 6760

- **Burgh Primary School Nursery Class**
  41 King Street
  Rutherglen
  G73 1JY
  ☎ 0141 647 6760

- **Burnside Primary School**
  Glenlui Avenue
  Rutherglen
  G73 4JE
  ☎ 0141 634 1916

- **Cairns Primary School**
  Cairnswell Avenue
  Cambuslang
  G72 8SW
  ☎ 0141 641 2218

- **Cairns Primary School Nursery Class**
  Cairnswell Avenue
  Halfway
  Cambuslang
  G72 8SW
  ☎ 0141 641 2218

- **Calderwood Primary School**
  Buchanan Drive
  Rutherglen
  G73 3PQ
  ☎ 0141 647 1277

- **Canberra Primary School**
  Belmont Drive
  East Kilbride
  G75 8HD
  ☎ 01355 224362

- **Carluke Primary School**
  Belstane Road
  Carluke
  ML8 4BG
  ☎ 01555 771621

- **Carluke Primary School Nursery Class**
  Belstane Road
  Carluke
  ML8 4BG
  ☎ 01555 771621

- **Carmichael Primary School**
  Carmichael
  Biggar
  ML12 6PG
  ☎ 01555 880216

- **Carnwath Primary School**
  Couthally Terrace
  Carnwarth
  Lanark
  ML11 8HY
  ☎ 01555 840263

- **Carnwarth Primary School Nursery Class**
  Couthally Terrace
  Carwarth
  Lanark
  ML11 8HY
  ☎ 01555 840263

- **Carstairs Junction Primary School**
  Coronation Street
  Carstairs Junction
  ML11 8QY
  ☎ 01555 870301

- **Carstairs Junction Primary School Nursery Class**
  Coronation Street
  Carstairs Junction
  ML11 8QY
  ☎ 01555 870301

- **Carstairs Primary School**
  Avenue Road
  Lanark
  ML11 8QF
  ☎ 01555 870462

- **Castlefield Primary School**
  Maple Terrace
  East Kilbride
  G75 9EG
  ☎ 01355 230810

- **Castlefield Primary School Nursery Class**
  Maple Terrace
  East Kilbride
  G75 9EG
  ☎ 01355 247236

- **Cathkin Primary School**
  Burnside Road
  Rutherglen
  G73 4AA
  ☎ 0141 634 4569

- **Cathkin Primary School Nursery Class**
  Burnside Road
  Rutherglen
  G73 4LY
  ☎ 0141 634 4569

- **Cathkin Community Nursery**
  c/o Cathkin High School
  Whitlawburn
  Cambuslang
  G72 8YS
  ☎ 0141 641 6125

- **Chapelton Primary School**
  Glasgow Road
  Strathaven
  ML10 6RS
  ☎ 01357 300243

- **Chatelherault Primary School**
  Silvertonhill Avenue
  Hamilton
  ML3 7NT
  ☎ 01698 282929

- **Chatelherault Primary School Nursery Class**
  Silvertonhill Avenue
  Hamilton
  ML3 7NT
  ☎ 01698 282929

- **Coalburn Primary School**
  Coalburn Road
  Lanark
  ML11 0LH
  ☎ 01555 820221

- **Coalburn Primary School Nursery Class**
  Coalburn Road
  Coalburn
  Lanark
  ML11 0LH
  ☎ 01555 820221

- **Coulter Primary School**
  Coulter
  Biggar
  ML12 6PZ
  ☎ 01899 220255

- **Craigbank Primary School**
  Avon Road
  Larkhall
  ML9 1PZ
  ☎ 01698 882513

- **Crawford Primary School**
  Carlisle Road
  Biggar
  ML12 6TP
  ☎ 01864 502686

- **Crawforddyke Primary School**
  Eastfield Road
  Carluke
  ML8 4NZ
  ☎ 01555 771215

- **Crawfordjohn Primary School**
  Crawfordjohn
  Biggar
  ML12 6SR
  ☎ 01864 504249

- **Crosshouse Primary School**
  Plover Drive
  East Kilbride
  G75 8UX
  ☎ 01355 245300

- **Crosshouse Primary School Nursery Class**
  Plover Drive
  East Kilbride
  G75 8UX
  ☎ 01355 245300

- **Dalserf Primary School**
  Douglas Drive
  Larkhall
  ML9 3AQ
  ☎ 01698 882680

- **David Livingstone Memorial Primary School**
  Morven Avenue
  Blantyre
  G72 9JY
  ☎ 01698 823680

- **David Livingstone Memorial Primary School Nursery Class**
  Morven Avenue
  Blantyre
  G72 9JY
  ☎ 01698 823680

- **Douglas Primary School**
  Ayr Road
  Douglas
  ML11 0QA
  ☎ 01555 851224

- **Douglas Primary School Nursery Class**
  Ayr Road
  Douglas
  ML11 0QA
  ☎ 01555 851224

- **Early Learning Unit**
  Carlisle Road
  Hamilton
  ML3 7EW
  ☎ 01698 281228

- **Earnock Parent and Children Centre**
  Earnock High School
  Wellhall Road
  Hamilton
  ML3 9UE
  ☎ 01698 425755

- **East Milton Primary School**
  Vancouver Drive
  East Kilbride
  G75 8LG
  ☎ 01355 222346

- **East Milton Primary School Nursery Class**
  Vancouver Drive
  East Kilbride
  G75 8LG
  ☎ 01355 222346

- **First Step Community Nursery**
  Udston Community Centre
  Fleming Way
  Hamilton
  ML3
  ☎ 01698 712643

- **Forth Primary School**
  Main Street
  Forth
  ML11 8AE
  ☎ 01555 811205

- **Forth Primary School Nursery Class**
  Main Street
  Forth
  ML11 8AE
  ☎ 01555 811205

- **Gilmourton Primary School**
  Drumclog
  Strathaven
  ML10 6QF
  ☎ 01357 440331

- **Glassford Primary School**
  Alston Street
  Strathaven
  ML10 6TG
  ☎ 01357 521124

- **Glengowan Primary School**
  Academy Street
  Larkhall
  ML9 2BJ
  ☎ 01698 882208

- **Glenlee Primary School**
  Reid Street
  Hamilton
  ML3 0RQ
  ☎ 01698 823343

- **Glenlee Primary School Nursery Class**
  Reid Street
  Hamilton
  ML3 0RQ
  ☎ 01698 823343

- **Greenhills Primary School**
  Cedar Drive
  East Kilbride
  G75 9JD
  ☎ 01355 241646

- **Greenhills Primary School Nursery Class**
  Cedar Drive
  East Kilbride
  G75 9JD
  ☎ 01355 241646

- **Halfmerke Primary School**
  Logie Park
  East Kilbride
  G74 4BU
  ☎ 01355 221982

- **Halfmerke Community Nursery**
  Logie Park
  East Kilbride
  G74 4BU
  ☎ 01355 243156

- **Hallside Primary School**
  Overton Road
  Cambuslang
  G72 7XA
  ☎ 0141 641 3289

- **Hamilton School for the Deaf Nursery Class**
  Earnock High School
  Wellhall Road
  Hamilton
  ML3 9UE
  ☎ 01698 286618

- **Hareleeshill Primary School**
  Myrtle Lane
  Larkhall
  ML9 2RQ
  ☎ 01698 883155

- **Hareleeshill Community Nursery**
  Myrtle Lane
  Larkhall
  ML9 2RQ
  ☎ 01698 883155

- **Heathery Knowe Primary School**
  Whitehill Terrace
  East Kilbride
  G75 0NG
  ☎ 01355 221042

- **Heathery Knowe Primary School**
  Nursery Class
  Whitehill Terrace
  East Kilbride
  G75 0NG
  ☎ 01355 221042

- **High Blantyre Primary School**
  Broompark Road
  High Blantyre
  G72 9SH
  ☎ 01698 827670

- **High Blantyre Primary School Nursery Class**
  Broompark Road
  High Blantyre
  G72 9SH
  ☎ 01698 827670

- **High Mill Primary School**
  Market Road
  Carluke
  ML8 4BE
  ☎ 01555 772580

- **High Mill Primary School Nursery Class**
  Market Road
  Carluke
  ML8 4BE
  ☎ 01555 772580

- **Hollandbush Nursery School**
  Mill Road
  Hamilton
  ML3 8AA
  ☎ 01698 284005

- **Hunter Primary School**
  Crawford Drive
  East Kilbride
  G74 3YB
  ☎ 01355 221076

- **James Aiton Primary School**
  Morrison Street
  Cambuslang
  G72 7HZ
  ☎ 0141 641 2472

- **Kirkfieldbank Primary School**
  Kirkfieldbank
  Lanark
  ML11 9JJ
  ☎ 01555 662620

- **Kirklandpark Primary School**
  Kirklandpark Avenue
  Strathaven
  ML10 6DY
  ☎ 01357 520177

- **Kirklandpark Primary School Nursery Class**
  Kirklandpark Avenue
  Strathaven
  ML10 6DY
  ☎ 01357 520177

- **Kirkton Primary School**
  Kirkton Avenue
  Carluke
  ML8 5AB
  ☎ 01555 772466

- **Kirtonholme Primary School**
  Dornoch Place
  East Kilbride
  G74 1DY
  ☎ 01355 222050

- **Kirtonholme Primary School Nursery Class**
  Dornoch Place
  East Kilbride
  G74 1DY
  ☎ 01355 222050

- **Laighstonehall Childrens Centre**
  (c/o St Peter's Primary School)
  Highstonehall Road
  Hamilton
  ☎ 01698 420421

- **Lamington Primary School**
  Lamington
  Biggar
  ML12 6HW
  ☎ 01899 850249

- **Lanark Primary School**
  Rhyber Avenue
  Lanark
  ML11 7HQ
  ☎ 01555 662806

- **Lanark Primary School Nursery Class**
  Rhyber Avenue
  Lanark
  ML11 7QH
  ☎ 01555 662806

- **Larkhall Children's Centre**
  c/o Larkhall High School
  Cherryhill
  Larkhall
  ML9 1QN
  ☎ 01698 886560

- **Law Primary School**
  Lawhill Road
  Carluke
  ML8 5HA
  ☎ 01698 350816

- **Law Primary School Nursery Class**
  Lawhill Road
  Carluke
  ML8 5HA
  ☎ 01698 350816

- **Leadhills Primary School**
  Main Street
  Biggar
  ML12 6XR
  ☎ 01659 74202

- **Libberton Primary School**
  Libberton
  Biggar
  ML12 6NB
  ☎ 01899 308281

- **Loch Primary School**
  Lochaber Drive
  Rutherglen
  G73 5HX
  ☎ 0141 634 7217

- **Loch Primary School Nursery Class**
  Lochaber Drive
  Rutherglen
  G73 5HX
  ☎ 0141 634 7217

- **Long Calderwood Primary School**
  Bosworth Rd
  East Kilbride
  G74 3QT
  ☎ 01355 224414

- **Machanhill Primary School**
  Machanhill
  Larkhall
  ML9 2HG
  ☎ 01698 882101

- **Machanhill Primary School Nursery Class**
  Machanhill
  Larkhall
  ML9 2HG
  ☎ 01698 882101

- **Maxwellton Primary School**
  Maxwellton Avenue
  East Kilbride
  G74 3DU
  ☎ 01355 222521

- **Maxwellton Primary School Nursery Class**
  Maxwellton Avenue
  East Kilbride
  G74 3DU
  ☎ 01355 222521

- **Milton Primary School**
  Strathaven Road
  Lesmahagow
  ML11 0DN
  ☎ 01555 894282

- **Mossneuk Primary School**
  Mossneuk Drive
  East Kilbride
  G75 8XQ
  ☎ 01355 239777

- **Mossneuk Nursery**
  Mossneuk Drive
  East Kilbride
  G75 8XQ
  ☎ 01355 268490

- **Mount Cameron Primary School**
  Blacklaw Drive
  East Kilbride
  G74 2EX
  ☎ 01355 232062

- **Mount Cameron Nursery Class**
  Blacklaw Drive
  East Kilbride
  G74 2EX
  ☎ 01355 232062

- **Mount Cameron Primary School Gaelic Unit Nursery**
  Blacklaw Drive
  St Leonard's
  East Kilbride
  G74 2EX
  ☎ 01355 232062

- **Muiredge Primary School**
  Watson Street
  Uddingston
  G71 7JL
  ☎ 01698 813852

- **Muiredge Primary School Nursery Class**
  Watson Street
  Uddingston
  G71 7JL
  ☎ 01698 813852

- **Murray Primary School**
  Napier Hill
  East Kilbride
  G75 0JP
  ☎ 01355 222566

- **Murray Primary School Nursery Class**
  Napier Hill
  East Kilbride
  G75 0JP
  ☎ 01355 222566

- **Neilsland Primary School**
  Highstonehall Road
  Hamilton
  ML3 8LU
  ☎ 01698 286405

- **Netherburn Primary School**
  Draffan Road
  Larkhall
  ML9 3DE
  ☎ 01698 882484

- **Netherburn Primary School Nursery Class**
  Draffan Road
  Larkhall
  ML9 3DE
  ☎ 01698 882484

- **New Lanark Primary School**
  64 New Lanark Road
  Lanark
  ML11 9BY
  ☎ 01555 663069

- **Newfield Primary School**
  Muirhead
  Stonehouse
  ML9 3HG
  ☎ 01698 792084

- **Newfield Primary School Nursery Class**
  Muirehead
  Stonehouse
  ML9 3HG
  ☎ 01698 792084

- **Our Lady of Lourdes Primary School**
  Carnegie Hill
  East Kilbride
  G75 0AG
  ☎ 01355 221983

- **Our Lady of Lourdes Primary School Nursery Class**
  Carnegie Hill
  East Kilbride
  G75 0AG
  ☎ 01355 221983

- **Quarter Primary School**
  Limekilnburn Road
  Hamilton
  ML3 7XA
  ☎ 01698 424410

- **Quarter Primary School Nursery Class**
  Limekilnburn Road
  Hamilton
  ML3 7XA
  01698 424410

- **Rigside Primary School**
  Muirfoot Road
  Lanark
  ML11 9LP
  ☎ 01555 880252

- **Rigside & Rural Communities Nursery**
  Muirfoot Road
  Lanark
  ML11 9LP
  ☎ 01555 880689

- **Robert Owen Memorial Primary School**
  Smyllum Road
  Lanark
  ML11 7BZ
  ☎ 01555 662486

- **Robert Owen Nursery**
  Smyllum Road
  Lanark
  ML11 7BZ
  ☎ 01555 662486

- **Robert Smillie Memorial Primary School**
  Glen Avenue
  Larkhall
  ML9 1NJ
  ☎ 01698 882636

- **Robert Smillie Memorial Primary School Nursery Class**
  Glen Avenue
  Larkhall
  ML9 1NJ
  ☎ 01698 882636

- **Rutherglen Day Nursery**
  McDonald Centre
  245–7 King Street
  Rutherglen
  ☎ 0141 647 8914

- **Sandford Primary School**
  Stonehouse Road
  Strathaven
  ML10 6PD
  ☎ 01357 520345

- **South Park Primary School**
  Netherton Road
  East Kilbride G75 9DU
  ☎ 01355 224748

- **South Park Primary School Nursery Class**
  Netherton Road
  East Kilbride
  G75 9DU
  ☎ 01355 224748

- **Spittal Primary School**
  Lochlea Road
  Rutherglen
  G73 4QJ
  ☎ 0141 634 5861

- **Spittal Primary School Nursery Class**
  Lochlea Road
  Rutherglen
  G73 4QJ
  ☎ 0141 634 5861

- **Springwell Pre-5 Centre**
  32–8 Auchinraith Terrace
  Blantyre
  G72 0LT
  ☎ 01698 829050

- **St Anne's Primary School**
  Hall Street
  Hamilton
  ML3 6RZ
  ☎ 01698 283928

- **St Anthony's Primary School**
  Lochaber Drive
  Rutherglen
  G73 5HX
  ☎ 0141 634 7353

- **St Athanasius Primary School**
  John Street
  Carluke
  ML8 4DD
  ☎ 01555 771418

- **St Athanasius' Primary School Nursery Class**
  John Street
  Carluke
  ML8 4DD
  ☎ 01555 771418

- **St Blane's Primary School**
  Fernslea Avenue
  Blantyre
  G72 3PT
  ☎ 01698 823679

- **St Bride's Primary School**
  Ailsa Road
  Bothwell
  G71 8LP
  ☎ 01698 853709

- **St Bride's Primary School Nursery Class** (Bothwell)
  Ailsa Road
  Bothwell
  G71 8LP
  ☎ 01698 853709

- **St Bride's Primary School**
  Tabernacle Street
  Cambuslang
  G72 8JN
  ☎ 0141 641 3344

- **St Bride's Primary School Nursery Class** (Cambuslang)
  Tabernacle Street
  Cambuslang
  G72 8JN
  ☎ 0141 641 3344

- **St Cadocs's Primary School**
  Ivybank Avenue
  Cambuslang
  G72 8SQ
  ☎ 0141 641 3088

- **St Charles' Primary School**
  Newton Brae
  Cambuslang
  G72 7UW
  ☎ 0141 641 1483

- **St Columbkille's Primary School**
  Clincarthill Road
  Rutherglen
  G73 2LG
  ☎ 0141 647 5932

- **St Cuthbert's Primary School**
  Greenfield Road
  Hamilton
  ML3 0RG
  ☎ 01698 282175

- **St Cuthbert's Primary School Nursery Class**
  Greenfield Road
  Hamilton
  ML3 0RG
  ☎ 01698 282175

- **St Elizabeth's Primary School**
  William Drive
  Hamilton
  ML3 7RQ
  ☎ 01698 285080

- **St. Elizabeth's Primary School Nursery Class**
  William Drive
  Hamilton
  ML3 7RQ
  ☎ 01698 285080

- **St Hilary's Primary School**
  High Common Road
  East Kilbride
  G74 2AV
  ☎ 01355 232066

- **St Hilary's Primary School Nursery Class**
  High Common Road
  East Kilbride
  G74 2AV
  ☎ 01355 232066

- **St John the Baptist Primary School**
  North British Road
  Uddingston
  G71 6NW
  ☎ 01698 813540

- **St John's Primary School**
  Carlisle Road
  Kirkmuirhill
  ML11 9RZ
  ☎ 01555 892491

- **St John's Primary School**
  Dixon Street
  Hamilton
  ML3 6PZ
  ☎ 01698 283401

- **St Joseph's Primary School**
  Glasgow Road
  Blantyre
  G72 0YJ
  ☎ 01698 825121

- **St Joseph's Primary School Nursery Class**
  Glasgow Road
  Blantyre
  G72 0YJ
  ☎ 01698 825121

- **St Kenneth's Primary School**
  West Mains Road
  East Kilbride
  G74 1PU
  ☎ 01355 224741

- **St. Kenneth's Primary School Nursery Class**
  West Mains Road
  East Kilbride
  G74 1PU
  ☎ 01355 224741

- **St Leonard's Primary School**
  Brancumhall
  East Kilbride
  G74 3YA
  ☎ 01355 224800

- **St. Leonard's Primary School Nursery Class**
  Brancumhall
  East Kilbride
  G74 3YA
  ☎ 01355 224800

- **St Louise's Primary School**
  Whitehills Terrace
  East Kilbride
  G75 0NF
  ☎ 01355 230804

- **St Mark's Primary School**
  Sherry Drive
  Hamilton
  ML3 8XF
  ☎ 01698 283727

- **St Mark's Primary School**
  Kirkriggs Avenue
  Rutherglen
  G73 4LY
  ☎ 0141 634 4238

- **St. Marks's Primary School Nursery Class** (Rutherglen)
  Kirkriggs Avenue
  Rutherglen
  G73 4LY
  ☎ 0141 634 4238

- **St Mary's Primary School**
  Cadzow Street
  Hamilton
  ML3 6JT
  ☎ 01698 282850

- **St Mary's Primary School**
  Whitelees Road
  Lanark
  ML11 7LE
  ☎ 01555 663480

- **St. Mary's Primary School Nursery Class** (Lanark)
  Whitelees Road
  Lanark
  ML11 7LE
  ☎ 01555 663480

- **St Mary's Primary School**
  Raploch Road
  Larkhall
  ML9 1AN
  ☎ 01698 881121

- **St Ninian's Primary School**
  13 St Ninian's Road
  Hamilton
  ML3 9TS
  ☎ 01698 823656

- **St Patrick's Primary School**
  Commercial Road
  Strathaven
  ML10 6JW
  ☎ 01357 521317

- **St. Patrick's Primary School Nursery Class**
  Commercial Road
  Strathaven
  ML10 6JW
  ☎ 01357 521317

- **St Paul's Primary School**
  Blackmuir Road
  Hamilton
  ML3 0PX
  ☎ 01698 284777

- **St. Paul's Primary School Nursery Class**
  Blackmuir Road
  Hamilton
  ML3 0PX
  ☎ 01698 284777

- **St Peter's Primary School**
  Highstonehall Road
  Hamilton
  ML3 8LU
  ☎ 01698 281277

- **St Vincent's Primary School**
  Crosshouse Road
  East Kilbride
  G75 9DG
  ☎ 01355 241649

- **Stablestone Primary School**
  Ayr Road
  Douglas
  ML11 0SF
  ☎ 01555 851203

- **Stablestone Primary School Nursery Class**
  Ayr Road
  Douglas
  ML11 0SF
  ☎ 01555 851203

- **Stonehouse Primary School**
  Townhead Street
  Stonehouse
  ML9 3EL
  ☎ 01698 792377

- **Tinto Primary School**
  Main Street
  Biggar
  ML12 6LL
  ☎ 01899 308279

- **Tinto Primary School Nursery Class**
  Main Street
  Biggar
  ML12 6LL
  ☎ 01899 308279

- **Townhill Primary School**
  Melfort Road
  Hamilton
  ML3 9UR
  ☎ 01698 284776

- **Udson Primary School**
  Thornhill Road
  Hamilton
  ML3 9PS
  ☎ 01698 823677

- **Underbank Primary School**
  154 Lanark Road
  Carluke
  ML8 5QQ
  ☎ 01555 860289

- **Waltson Primary School**
  Walston
  Biggar
  ML12 6RA
  ☎ 01899 810234

- **Waltson Primary School Nursery Class**
  Walston
  Biggar
  ML12 6RA
  ☎ 01899 810234

- **Westburn Nursery School**
  50 Birch Road
  Cambuslang
  Glasgow
  G72 7LY
  ☎ 0141 641 7182

- **West Coats Primary School**
  Brownside Road
  Cambuslang
  G72 8NH
  ☎ 0141 641 1384

- **Wester Overton Primary School**
  Ashkirk Road
  Strathaven
  ML10 6JT
  ☎ 01357 521870

- **Wester Overton Primary School Nursery Class**
  Ashkirk Road
  Strathaven ML10 6JT
  ☎ 01357 521870

- **Whitehill Pre-5 Centre**
  c/o St Paul's Primary School
  Hamilton
  ML3 0PX
  ☎ 01698 284196

- **Wiston Primary School**
  Wiston
  Biggar
  ML12 6HT
  ☎ 01899 850634

- **Woodhead Primary School**
  Woodhead Crescent
  Hamilton
  ML3 8TB
  ☎ 01698 457669

- **Woodpark Primary School**
  Priory Avenue
  Lesmahagow
  ML11 0AD
  ☎ 01555 892251

- **Woodpark Primary School Nursery Class**
  Priory Avenue
  Lesmahagow
  ML11 0AD
  ☎ 01555 892251

- **Woodside Primary School**
  Johnstone Road
  Hamilton
  ML3
  ☎ 01698 427811

Nursery Schools (Private & Partnership)

Please find in the following section listings of private nurseries in and around the Glasgow area.

Many of the private nurseries enjoy partnership status with Glasgow City Council, South Lanarkshire Council, East Renfrewshire Council, North Lanarkshire Council and East Dunbartonshire Council.

- **Alba Childcare Supply Agency**
  ☎ 01738 635387 / 07713 121677

Alba Childcare Supply Agency is a business supplying qualified and experienced Nursery Nurses and Assistants to Nurseries, Playgroups, Out of School Clubs and other Childcare Settings.

We can help maintain the quality of care provided by these settings on a temporary or permanent basis. We have to adhere to strict regulations, all our staff are interviewed, references and qualifications checked as well as Enhanced Disclosure checked.

Working with Alba Childcare Supply Agency could not be easier, simply phone 07713 121677 and state what your staffing needs are, you will be invoiced monthly in a clear and simple format.

So, relax and rely on us.

We cover a wide area from Dundee, Perth, Fife, Edinburgh, Glasgow and surrounding areas. We attract high calibre staff to work for the agency and maintain a caring and dedicated workforce with equal opportunities. If you would like to become one of our team then just give us a call for an application form. The Alba Childcare Supply Agency commitment is to work closely with our clients, constantly seeking to improve the quality and efficiency of everything we do.

- **3 Bears Nursery (Private)**
  2 Wellshot Drive
  Cambuslang
  G72 8PP
  ☎ 0141 641 2811

Opening Times:
Mon – Fri 8.00am–6.00pm
This nursery provides care for children age 0 to 5yrs and has garden facilities and works in partnership with South Lanarkshire Council.

- **ABC / Crosslees Nursery (Thornliebank) Ltd**
  Crosslees Drive
  Thornliebank
  Glasgow
  G46 7DZ
  ☎ 0141 620 3280

Opening Times:
Mon – Fri 8.00am–6.00pm
This nursery provides care for children age 6 wks to 5 yrs, has garden facilities and works in partnership with East Renfrewshire Council

- **Acorn Park Nursery & Kindergarten**
  Beresford House
  6 Claremont Terrace
  G3 7XR
  ☎ 0141 332 2461

Opening Times:
Mon – Fri 8.00am–6.00pm
This nursery provides care for children age 0 to 5 yrs, has garden facilities and works in partnership with Glasgow City Council.

- **Adelaide's Nursery School**
  209 Bath Street
  Glasgow
  G2 4HZ
  ☎ 0141 248 4970
  www.adelaides.co.uk

Opening Times:
Mon – Fri 8.15am–6.00pm
This nursery provides care for children age 6 wks to 5 yrs, has garden facilities and works in partnership with Glasgow City Council.

- **Adventure Playgroup**
  (within Lammermoor Play Centre)
  Kenilworth
  East Kilbride
  Glasgow
  G74 3PG
  ☎ 01355 241458

Opening Times:
Mon – Fri 9.30am–12.00pm
This nursery provides care for children age $2\frac{1}{2}$ to 5yrs, has garden facilities and works in partnership with South Lanarkshire Council.

- **Asquith Nursery**
  c/o David Lloyd Club
  Arkleston Road
  Cockleshill Park
  Renfrew
  PA4 ORA
  ☎ 0141 842 1370

Opening Times:
Mon – Fri 8.00am–6.00pm
This nursery provides care for children age 3 mths – 5yrs, has garden facilities and works in partnership with Renfrewshire Council.

- **Bardykes Farm Nursery School**
  Bardykes Road
  Blantyre
  G72 9UJ
  ☎ 01698 822212

Opening Times:
Mon – Fri 9.00am–12.00pm and 1.00pm–4.00pm
This nursery provides care for children age 2½ to 5yrs, has garden facilities and works in partnership with South Lanarkshire Council.

- **Bishopbriggs Childcare Centre Limited S.I.N.A.**
  South Crosshill Road
  Bishopbriggs
  G64 2NZ
  ☎ 0141 563 0080
  Fax 0141 762 0080

Opening Times:
Mon – Fri 7.45am–6.00pm
This nursery provides care for children age 12 wks to 12 yrs, has garden facilities and works in partnership with East Dunbartonshire Council.
This nursery provides other nursery and out of schools services please contact directly for further details.

- **Blairhall Private Nursery**
  22 Blairhall Avenue
  Glasgow
  G41 3BA
  ☎ 0141 632 1066

Opening Times:
Mon – Fri 8.00am–6.00pm
This nursery provides care for children age 0 to 5 yrs and has garden facilities.

- **Bothwell Montessori Nursery**
  53 Main Street
  Bothwell
  ☎ 01698 850000

Opening Times:
Mon – Fri 8.00am–6.00pm
This nursery provides care for children age 2 yrs to 5 yrs, has garden facilities and works in partnership with Glasgow City Council, North Lanarkshire Council & South Lanarkshire Council.

- **Braidfield Nursery** (Kidcare Ltd)
  Braidfield High School
  Queen Mary Avenue
  Drumry
  G81 2LS
  ☎ 0141 951 2159

Opening Times:
Mon – Fri 8.30am–5.30pm
This nursery provides care for children age 0 to 5 yrs has outdoor facilities and works in partnership with West Dunbartonshire Council

- **Brookland Private Nursery School S.I.N.A.**
  87 Duntocher Road
  Clydebank
  G81 3LP
  ☎ 0141 952 7686

Opening Times:
Mon – Fri 8.00am–6.00pm
This nursery provides care for children age 0–5yrs, has garden facilities and works in partnership with West Dunbartonshire Council.

- **Broomhill Kindergarten**
  137–9 Crow Road
  Glasgow
  G11 7SG
  ☎ 0141 339 3024

Opening Times:
Mon – Fri 8.00am–6.00pm
This nursery provides care for children age 2 yrs to 5 yrs, has garden facilities and works in partnership with Glasgow City Council.

- **Buchanan Private Nursery Ltd**
  3 Grampian Way
  Bearsden
  G61 4SP
  ☎ 0141 570 0133

Opening Times:
Mon – Fri 8.00am–6.00pm
This nursery provides care for children age 0–5 yrs, has garden facilities and works in partnership with East Dunbartonshire City Council

- **Cambuslang Childcare Project**
  Ivybank Avenue
  Halfway
  Cambuslang
  G72 8SQ
  ☎ 0141 641 6791

Opening Times:
Mon – Fri 9.00am–4.00pm
This nursery provides care for children age 6 wks to 5 yrs and works in partnership with South Lanarkshire Council

- **Careshare at Oaklands**
  Lymekilns Road
  Stewartfield
  East Kilbride
  G74 4RR
  ☎ 01355 260665

Opening Times:
Mon – Fri 7.45am–5.45pm
This nursery provides care for children age 6 wks to 5 yrs, has garden facilities and works in partnership with South Lanarkshire Council

■ **Careshare at Netherton**
Next Generation Club
236 Netherton Road
Glasgow
G13 1BJ
☎ 0141 950 2450

Opening Times:
Mon – Fri 8.00am–6.00pm
This nursery provides care for children age 6 wks to 5 yrs, has garden facilities and works in partnership with Glasgow City Council

■ **Carlton Nursery**
78 Carlton Place
Glasgow
G5 9TH
☎ 0141 429 6177

Opening Times:
Mon – Fri 8.15am–6.00pm
This nursery provides care for children age 6 wks to 5 yrs, has access to garden facilities and works in partnership with Glasgow City Council.

■ **Carnwadric & Kennishead Pre 5 Unit**
32 Kiloran Street
Thornliebank
G46 8LT
☎ 0141 638 8597

Opening Times:
Mon – Fri 8.30am–11.30pm & 1.00pm–4.00pm
This nursery provides care for children age 3 yrs to 5 yrs, has garden facilities and works in partnership with Glasgow City Council.

■ **Carrickstone Farm Private Day Nursery**
5 Gailes Road
Cumbernauld
Glasgow
G68 0JJ
☎ 01236 732023

Opening Times:
Mon – Fri 7.30am–6.00pm
This nursery provides care for children age 6 wks to 5 yrs, has garden facilities and works in partnership with North Lanarkshire Council.

■ **Cathcart Kindergarten**
23 Garry Street
Glasgow
G44 4AZ
☎ 0141 632 7244 / 0141 633 3403

Opening Times:
Mon – Thurs 8.00am–6.00pm
This nursery provides care for children age 2 yrs to 5 yrs and has garden facilities.

■ **ChIS**
Children's Information Service
☎ Freephone 0800 032 0323

Choosing childcare and early education or finding suitable services that meet your child's needs can be a big step for parents, carers and their children and there are many options to consider. Visit the ChIS website at www.childcarelink.gov.uk or call freephone 0800 032 0323 if you want to know more about services for children and families in your area.

- **Clever Cloggs Nursery**
  133 Balornock Road
  Balornock
  Glasgow
  ☎ 0141 558 8188

Opening Times:
Mon – Fri 7.00am–6.00pm
This nursery provides care for children age 6 wks to 5 yrs, has garden facilities and works in partnership with Glasgow City Council.

- **Clydebank College Nursery** (Kidcare Ltd)
  Clydebank College
  Kilbowie Road
  Clydebank
  G81 2AA
  ☎ 0141 951 4458

Opening Times:
Mon – Fri 8.30am–5.00pm
This nursery provides care for children age 0 to 5 yrs, has outdoor facilities and works in partnership with West Dunbartonshire District Council.

- **Craigholme Nursery**

For **Craigholme Nursery** *see* EDUCATION (INDEPENDENT SCHOOLS & NURSERIES)

- **First Stepp Community Nursery**
  Fleming Way
  Hamilton
  ML3 9PQ
  ☎ 01698 712643

Opening Times:
Mon – Fri 8.00am–6.00pm
This nursery provides care for children age 0 to 5 yrs, has garden facilities and works in partnership with South Lanarkshire Council.

- **Firtrees Nursery**
  Dalzell Drive
  Motherwell
  ☎ 01698 232285

Opening Times:
Mon – Fri 8.00am–6.00pm has garden facilities and works in partnership with North Lanarkshire Council.
For **Firtrees Nursery (Out of School Care)** *see* EDUCATION (AFTER SCHOOL CARE)

- **Four Seasons Nurseries**
  City Centre Child Care
  3 Cadogan Street
  Glasgow
  G2 6QE
  ☎ 0141 248 9344

Opening Times:
Mon – Fri 7.00am–7.30pm & Sat crèche 9.00am–1.00pm
This nursery provides care for children age 3 mnths to 8 yrs, has garden facilities and works in partnership with Glasgow City Council.

- **Glasgow University Nursery**
  (Kidcare Ltd)
  28 Hillhead Street
  Hillhead
  Glasgow
  G12 8PZ
  ☎ 0141 334 4650

Opening Times:
Mon – Fri 8.00am–6.00pm
This nursery provides care for children age 0 to 5 yrs has outdoor facilities and works in partnership with Glasgow City Council

- **Glenburn House Private Day Nursery**
  19A Glenburn Road
  College Milton
  East Kilbride
  ☎ 01355 244448

Opening Times:
Mon - Fri 7.30am - 6.00pm
This nursery provides care for children age 6 wks to 5 yrs, has garden facilities and works in partnership with South Lanarkshire Council.

- **Gowanlea Private Day Nursery School**
  37–9 Garscadden Road
  Glasgow
  G15 6UH
  ☎ 0141 944 3877

Opening Times:
Mon – Fri 8.00am–5.45pm
This nursery provides care for children age 3 mnths to 5 yrs has an outside play area and works in partnership with Glasgow City Council.

- **Greenbank Playgroup**
  Greenbank Church
  Eaglesham Road
  Glasgow
  ☎ 0141 644 4878

Opening Times:
Mon – Fri 9.10am–11.40pm
This playgroup provides care for children from 2½ yrs

- **Happy Days Too**
  9 East Kilbride Road
  Busby
  Glasgow
  G76 8JY
  ☎ 0141 644 5858
  Fax 0141 644 5863

Opening Times:
Mon – Fri 7.45am–6.00pm
This nursery provides care for children age 3 mnths to 12 yrs, has garden facilities, has an after school care facility and works in partnership with East Renfrewshire Council
For **Happy Days Too After School Care** *see* EDUCATION (AFTER SCHOOL CARE)

- **Harlequin Kindergarten**
  Private Nursery
  Murray Road
  East Kilbride
  ☎ 01355 227711

  Opening Times:
  Mon – Fri 8.00am–6.00pm
  This nursery provides care for children age 0 to 5 yrs, has garden facilities and works in partnership with South Lanarkshire Council.

- **Harlequin Little Jesters**
  59 Barrhead Road
  Newton Mearns
  Glasgow
  G77
  ☎ 0141 616 2315

  Opening Times:
  Mon – Fri 8.00am–6.00pm
  This nursery provides care for children age 0 to 5 yrs, has garden facilities and works in partnership with East Renfrewshire Council

- **Harlequin Nurseries**
  15 Hillside Road
  Mansewood
  Glasgow
  G43 1DB
  ☎ 0141 649 1557

  Opening Times:
  Mon – Fri 8.00am–6.00pm
  This nursery provides care for children age 0 to 3 yrs, has garden facilities and works in partnership with Glasgow City Council

- **Harlequin Nurseries Gold**
  3 Hillside Road
  Mansewood
  Glasgow
  G43 1DB
  ☎ 0141 649 1557

  Scotland's only 24 hour, 7 days a week nursery can provide care for children age 0 to 8 yrs, has garden facilities and works in partnership with Glasgow City Council

- **Head Start Nursery**
  Partick Trinity Church
  20 Lawrence Street
  Glasgow
  ☎ 0141 337 3145

  Opening Times:
  Mon – Fri 8.00am–6.00pm
  This nursery provides care for children age 0 to 5 yrs and has garden facilities.

- **Heathdene Private Nursery**
  124 Carmunnock Road
  Glasgow
  G44 5UU
  ☎ 0141 637 8953

  Opening Times:
  Mon – Fri 8.00am–6.00pm
  This nursery provides care for children age 6 wks to 5 yrs, has garden facilities and works in partnership with Glasgow City Council.

- **Hickory Dickory House**
  15 Bengal Street
  Pollokshaws
  G43 1NL
  ☎ 0141 636 0000

Opening Times: 8.00am–6.00pm
This nursery provides care for children age 0 to 5yrs and has an outside play area

- **Hopscotch Nurseries**
  4-8 Morgan Street
  Hamilton
  ML3 6RJ
  ☎ 01698 426800

Opening Times: 8.00am–6.00pm
This nursery provides care for children age 0 to 3yrs, has garden facilities and works in partnership with South Lanarkshire Council.

- **Hopscotch Kindergarten**
  58 Tuphall Road
  Hamilton
  ML3 6TB
  ☎ 01698 426800

Opening Times: 8.00am–6.00pm
This nursery provides care for children age 3 yrs to 5 yrs, has garden facilities and works in partnership with South Lanarkshire Council.
For Hopscotch After School Care *see* EDUCATION (AFTER SCHOOL CARE)

- **Hullabaloo Day Nursery**
  38 Ibrox Terrace
  Glasgow
  G51 2TB
  ☎ 0141 427 0122

Opening Times:
Mon – Fri 8.00am–6.00pm
This nursery provides care for children age 3 mnths to 5 yrs, has garden facilities and works in partnership with Glasgow City Council.

- **Jack & Jill Nursery**
  266 Saracen Street
  Glasgow
  G22
  ☎ 0141 336 3434

Opening Times:
Mon – Fri 8.00am–6.00pm
This nursery provides care for children age 0 to 5 yrs, has garden facilities and works in partnership with Glasgow City Council.

- **Jack & Jill's Nursery**
  11 South Avenue
  Clydebank Business Park
  Glasgow
  G81 2NR
  ☎ 0141 562 0056

Opening Times:
Mon – Fri 7.30am–6.00pm
This nursery provides care for children age 6 wks to 5 yrs, has garden facilities and works in partnership with West Dunbartonshire Council.

- **Jack & Jill's Pre-5's Group**
  St Hilary's Primary School
  High Common Road
  St Leonard's
  East Kilbride
  ☎ 07952 373583

Opening Times:
Mon – Fri 9.00am–11.45pm
This nursery provides care for children age 2 yrs 10 mnths to 5 yrs and works in partnership with South Lanarkshire Council and has access to a playground.

- **Kilmardinny Nursery School**
  (within West of Scotland Rugby Club)
  Glasgow Road
  Milngavie
  ☎ 0141 956 2891

Opening Times:
Mon – Fri 8.30am–5.30pm
This nursery provides care for children age 3 yrs to 5 yrs, has garden facilities, can provide after school care and works in partnership with East Dunbartonshire Council.

- **Kirkhillgait Nursery**
  82–4 Broom Road East
  Newton Mearns
  Glasgow
  G77 5SR
  ☎ 0141 639 8000

Opening Times:
Mon – Fri 8.00am–6.00pm
This nursery provides care for children age 6 wks to 5 yrs and works in partnership with East Renfrewshire Council.

- **Kirktonholme Private Nursery**
  401 Kirktonholme Road
  East Kilbride
  G74 1RS
  ☎ 01355 222000

Opening Times:
Mon – Fri 8.00am–6.00pm
This nursery provides care for children age 6 wks to 12 yrs, has garden facilities, can provide after school care and works in partnership with South Lanarkshire Council.

- **Learning Tree Nursery**
  3 Claremont Terrace
  Glasgow
  G3 7XR
  ☎ 0141 353 1234

Opening Times:
Mon – Fri 7.30am–6.30pm
This nursery provides care for children age 0 to 5 yrs, has garden facilities and works in partnership with Glasgow City Council.

- **Leisuredrome Nursery** (Kidcare Ltd)
147 Balmuidy Road
Bishopbriggs
Glasgow
G64 3HD
☎ 0141 762 0022

Opening Times:
Mon – Fri 8.00am–6.00pm
This nursery provides care for children age 2 yrs to 5 yrs, has garden facilities and works in partnership with East Dunbartonshire Council.

- **Lilybank Private Nursery & Pre-School**
7A Lilybank Street
Hamilton
ML3 6NN
☎ 01698 428699

Opening Times:
Mon – Fri 8.15am–5.30pm
This nursery provides care for children age 3 yrs to 5 yrs, has garden facilities and works in partnership with North and South Lanarkshire Council.

- **Little Acorns Nursery School**
39 Shawhill Road
Shawlands
☎ 0141 632 3469

Opening Times:
Mon – Fri 8.00am–6.00pm
This nursery provides care for children age 2 yrs to 5 yrs, has garden facilities and works in partnership with Glasgow City Council

- **Little Gems Nursery & After School Care Ltd (Little Gems Baby Unit)**
10 North View Lane
Westerton
Glasgow
G61 1NY
☎ 0141 931 5330

Opening Times:
Mon – Fri 8.00am–6.00pm
This baby unit provides care for children age 3 mnths to 3 yrs and has its own garden facilities. For **Little Gems After School Care** *see* EDUCATION (AFTER SCHOOL CARE)

- **Little Gems Nursery & After School Care Ltd**
57 Stockiemuir Avenue
Bearsden
Glasgow
G61 3JJ
☎ 0141 931 5333

Opening Times:
Mon – Fri 8.00am–6.00pm
This nursery provides care for children age 3 yrs to 5 yrs, has access to local gardens and works in partnership with East Dunbartonshire Council.
For **Little Gems After School Care** *see* EDUCATION (AFTER SCHOOL CARE)

- **Little Lambs Nursery**
Crossbasket House
Stoneymeadow Road
High Blantyre
G72 9UE
☎ 01698 821145

Opening Times:
Mon – Fri 8.00am–6.00pm
This nursery provides care for children age 0 to 5 yrs, has garden facilities and works in partnership with South Lanarkshire Council.

- **Manor Park Nursery**
  46 Lefroy Street
  Coatbridge
  ML5 1NB
  ☎ 01236 602929

  Opening Times:
  Mon – Fri 8.00am–6.00pm
  This nursery provides care for children age 2 yrs to 5 yrs, has garden facilities and works in partnership with North Lanarkshire Council.

- **Mayfield Private Nursery School S.I.N.A.**
  148 Albert Road
  Glasgow
  G42 8UF
  ☎ 0141 423 4723

  Opening Times:
  Mon – Fri 8.00am–6.00pm
  This nursery provides care for children age 0 to 5 yrs, has garden facilities and works in partnership with Glasgow City Council.

- **Meadow Club Pre 5 Group**
  (within Baird Memorial Primary School)
  Glenacre Road, North Carbrain
  Cumbernauld
  G67
  ☎ 01236 617003

  Opening Times:
  Mon – Fri 9.15am–11.45 & 12.45pm–3.15pm
  This nursery provides care for children age 3 to 5 yrs, has garden facilities and is run by a committee.

- **Mearnswood Nursery School**
  60a Stewarton Road
  Newton Mearns
  G77 6NP
  ☎ 0141 639 5292

  Opening Times:
  Mon – Fri 8.00am–6.00pm
  This nursery provides care for children age 6 wks to 5 yrs, has garden facilities and works in partnership with East Renfrewshire Council.

- **Merkland Private Nursery**
  27 Crow Road
  Glasgow
  G11 7RT
  ☎ 0141 337 1732

  Opening Times:
  Mon – Fri 8.00am–6.00pm
  This nursery provides care for children age 0 to 5 yrs, has garden facilities and works in partnership with Glasgow city Council.

- **Mulberry Kindergarten**
  4 Park Gardens
  Glasgow
  G3 7YE
  ☎ 0141 353 0003

  Opening Times:
  Mon – Fri 8.00am–6.00pm
  This nursery provides care for children age 0 to 5 yrs, has garden facilities and works in partnership in Glasgow City Council.

- **Munro House Nursery**
  Munro Place
  Anniesland
  G13 2UW
  ☎ 0141 959 0438

Opening Times:
Mon – Fri 7.30am–6.00pm
This nursery provides care for children age 6 wks to 3 yrs, has garden facilities and works in partnership with Glasgow City Council.

- **Munro Kindergarten**
  Munro Place
  Anniesland
  G13 2UW
  ☎ 0141 959 8885

Opening Times:
Mon – Fri 7.30am–6.00pm
This nursery provides care for children age 3 yrs to 5 yrs, has garden facilities and works in partnership with Glasgow City Council.

- **Newlands Kindergarten**
  100 Merrylee Road
  Glasgow
  G43 4EZ
  ☎ 0141 637 5528
  www.newlandskindergarten.co.uk

Opening Times:
Mon – Fri 8.00am–5.45pm
This nursery provides care for children age 2 yrs to 5 yrs, has garden facilities, can provide after school care and works in partnership with Glasgow City Council.

- **Nightingales Nursery**
  Block 1 Yorkhill Court
  Dalnair Street
  Glasgow
  G3 8SG
  ☎ 0141 337 6133

Opening Times:
Mon – Fri 7.00am–6.00pm
This nursery provides care for children age 3 mnths to 5 yrs, has garden facilities.and works in partnership with Glasgow City Council.

- **Oakwood House Pre School Centre**
  6 Upper Bourtree Drive
  Rutherglen
  Glasgow
  G73
  ☎ 0141 631 3331

Opening Times:
Mon – Fri 8.00am–6.00pm
This nursery provides care for children age 0 to 3 yrs, and has garden facilities.
For **Oakwood Out of School Care** *see* EDUCATION (AFTER SCHOOL CARE)

- **Oakwood House Pre School Centre**
  11 Crosshill Drive
  Rutherglen
  Glasgow
  G73
  ☎ 0141 613 1187

Opening Times:
Mon – Fri 8.00am–6.00pm
This nursery provides care for children age 3 yrs to 5 yrs, has garden facilities and works in partnership with South Lanarkshire Council.
For **Oakwood Out of School Care** *see* EDUCATION (AFTER SCHOOL CARE)

- **The Park Nursery**
  7 Woodside Crescent
  Glasgow
  G3 7UL
  ☎ 0141 332 0366

  Opening Times:
  Mon – Fri 8.00am–6.00pm
  This nursery provides care for children age 0 to 5 yrs, has garden facilities and works in partnership in Glasgow City Council.

- **Park Private Nursery**
  Montessori Education
  4 Hillington Park Circus
  Glasgow
  ☎ 0141 882 4332

  Opening Times:
  Mon – Fri 8.30am–5.00pm
  This nursery provides care for children age 3 yrs to 5 yrs, has garden facilities and works in partnership with Glasgow City Council.

- **Piccolo Pre School Nursery**
  57 Blair Road
  Coatbridge
  ☎ 01236 422800

  Opening Times:
  Mon – Fri 7.45am–5.45pm
  This nursery provides care for children age 0 to 5 yrs, has garden facilities and works in partnership with North Lanarkshire Council.

- **Pied Piper Nursery**
  25 Hector Road
  Shawlands
  Glasgow
  G41 3RJ
  ☎ 0141 649 2715

  Opening Times:
  Mon – Fri 8.00am–6.00pm
  This nursery provides care for children age 6 wks to 5 yrs, has garden facilities and works in partnership with Glasgow City Council.

- **Play House**
  959 Crookston Road
  Glasgow
  G53 7DT
  ☎ 0141 810 5777

  Opening Times:
  Mon – Fri 8.00am–5.30pm
  This nursery provides care for children age 2 yrs to 5 yrs, has garden facilities and works in partnership with Glasgow City Council.

- **Poppins Kindergarten**
  172 Queens Drive
  Glasgow
  G42 8QZ
  ☎ 0141 424 1333

  Opening Times:
  Mon – Fri 8.00am–6.00pm
  This nursery provides care for children age 6 wks to 5 yrs, has garden facilities and works in partnership with Glasgow City Council.

- **Sinclair Nursery**
  6 Sinclair Drive
  Glasgow
  G42 9QE
  ☎ 0141 636 1212

Opening Times:
Mon – Fri 8.00am–6.00pm
This nursery provides care for children age 6 wks to 5 yrs, has garden facilities and works in partnership with Glasgow City Council.

- **Small World Day Nursery**
  105 New City Road
  Cowcaddens
  ☎ 0141 353 2626

Opening Times:
Mon – Fri 8.00am–6.00pm
This nursery provides care for children age 0 to 12 yrs, has garden facilities, can provide after school care and works in partnership with Glasgow City Council. For **Small World Day Nursery (After School Care)** *see* EDUCATION (AFTER SCHOOL CARE)

- **Smarties Pre-School Group**
  Clarkston Baptist Church Hall
  Arthur Street
  Clarkston
  G76 7BD
  ☎ 0141 638 0692

Opening Times:
Mon – Fri 9.15am–11.45pm
This nursery provides care for children age 3½ to 5 yrs and works in partnership with East Renfrewshire Council.

- **Somerset Nursery (Head Office)**
  6 Fitzroy Place (on Sauchiehall Street)
  Glasgow
  G3 7RH
  ☎ 0141 204 3399

Opening Times:
Mon – Fri 8.00am–6.00pm
This nursery provides care for children age 6 wks to 3 yrs and has garden facilities.

- **Somerset Nursery**
  4a Clairmont Gardens
  Glasgow
  G3 7LW
  ☎ 0141 353 0001

Opening Times:
Mon – Fri 8.00am–6.00pm
This nursery provides care for children age 3 to 5 yrs, has garden facilities and works in partnership with Glasgow City Council.

- **Somerset Nursery**
  229 Woodlands Road
  Glasgow
  G3 6LW
  ☎ 0141 333 1296

Opening Times:
Mon – Fri 8.00am–6.00pm
This nursery provides care for children age 6 wks to 3 yrs and has garden facilities.

- **Somerset Nursery**
  2 Parkgrove Terrace
  Glasgow
  G3 7SD
  ☎ 0141 337 6655

Opening Times:
Mon – Fri 8.00am–6.00pm
This nursery provides care for children age 6 wks to 3 yrs and has garden facilities.

- **Happy Days Too (Southfield House)**
  Mearns Kirk
  Glasgow
  ☎ 0141 639 9191

Opening Times:
Mon – Fri 7.45am–6.00pm
This nursery provides care for children age $2^1/_2$ to 5yrs, has garden facilities, has an after school care service and works in partnership with East Renfrewshire Council.
For **Happy Days Too After School Care** *see* EDUCATION (AFTER SCHOOL CARE)

- **SPPA**
  Scottish Pre-school Play Association
  14 Elliot Place
  Glasgow
  G3 8EP
  ☎ 0141 221 4148

- **Stepping Stones for Families**
  55 Renfrew Street
  Glasgow
  G2 3BD
  ☎ 0141 331 2828

Registered Office: for advice on any of the Stepping Stones for Families units

- **Stonefield Private Day Nursery**
  75 Stonefield Road
  Blantyre
  G72 9SA
  ☎ 01698 825549

Opening Times:
Mon – Fri 8.00am–6.00pm
This nursery provides care for children age 2 yrs to 5 yrs, has garden facilities, can provide after school care and works in partnership with South Lanarkshire Council.
For **Stonefield Out of School Care** *see* EDUCATION (AFTER SCHOOL CARE)

- **Strathclyde University Nursery**
  (Kidcare Ltd)
  Weaver Street
  Rottenrow
  Glasgow
  G4 0NG
  ☎ 0141 553 4125

Opening Times:
Mon – Fri 8.00am–6.00pm
This nursery provides care for children age 0 to 5 yrs, has garden facilities and works in partnership with Glasgow City Council.

- **Sunflower Private Nursery**
  31 Glasgow Road
  Clydebank
  G81 5PJ
  ☎ 01389 800329

Opening Times: Mon – Fri 8.00am–6.00pm
This nursery provides care for children age 6 wks to 5 yrs, has garden facilities and works in partnership with all local authorities.

- **Sunflower Private Nursery**
  26 Beardmore Way
  Clydebank Industrial Estate
  Glasgow
  ☎ 0141 952 4415

Opening Times: Mon – Fri 8.00am–6.00pm
This nursery provides care for children age 6 wks to 5 yrs, has garden facilities and works in partnership with all local authorities.

- **Sweetie Brae Nursery**
  101 Glasgow Road
  Strathaven
  ML10 6NF
  ☎ 01357 529200

Opening Times:
Mon – Fri 8.00am–6.00pm
This nursery provides care for children age 0 to 5 yrs, has a small garden and works in partnership with South Lanarkshire Council.

- **Task Childcare Service**
  192 McNeil Street
  Glasgow
  ☎ 0141 429 1140

This nursery provides care for children age 0 to 3 yrs & provides a wraparound service for 3–5 yr olds
For Task After School Care *see* EDUCATION (AFTER SCHOOL CARE)

- **Technotots (Childcare) Ltd**
  Transfer House
  Scottish Enterprise Technology Park
  Rankine Avenue
  East Kilbride
  ☎ 01355 272255

Opening Times:
Mon – Fri 7.45am–6.00pm
This nursery provides care for children age 0 to 5 yrs, has garden facilities, can provide after school care and works in partnership with South Lanarkshire Council.

- **Tinkerbell Kindergarten**
Block 4 Traction House
Tinkers Lane
Motherwell
☎ 01698 258887

Opening Times:
Mon – Fri 8.00am–6.00pm
This nursery provides care for children age 6 wks to 5 yrs and has access to a local park.

- **Treehouse Day Nursery**
65 Old Mill Road
Uddingston
G71 7PF
☎ 01698 323200

Opening Times:
Mon – Fri 8.00am–6.00pm
This nursery provides care for children age 6 wks to 5 yrs and works in partnership with South Lanarkshire Council. This nursery has a park opposite.

- **Wellpark Nursery** (Kidcare Ltd)
Wellpark Business Centre
120 Sydney Street
Glasgow
G31 1JF
☎ 0141 550 7511

Opening Times:
Mon – Fri 8.00am–6.00pm
This nursery provides care for children age 0 to 5 yrs, has garden facilities and works in partnership with Glasgow City Council.

- **West End Montessori Pre-School**
300 Great Western Road
Glasgow
G4 9JB
☎ 0141 339 4346

Opening Times:
Mon – Fri 8.30am–4.00pm
This nursery provides care for children age 2 yrs to 5 yrs, has garden facilities and works in partnership with Glasgow City Council.

- **Westbourne Gardens Nursery School**
69 Hyndland Road
Glasgow
G12 9UX
☎ 0141 337 1361

Opening Times:
Mon – Fri 8.30am–12.00pm &
1.00pm–4.00pm,
Lunch Club 12.00pm–1.00pm
This nursery provides care for children age 2 yrs to 5 yrs, has garden facilities and works in partnership with Glasgow City Council.

- **Windmill Nursery**
Baptist Church
Windmillhill Street
Motherwell
ML1 1RY
☎ 01698 254177

Opening Times:
Mon – Fri 8.00am–6.00pm
This nursery provides care for children age 0 to 5 yrs and works in partnership with North Lanarkshire Council.

SCOTTISH CHILDMINDING ASSOCIATION

Please find details of quality childminding services throughout Glasgow City.

"Quality childminding ... building confident children within a family childcare experience"

The **Scottish Childminding Association** is the only dedicated support organisation in Scotland for registered childminding. The Association is committed to the development needs of registered childminders and actively promotes childminding as a quality childcare choice.

Our vision is for childminding to be recognised as a unique, family-based childcare service and for childminders to receive the support and advice that they need to continue to meet the National Childcare Standards.

Scottish Childminding Association is proud to work in partnership with Glasgow City Council to develop and deliver quality childminding services throughout Glasgow City.

- **Scottish Childminding Association**
  ☎ 01786 449063
  www.childminding.org

Glasgow

Committed to Quality Childcare

Family Breaks

Please find in the following section listings of:

- **Crieff Hydro**
- **County Wexford**
- **Hilton Coylumbridge, Aviemore**

Family Breaks

Please find in the following section information on Family Breaks.

- **County Wexford**
  Ireland
  ☎ 00353 1 4947086

See opposite.

- **Crieff Hydro**
  Crieff
  Perthshire
  Scotland
  ☎ 01764 65 5555

Facilities include crèche, children's club for children aged 2 yrs to 8 yrs, which is open for 3 sessions daily, all year. A children's three-course menu is also available in a unsupervised area away from the bar, baby food & bottles can also be heated and highchairs are available

FOR RENT: County Wexford, Ireland - beautiful new detached bungalow in private estate with large secure garden 3 dbl bedrooms (one ensuite). Very close to beach. Ideally suited for young children. Playground facility. Located 3 miles from Courtown - a popular seaside town with leisure facilities.
2h 30m drive from Dublin Airport, or 1h 30m from Dun Laoghaire ferry.
Tel 00353 1 4947086 for details/

- **Hilton Coylumbridge**
  Aviemore
  Tel 01479 811 811 or
  Hilton Reservations Worldwide on
  ☎ 08705 90 90 90

Whether you are looking for a family get-together or somewhere to escape everyday life, we can offer all the ingredients you need for a wonderful Family holiday. Set deep in the heart of the Cairngorm National Park, **Hilton Coylumbridge** offers the ideal setting for that much earned break.

Set within its own 65 acre wooded estate, Hilton Coylumbridge is a place the whole family will enjoy. The hotel offers 175 comfortable bedrooms all equipped with the usual amenities you would expect from a Hilton hotel. Surrounded by an endless choice of attractions and activities, the hotel is a year round leisure base with something for everyone.

The Grant Room, the main restaurant serves traditional Scottish cuisine that's freshly prepared using local produce. It is also the venue for the fabulous Hilton Family breakfast.

You'll love Café Cino – bringing a taste of the continent to Coylumbridge, with speciality coffees, carefully crafted sandwiches, paninis and fresh pastries. Or why not try Terracotta's – The hotel's Mediterranean style restaurant with an eclectic menu that shows influences all over Europe? The contrasting colours and modern art make for a warm and relaxed experience. And that's before you even taste the food.

The Fun House isn't just for kids – especially if you fancy an authentic hotdog from our American style diner, a quick game of air hockey, ten pin bowling or a round of all weather adventure mini-golf.

Of course it's always a good idea to take time to relax and ease the stresses of the day away. Do this with a visit to the leisure facilities where you can refresh with a swim, relax in the bubble pool or take a massage. Within the grounds of the Hilton Coylumbridge itself there also two outdoor tennis courts and Children's Play park. Live Entertainment each evening in the foyer lounge bar makes this a truly memorable holiday for all the family.

THE GLASGOW GUIDE

FOR PARENTS AND CARERS

2005 edition

NOTE TO ADVERTISERS

If you were not listed in ***The Glasgow Guide for Parents and Carers*** 2004 (2nd) edition, don't worry. Have your business or service listed in ***The Glasgow Guide for Parents and Carers*** 2005 (3rd) edition. Fill in your details below and return by the 30th September 2004 to:

Glasgow Under 6's Ltd
48 Flenders Avenue
Clarkston
Glasgow, G76 7XZ
Tel/Fax 0141 616 3661
E: glasgowunder6s@fsmail.net

Name of Business & Contact Name . . . .

Address . . . .

. . . .

Postcode . . . . Tel/Fax No. . . . .

Email . . . . www . . . .

PLEASE TICK BELOW

Free Listing ❑

Request advertising details ❑

NOTE TO READERS

We would like to hear your comments and suggestions for our 2005 edition. These should be sent to **Glasgow Under 6's Ltd** at the address above.

HEALTH

Please find included in the following section listings of:

- **Helplines**
- **Pharmacies** (with extended opening hours)
- **Services**
- **Support for Parents**
- **Vaccinations**
  (babies & young children)

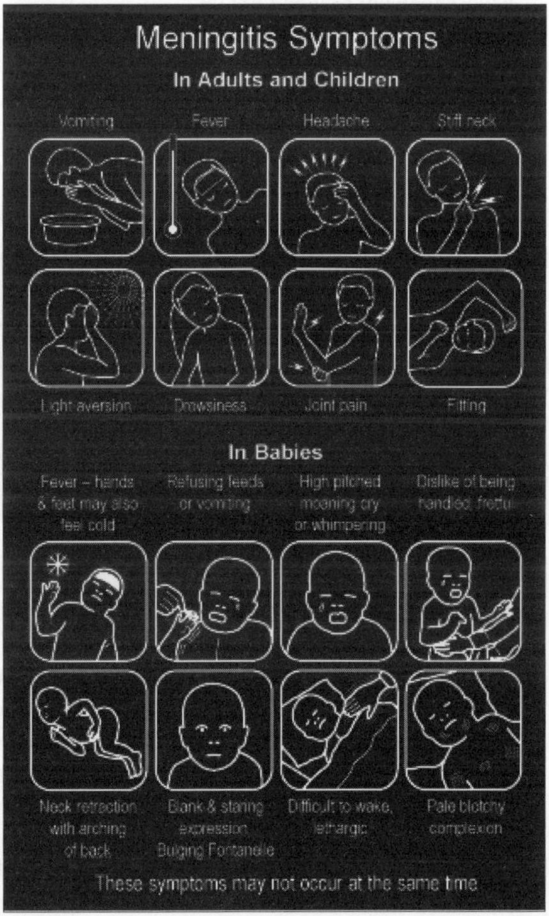

Helplines

Please find below listings of helplines in and around the Glasgow area.

- **Birthlink at Family Care**
  21 Castle Street
  Edinburgh
  EH2 3DN
  ☎ 0131 225 6441

  Post-adoption counselling centre
  Mon – Thurs 9.00am–4.00pm
  Fri 9.00am–4.30pm
  Sat & Sun closed

- **Capability Scotland Advice** (ASCS)
  ☎ 0131 313 5510
  Email: ascs@capability-scotland.org.uk
  www.capability-scotland.org.uk

  Mon – Fri 9.00am–5.00pm
  Sat & Sun closed
  Provides information on all disability issues

- **Careline**
  ☎ 020 8514 1177

  Confidential crisis telephone counselling on any subject
  Mon – Fri 10.00am–4.00pm & 7.00pm–10.00pm

- **Chas**
  Children's Hospice Association Scotland
  ☎ 0141 248 3103

  The **Children's Hospice Association Scotland** provides children's hospice services for children with life limiting conditions and for their families

- **Child Death Helpline**
  ☎ Freephone 0800 282986

  Telephone helpline for anyone affected by the death of a child

- **ChildLine Scotland**
  ☎ Freephone 0800 1111
  www.childline.org.uk

  In addition to the above service ChildLine Scotland operates:

  A **Bullying Line** for children and young people concerned about bullying on Freephone 0800 44 11 11. This line is open Mon–Fri from 3.30pm–10.30pm.

  ChildLine Scotland is the free, confidential, telephone counselling service for children and young people.

  ChildLine Scotland aims to protect children who are at risk or harm and to help children resolve or alleviate their problems and worries. Although ChildLine Scotland answers calls during afternoons and evenings, the peak calling times, a 24hour service is maintained through the London base using the same Freephone 0800 1111 number.

The Line – for children and young people living away from home on Freephone 0800 88 44 44. This service operates Mon–Fri 3.30pm–10.30pm and on Sat & Sun 2.00pm–8.00pm. This service is for young people who live in residential or foster care, boarding school, hospital or secure accommodation.

A textphone (Minicom) service for children and young people with hearing or speech impairment on Freephone 0800 400 222. This line is open Mon–Fri from 9.30am–10.30pm, Sat &Sun 9.30am–8.00pm

- **Contact a Family**
  ☎ Freephone 0808 808 3555

Mon – Fri 10.00am–4.00pm
Provides advice & information on all issues affecting families of children with disabilities, special needs or rare disorders

- **Contact a Family Scotland**
  ☎ 0131 475 2608
  ☎ Freephone 0808 808 3555
  www.cafamily.org.uk

- **Cystic Fibrosis Trust**
  ☎ 0845 859 1000

Providing information & advice on cystic fibrosis
Mon – Fri 9.00am–5.00pm An answering machine is available out of hours

- **Diabetes UK**
  ☎ 0207 424 1030

Provides people with support & information on all aspects and care of diabetes

- **Downs Syndrome Scotland**
  ☎ 0131 313 4225

Provides support, training, education and health advice. Provides a quarterly newsletter and general parent and family support.

■ **Epilepsy Action** ☎ Freephone 0808 8005050 www.epilepsy.org.uk	Provides help, advice and information Opening Hours: Mon – Thurs 9.00am–4.30pm, Fri 9.00am–4.00pm
■ **Gingerbread Scotland** ☎ 0141 576 5085	Association for lone parents & their children Provides information, advice & counselling This is a voluntary run organisation
■ **Guide Dogs for the Blind Association** National call line ☎ 0870 600 2323	Provides information, support and advise for the visually impaired
■ **Home-Start Glasgow North West** ☎ 0141 948 0441 **Home-Start Glasgow South** ☎ 0141 585 6712	**HOME-START** is a voluntary organisation in which volunteers offer regular support, friendship and practical help to young families under stress in their own homes, helping to prevent family crisis and breakdown, and emphasising the pleasures of family life. HOME-START provides a breathing space for parents and elbowroom for many professional workers who refer any family with at least one child under school age to the scheme
■ **Hyperactive Children's Support Group** ☎ 01243 551313 www.hacsg.org.uk	Mon – Fri 10.00am–1.00pm Provides information for parents and carers who have children with ADHD

meningitis trust

The Meningitis Trust is available 24 hours a day to answer all your questions and provide support. Call us on 0845 6000 800.

Come along and join in some fun events with our Monty the duck mascot. There's plenty to choose from! Your help can allow us to increase awareness of the disease and provide the following essential services

- **A 24 hour helpline** staffed by nurses trained in meningitis and meningococcal disease providing information and support: **0845 6000 800**
- **Professional counselling service** available for those requiring more intense support as a direct result of meningitis and septicaemia
- **Financial grants** to help improve the quality of life for meningitis sufferers and their families
- **A Home visiting service** providing support and advice from a health professional
- **A one to one contact service** offering people the opportunity to share their experience with someone who has been in a similar situation
- **Education and training** available for childcare, education and health professionals

For further information on events or our support services, please contact:

0845 6000 800 or email **scotland@meningitis-trust.org**

- **The Meningitis Trust**
  UK 24 Hr Helpline
  ☎ 0845 6000 800

B aware of Meningitis

Meningitis is the disease parents fear most, and still kills more children in the UK than any other infectious disease. So what exactly is it?

Meningitis is inflammation of the meninges, the lining surrounding the brain; it can be caused by bacteria, viruses and fungi. Bacterial Meningitis is a very serious condition and can be fatal. The most common cause of bacterial meningitis in the UK is meningococcal and this can also cause another very serious illness called septicaemia (blood poisoning).

If you suspect meningitis, every second counts, see medical help immediately as early treatment with antibiotics is vital. Be safe, be vigilant and remember the symptoms.

In babies and children symptoms can be a high temperature, possibly with cold hands and feet, vomiting or refusing feeds, high pitched or moaning whimpering cry, blank staring expression, pale blotchy complexion, floppy, fretful or dislike of being handled, difficult to wake, a babies soft spot on the head (fontanelle) may become raised, tense or bulging. Older children may complain of headaches, neck stiffness, dislike of bright lights, joint or muscle pains.

If septicaemia is present there may be a rash and this can start anywhere on the body. It may initially appear as tiny pin pricks. If left untreated these little spots will join together to give the appearance of fresh bruising. The rash will not fade under the pressure of a glass when firmly pressed against the skin. Do not wait for a rash, it may be the last symptom to appear if at all.

- **The Miscarriage Association**
  ☎ 01924 200799
  www.miscarriageassociation.org.uk

  Mon – Fri 9.00am–4.00pm
  Information & support on pregnancy loss

- **Multiple Sclerosis Society Scotland**
  ☎ Freephone 0808 800 8000

Offers advise & support

- **Muscular Dystrophy Campaign**
  ☎ 0207 720 8055
  www.muscular-dystrophy.org

Mon – Thurs 10.00am–4.00pm

- **National Autistic Society**
  ☎ 0870 600 8585

Mon – Fri 10.00am–4.00pm
Advice and support for people with autistic spectrum disorders and an advice line for parents & carers

- **National Deaf Children's Society**
  ☎ Freephone 0808 800 8880

Information for parents & professionals on any issues to do with deaf children

- **National Society for Epilepsy**
  ☎ 01494 601400

Information & confidential support Mon – Fri 10.00am–4.00pm, except bank holidays, with any issues relating to epilepsy

- **NCT**
  ☎ enquiry line 0870 444 8707
  www.nctpregnancyandbabycare.com
  Maternity Sales Mail Order
  ☎ 0870 112 1120
  Website www.nctms.co.uk
  Breastfeeding Helpline
  ☎ 0870 444 8708
  Local Contacts
  Glasgow North
  ☎ Rachel 0141 339 1449
  Glasgow South
  ☎ Rosemary 0141 631 4158
  East Kilbride
  ☎ Gillian 0700 5802566
  Lomond
  ☎ Jackie 01389 755 982

The **National Childbirth Trust** offers information and support in pregnancy, childbirth and early parenthood. It aims to give every parent the chance to make informed choices. It tries to make sure that its services, activities and membership are fully accessible to everyone.
(Charity number 801395)

8.00am–10.00pm, 7 days

For NCT Maternity Sales *see* SHOPPING (MATERNITY WEAR)

- **NSPCC Child Protection Helpline**
  ☎ Freephone 0808 800 5000

- **One Parent Families Scotland**
  ☎ Freephone 0800 018 5026 (can only be dialled from a landline)
  If calling from a mobile please call 0131 556 3899
  www.opfs.org.uk

One Parent Families Scotland has a long history of helping lone parents with expert advice and information. With support from The Royal Bank of Scotland we now operate a free Lone Parent Helpline in partnership with One Plus. Callers to the 0800 018 5026 number can get advice on many issues such as childcare, benefits, legal matters, returning to work and housing. Free factsheets and booklets are also available to callers, along with details of local support agencies throughout Scotland. We aim to provide expert advice and information along with a sympathetic listening ear.

Through our web site at www.opfs.org.uk you can find out more about issues affecting lone parents and download copies of our publications. We can be contacted by email on info@opfs.org.uk

lone parent helpline

0800 018 5026

Information and free publications on benefits, money, legal rights, childcare, holidays, work, education, maintenace

- **One Plus**
  55 Renfrew Street
  Glasgow
  ☎ 0141 333 1450

Advice sessions available:
Tues & Fri 11.00am–1.00pm & 2.00–3.00pm
Thurs 12.30–3.30pm

To offer advice and counselling for individual lone parents

- **ParentLine Scotland**
  ☎ Freephone 0808 800 2222

ParentLine Scotland 0808 800 2222 is the free confidential helpline for anyone caring for a child to call. Our service reaches out to parents in every part of Scotland, including the most isolated communities. We are there to help parents talk through concerns and to get the information and support they need, exactly when they need it. The service is available to everyone and all calls are free.

- **RNIB Helpline**
  ☎ 0845 766 9999

Mon – Fri 9.00am–5.00pm
Information, support & advice for anyone with a sight problem

- **Samaratins**
  ☎ National 0845 7 90 90 90 (24hrs)
  ☎ Glasgow 0141 248 4488 (24hrs)
  www.samaratins.org

Anyone can visit their local Samaratins office daily from 9.30am–10.00pm
Provides a confidential telephone support service on all matters affecting individuals

- **Scottish Cot Death Trust**
  Royal Hospital for Sick Children
  ☎ 0141 357 3946

The **Scottish Cot Death Trust** provide support for bereaved families

They also offer advice & information about safe infant care practices, for parents and professionals

Key Steps to reduce the risks for your baby

- Place baby on the back to sleep
- Don't smoke during pregnancy
- Keep baby in a smoke-free zone after birth
- Don't let baby get too hot
- Keep baby's head uncovered – place in the 'feet to foot' position

- **The Scottish Society for Autism**
  ☎ 012597 200 44
  www.autism-in-scotland.org.uk

Mon – Thurs 9.00am–5.00pm &
Fri 9.00am–4.30pm
Providing a comprehensive range of expertise in care, support & education for people with autism, their families and carers

- **Stepfamily Scotland**
  ☎ Helpline 0131 225 5800

Call Mon – Fri
Support & information for all members of stepfamilies (including grandparents)

PHARMACIES

Please find in the following section listings of pharmacies in and around the Glasgow area, some with extended opening hours.
Please note that Munro Pharmacies have a drive-thru pharmacy in East Kilbride that has extended opening hours.
You can also contact your local police station for pharmacies with extended opening hours.

- **J B Pharmacy**
  106 North Road
  Bellshill
  ☎ 01698 841950

  Opening Times: 7 days 9.00am–9.00pm
  Christmas Day & Boxing Day approx opening times: 10.00am–4.00pm
  New Years Day & 2nd of January approx opening times: 10.00am–4.00pm

- **J P Mackie**
  1067 Pollokshaws Road
  Shawlands
  Glasgow
  ☎ 0141 649 8915

  Opening Times:
  Mon – Fri 9.00am–8.00pm, Sat & Sun 9.00am–6.00pm,
  9.00am–3.00pm on Bank Holidays

- **Monklands Pharmacy**
  108–112 Deedes Street
  Airdrie
  ☎ 01236 753252

  Opening Times:
  7 days 9.00am–9.00pm
  This pharmacy is open on Christmas Day, Boxing Day, 1st & 2nd January (varied hours, please call)

- **Munro Pharmacy**
  263 Alderman Road
  Knightswood
  Glasgow
  G13 3AY
  ☎ 0141 959 1914

  Opening Times:
  Mon – Sun 9.00am–11.00pm

- **Munro Pharmacy**
  182–184 Main Street
  Barrhead
  G78 1SL
  ☎ 0141 881 5686

  Opening Times:
  Mon – Fri 9.00am–6.00pm,
  Sat 9.00am–5.30pm

- **Munro Pharmacy**
  764 Anniesland Road
  Knightswood
  Glasgow
  G14 0YU
  ☎ 0141 959 0618

  Opening Times:
  Mon – Sat 9.00am–6.00pm

- **Munro Pharmacy**
  Unit 2
  Kwiksave
  Crown Street
  Gorbals
  Glasgow
  G5 0SD
  ☎ 0141 429 5037

  Opening Times:
  Mon – Fri 9.00am–6.00pm
  Sat 9.00am–5.00pm

- **Munro Pharmacy**
  16 Douglas Street
  Milngavie
  Glasgow
  G62 7PB
  ☎ 0141 956 5235

  Opening Times:
  Mon – Sat 9.00am–6.00pm

- **Munro Pharmacy**
  549 Maryhill Road
  Maryhill
  Glasgow
  G20 7UJ
  ☎ 0141 946 3212

  Opening Times:
  Mon – Fri 9.00am–5.30pm
  Sat 9.00am–1.00pm

- **Munro Pharmacy**
  199 Roxburgh Street
  Greenock
  PA15 4DA
  ☎ 01475 722733

  Opening Times:
  Mon – Fri 9.00am–5.30pm
  Sat 9.00am–5.00pm

- **Munro Pharmacy**
  1604 Paisley Road West
  Glasgow
  G52 3QN
  ☎ 0141 882 8769

  Opening Times:
  Mon – Fri 9.00am–6.00pm
  Sat 9.00am–5.30pm

■ **Munro Pharmacy** 186-188 Abercromby Street Glasgow G40 2RZ ☎ 0141 554 3281	Opening Times: Mon – Fri 9.00am–6.00pm Sat 9.00am–1.00pm
■ **Munro Pharmacy** 50 Hillington Road South Glasgow G52 2AA ☎ 0141 882 8829	Opening Times: Mon – Fri 9.00am–6.00pm Sat 9.00am–1.00pm
■ **Munro Pharmacy** 2 Alberta Ave Westwood East Kilbride G75 8BF ☎ 01355 222517	Opening Times: Mon – Sun 9.00am–11.00pm
■ **Munro Pharmacy** Unit 11 Clarkston Toll Clarkston G76 7BG ☎ 0141 638 8803	Opening Times: Mon – Fri 9.00am–6.00pm Sat 9.00am–5.30pm
■ **Munro Pharmacy** 30A Russell Street Chapelhall ML6 8SG ☎ 01236 755229	Opening Times: Mon – Fri 9.00am–6.00pm Sat 9.00am–5.00pm
■ **Munro Pharmacy** 25 Common Green Strathaven ML10 6AQ ☎ 01357 521163	Opening Times: Mon – Fri 9.00am–6.00pm Sat 9.00am–5.30pm

- **Munro Pharmacy**
  693 Great Western Road
  Glasgow
  G12 8RA
  ☎ 0141 339 0012

  Opening Times:
  Mon – Sun 9.00am–9.00pm

- **Munro Pharmacy**
  82 Portland Place
  Hamilton
  ML3 7LA
  ☎ 01698 286130

  Opening Times:
  Mon, Tues, Thurs, Fri 9.00am–7.15pm
  Wed & Sat 9.00am–5.00pm
  Sun 11.00am–2.00pm

- **Munro Pharmacy**
  147 Great Western Road
  Glasgow
  G4 9AW
  ☎ 0141 332 1478

  Opening Times:
  Mon – Fri 9.00am–5.45pm
  Sat 9.00am–1.00pm

- **Munro Pharmacy**
  9–11 St Marnock Street
  Kilmarnock
  KA1 1DZ
  ☎ 01563 541145

  Opening Times:
  Mon – Fri 9.00am–6.00pm
  Sat 9.00am–5.00pm

- **Munro Pharmacy**
  Kirk Road
  Houston
  PA6 7AR
  ☎ 01505 614739

  Opening Times:
  Mon – Fri 8.30am–5.30pm
  Sat 9.00am–12.30pm

- **Munro Pharmacy**
  46 Brandon Parade East
  Motherwell
  ML1 1LY
  ☎ 01698 264845

  Opening Times:
  Mon – Sat 9.00am–9.00pm

- **Munro Pharmacy**
  220 Dalmellington Road
  Crookston
  Glasgow
  G53 7FY
  ☎ 0141 882 8877

  Opening Times:
  Mon – Sat 9.00am–6.00pm

■ **Munro Pharmacy**
Station Plaza
Pennyburn Road
Kilwinning
Ayrshire
☎ 01294 559898

Opening Times:
Mon – Sat 9.00am–6.00pm

■ **Munro Pharmacy**
15 Livery Walk
Bridge of Weir
PA11 3NN
☎ 01505 613614

Opening Times:
Mon – Fri 9.00am–5.30pm
Sat 9.00am–5.00pm

■ **Munro Pharmacy**
Unit 7 Shopping Precinct
Houston Court
Johnstone
PA5 8DJ
☎ 01505 328810

Opening Times:
Mon – Fri 9.00am–5.30pm
Sat 9.00am–5.00pm

Opening Times:
Mon – Fri 9.00am–6.00pm
Sat 9.00am–2.00pm

- **Munro Pharmacy**
  298 Dyke Road
  Knightswood
  Glasgow
  G13 4QU
  ☎ 0141-959-2456

Opening Times:
Mon – Fri 9.00am–6.00pm
Sat 9.00am–1.00pm

- **Munro Pharmacy**
  48 North Elgin Street
  Whitecrook
  Clydebank
  G81 1BZ
  ☎ 0141-562-0310

Opening Times:
Mon – Fri 9.00am–9.00pm,
Sat 9.00am–6.00pm, Sun – closed

- **Sinclair Pharmacy**
  145 Spey Road
  Bearsden
  Glasgow
  G61 1LF
  ☎ 0141 942 6626

SERVICES

- **Adela Stockton**
  Birth Consultancy Services
  21 Kelvinside Gardens East
  Glasgow
  G20 6BE
  ☎ 0141 945 4986

- **Caring Touch**
  ☎ 01389 850237

Baby massage and yoga

Opening Times:
Mon – Sun 7.30am–9.00pm
Home Visits are also available

For some children, learning can be hard work for what seems like no apparent reason. Some of the symptoms of dyslexia can include reading difficulties, spelling problems, poor writing and grammar, poor mathematical skills, concentration and attention span problems, memory lapses, balance or problems with co-ordination, and underachieving or low self-esteem. This can often result in children being labelled 'thick', 'stupid' or 'lazy' when in reality, they are often far brighter than anyone realised. Famous people believed to have experienced dyslexia but not let it stand in their way, include Albert Einstein, Richard Branson, Steve Redgrave, Alexander Graham Bell and Winston Churchhill.

Now a revolutionary breakthrough in drug-free treatment made by the Dyslexia Treatment Centre's research team, means that virtually everyone with dyslexia or related learning difficulties can benefit from dramatic improvements.

Recognising that no two dyslexics are the same, the Dyslexia Treatment Centre's professionally trained staff structure tailor-made treatment solutions for each child. Typically, treatment takes six months.

Further services available at this centre are:
Couple Counselling without waiting
☎ 0141 354 8997
Scottish Phobia Society
☎ 0800 0837 824
Academy of NLP & Hypnosis
☎ 0800 0834 585

- **Dyslexia Treatment Centre**
  The Pentagon
  Washington Street
  Glasgow
  G3
  ☎ 0870 060 1549

Magical visit could be all your child needs

HAVE you ever felt the kind of immense all consuming pride that comes from being a parent whose child has just smiled their first smile, taken their first step, or appeared in the school nativity play as the back end of a donkey?

Well, multiply that feeling a hundred-fold and add pure joy and excitement, too and you will start to imagine how I felt as I heard the voice at the end of the phone.

"Dad, Dad, Dad — guess what? I've just got my school report", he said. Can I open it now?" It was the last day of my son, Jack's school term.

Pay a visit to the Centre and help your child enjoy learning again.

"Go ahead" I said.

His excitement, exhilaration and pride in himself was fully expressed in his voice as he squealed down the phone.

"I've got an "A" in... an "A" in... " and so it went on: nine As, three Bs and a C.

All of the teachers' comments went along the lines of how well Jack had progressed this term. One teacher said that she had never known Jack to be so motivated in his work.

So, am I just another proud parent?

You tell me ... three months earlier at Jack's parent-teacher meeting I had again refused to accept suggestions that he had "learning difficulties" and required special needs teaching.

He is an exceptionally bright, lively child and this just did not make sense to me.

Luckily, I knew about ***Jeffrey Goodwin*** a Dyslexia specialist working in Glasgow who had trained in London.

He developed the ***Magical Spelling and Dyslexia Treatment Centre*** training system, for training people with dyslexia and/or dyspraxia to overcome the symptoms of their learning difficulties.

FREEPHONE 0870 060 1549
So call now — and make that difference.

Jeffrey Goodwin's Magical Spelling and Dyslexia Treatment Centre could just have all the answers to your child's problems.

HOW IT WORKED

THE system worked by utilising discrete parts of Jack's brain through a series of mental and physical exercises.

The consultation took two hours and involved a period of approximately 45 minutes of puzzles and questions in a completely informal and relaxed setting — this was the diagnosis part of the consultation — a simple assessment of exactly how Jack was processing information and how effectively that worked for him.

Through the diagnosis Jeffrey was able to tell exactly what Jack's learning strategies were and proceeded to work through various "puzzles" which developed discrete parts of the brain.

Jack could spell "hippopotamus" forwards and backwards by the end of the session and recall a list of 20 objects forwards and backwards. He did all this and lots more and had great fun!

He came out of the two-hour session laughing and joking.

Is that it? No, it is a three- month programme visiting once a week or, for more severe cases, a six-month programme.

As you see your child's confidence grow daily you may wonder how you ever did
without it.

So am I a proud parent too? You bet! I'm delighted to be able to assist others unleash their potential too!

So exactly who can benefit from this?

- **Children from seven and above — who despite early signs of normal intelligence are showing signs of learning difficulties or attention problems.**

- **Adolescents — who have found schoolwork progressively more and more difficult and show signs of frustration when trying to keep up.**

- **Adults — who have often questioned why they are underachieving. They realise their thinking skills are more advanced than their ability to communicate their thoughts.**

Many of our students have never been officially diagnosed with dyslexia, dyspraxia or attention disorder but know they are not "realising their potential".

If you think you or a loved one may benefit from the *Dyslexia Treatment Centre* programme but are not sure, call our fully trained customer information team on *0870 060 1549* for advice.

Kids can benefit at the Centre

- **Elizabeth Quinn**
  Child Behaviour Specialist
  ☎ 0141 576 4252

Parents!

Are you struggling with:

- Toddler tantrums?
- Disobedience?
- Aggression?
- Poor sleeping habits?
- Poor eating habits?
- Poor concentration?

You are not alone. Let me help you.

Problematic behaviour in young children is a growing cause of major stress for parents. Many parents are seeking ways of dealing with this difficulty but often struggle alone.

I can provide personal, confidential consultations, assisting parents and child to develop plans to tackle behavioural difficulties and to encourage the positive behaviour which all children are capable of.

As a parent and grandparent I am well aware of the pressures on parents and I offer practical, common-sense strategies which will reduce your stress and help you to get your child back on track.

Call me on 0141 576 4252 or email me at liz@equinn.com. You can also check my website at www.equinn.com

SUPPORT FOR PARENTS

Westone & Riverside LHCCs provide primary care services to the west of the city and offer a wide range of support services for parents:

BREASTFEEDING

Thinking about breastfeeding...

If you need help Glasgow Breastfeeding Initiative can provide you with a volunteer helper from your local community to offer information and advice about breastfeeding. If you go on to breastfeed, the volunteer will provide you with ongoing support. For more information call the Breastfeeding Initiative on 0141 531 8227

Knightswood Breastfeeding Support Group

Alternatively, you may want to come along to our drop in group for information, support or advice. The group is currently meeting in Knightswood Community Centre on Monday's from 10.30–12pm...for more information call the pre-5 Family Service on 0141 314 6225

DENTAL HEALTH

Remember that you can register your baby with a dentist from birth and it is also important to attend for a dental check up every six months.

HEALTH ADVICE

For general help or information on your child's health speak to your health visitor who can be contacted through your GP practice.

PRE-5 FAMILY SERVICE

Baby Bounce & Rhyme Time (under 2's)

Action, rhyme, songs and storytelling to enhance early literacy in pre-5's.
Wednesday 10.30am–11.30am, Partick Library
Thursday 1.30pm–2.30pm, Whiteinch Library

Play & Share (2–5 year olds)

Parents and toddlers sharing the experience of play and development through curriculum-based activities
(Buddies Club) Friday 10.00am–12 noon, Netherton Community Centre

The service also provides a range of services that can be accessed through your health visitor or contact the pre-5 family service at William St Clinic on 0141 314 6225

- Infant Massage Groups
- 1st Time Parenting Classes
- Positive Parenting Classes
- Sleep Clinics

NHS Greater Glasgow

VACCINATIONS

Please find below details of your child's immunisations program (up to 15 months old). For an immunisations guide for 3 years to 5 year olds, see further on in this section. For more information on immunisation visit www.hebs.com

About Immunisation

Immunisation is a way of protecting ourselves from serious disease.

There are some diseases that can kill children or cause lasting damage to their health.

Your child should have their first immunisations at two months old.

They will be given further doses of these immunisations when they are three months old and four months old. Other immunisations are given at around 13 months old, then between three and five years old (before your child starts school), and in their teenage years.

You will be sent an appointment inviting you to bring your child for their immunisations.

Most doctor's surgeries and health centres run special immunisation or baby clinics. You can often drop in at other times if you can't get to the clinic during the day.

Very occasionally, children can have allergic reactions straight after immunisation. If they are treated quickly, they will recover completely. The people who give immunisations are trained to deal with allergic reactions.

There are very few reasons why a child should not be immunised. But you should let your health visitor, doctor or practice nurse know if your child:

- has a high fever
- has had a bad reaction to any other immunisation
- has had treatment for cancer
- has a severe allergy to eggs
- has a bleeding disorder
- has had convulsions (fits)

- has any illness which affects the immune system, for example HIV or AIDS; or
- is taking medicine which affects the immune system – for example, immunosuppressants (given after organ transplant or for cancer) or high-dose steroids.

Fever after Immunisation

A few children may develop a fever after immunisation.

A fever is a temperature over 37.5° C.

If your child's face feels hot to the touch and they look red or flushed, they probably have a fever. You could check their temperature with a thermometer.

Fevers are fairly common in children. They are usually mild, but it is important to know what to do if your child gets one.

How to treat a fever

1. Keep your child cool by gently sponging them with lukewarm (not cold) water and letting it dry on their skin; and making sure they don't have too many layers of clothes or blankets on.
2. Give them plenty of cool drinks.
3. Give them paracetamol liquid, such as Calpol, Disprol or Medinol. Read the instructions on the bottle carefully and give your child the correct dose for their age. You may need to give them a second dose four to six hours later.

Do not give aspirin to children under 12 years old.

Call your doctor immediately if your child:

- has a temperature of 39° C or above; or has
- a fit.

■ DTP-Hib vaccine

The DTP-Hib vaccine protects against four different diseases – Diphtheria, Tetanus and Pertussis (whooping cough) and Heamophilus influenza type b (Hib).

Your baby should have a DTP-Hib immunisation at two, three and four months old. They will be given a booster against diptheria, tetanus and pertussis before they start school. (They don't need a booster against Hib). They will get a tetanus and diptheria booster between the ages of 13 and 18 years.

What is diphtheria?

Diphtheria is a disease that usually begins with a sore throat and can quickly cause problems with breathing. It can damage the heart and nervous system and, in severe cases, it can kill.

What is tetanus?

Tetanus is a painful disease that affects the muscles and can cause breathing problems. Germs that are found in soil and manure and can get into the body through open cuts or burns cause it. Tetanus affects the nervous system and if not treated, it can kill.

What is pertussis (whooping cough)?

Whooping cough is a disease that can cause long bouts of coughing and choking which can make it hard to breathe. It can last for up to 10 weeks. It is not usually serious in older children, but it can be very serious in babies under one year old.

What is Hib?

Hib is an infection that can cause a number of major illnesses like blood poisoning, pneumonia and meningitis. All of these illnesses can kill if they are not treated quickly.

The Hib vaccine only protects your child against one type of meningitis (Hib). It does not protect against any other type of meningitis.

After immunisation

Your child may get some of the following side effects, which are usually mild.

- It is quite normal for your baby to be miserable within 48hrs of having the injection.
- Your baby may develop a fever.
- You may notice a small lump where your baby had the injection. This may last a few weeks.

If your child has a worse reaction to the DTP-Hib vaccine, talk to your doctor, nurse or health visitor.

Sometimes babies have fits a day or two after their DTB-Hib vaccination. If your baby has a fit, call your doctor immediately. Babies usually recover from fits quickly and completely. Young babies can have fits at any time, so having a fit after their vaccination may not necessarily be linked to the vaccine. Your doctor will decide whether your baby can have more doses of the vaccine. But if you delay the immunisation, it can increase the chances of fits after DTP-Hib. So it's important to make sure your child gets vaccinated at the right age.

■ Polio vaccine

Your baby should be immunised against polio at two, three and four months old. They will be given a booster before they start school and they will get another booster between the ages of 13 and 18. The polio vaccine protects against the disease poliomyelitis (polio). Unlike other immunisations, it is given as a liquid to swallow.

What is polio?

Polio is a virus that attacks the nervous system and can permanently paralyse the muscles. If it affects the chest muscle, polio can kill. The virus is passed in the faeces of people with polio or people who have just been immunised against polio.

After immunisation

Make sure anyone who changes your baby's nappy washes their hands thoroughly afterwards. The vaccine will continue to be passed into your baby's nappy for up to six weeks. People who have not been immunised against polio themselves could be infected by the tiny amount of virus in the vaccine if they come into contact with it. There is about one case of this each year in the UK.

Anyone who has not had the polio vaccine, including grandparents who might be looking after your baby, should talk to their doctor about it. They can arrange to have the vaccine at the same time as your baby.

There is an extremely small chance of developing polio from the vaccine- about one case in more than 1.5 million primary doses used.

How soon after their polio vaccine can I take my baby swimming?

You can take your baby swimming at any time, both before and after they have their polio vaccine. There is no risk of children catching, or passing on polio in swimming pools.

Your baby does not need any immunisations before they go swimming

■ MenC vaccine

Your baby should be immunised with the MenC vaccine at two, three and four months old.

This vaccine protects against infection by meningoccal group C. Meningococcal group C is a type of bacteria that can cause meningitis and septicaemia (blood poisoning). The MenC vaccine does not protect against meningitis caused by other bacteria or by viruses.

What is meningitis?

Meningitis is an inflammation of the lining of the brain. The same germs that cause meningitis may cause septicaemia (blood poisoning). Babies and young people aged 15 to 17 are most at risk of getting meningitis or septicaemia from meningococcal group C.

How effective is the MenC vaccine?

The MenC vaccine was introduced in Autumn 1999. In the year before the vaccine was introduced, there were 109 confirmed cases in Scotland of meningitis and septicaemia from meningococcal group C, and 11 people died. Since the MenC vaccine was introduced, there has been a drop of over 80% in the number of young people under 20 who get ill with this type of meningitis or septicaemia, and only one death in an unvaccinated patient has been reported.

Both meningitis and septicaemia are very serious in babies and young children. It is important that you know the signs and symptoms and what to do if you see them.

After immunisation

Your baby may have some redness and swelling where they had the injection. About half of all babies who have the vaccine may become irritable, and around one in 20 may get a mild fever.

MMR vaccine

Your baby should have their first dose of MMR vaccine at around 13 months old and a second dose before they start school.

MMR protects your child against Measles, Mumps and Rubella (German measles).

What is measles?
Measles is caused by a very infectious virus. It is often a mild disease but if there are complications, it can be dangerous. It causes a high fever and a rash and can go on to cause chest infections, fits and brain damage. About one in every 15 children who develop measles is at risk of complications. In serious cases, it can kill. We cannot tell which children may be seriously affected by measles.

What is mumps?
The mumps virus causes headache, fever and painful swollen glands in the face, neck or under the jaw. It can cause permanent deafness. It can also cause viral meningitis and encephalitis (inflammation of the brain). Very rarely, it causes painful swelling of the testicles in boys and the ovaries in girls.

What is rubella (German measles)?
Rubella usually causes a mild rash, swollen glands and a sore throat in children, but it is very serious for unborn babies. If a pregnant woman catches it early in her pregnancy, it can seriously harm her inborn baby's sight, hearing, brain, liver, lungs and bone marrow. This condition is called congenital rubella syndrome (CRS). In many cases, pregnant women catch rubella from their own, or their friend's children.

After the vaccine
The three separate vaccines in the MMR immunisation may have different side-affects at different times.

- Six to ten days after their MMR vaccine, some children may become feverish, develop a measles-like rash and go off their food as the measles part of the vaccine starts to work.
- In the six weeks after the vaccine, your child may (very rarely) get a rash of small bruise-like spots. If you see spots like these, show them to your doctor.
- Very rarely, children may get a mild form of mumps about three weeks after their immunisation. They will not be infectious and they can mix with other people as normal.

- About one child in every 1000 who have immunisation may have a fit, which is usually caused by a fever and is called a 'febrile convulsion'. But if a child has not been immunised and they get measles, they are 10 times more likely to have a fit.

Although encephalitis (inflammation of the brain) has been reported (one case in a million doses), the risk of children getting encephalitis after MMR vaccine is no higher than the risk of getting it they have not had the vaccine. However, the risk of a child developing encephalitis as a result of having measles is more common – about one in every 5000 cases.

Egg allergies

The MMR vaccine is made using eggs. If your child has a severe allergy to eggs (rashes on the face and body), a swollen mouth and throat, breathing problems and shock), tell your doctor or practice nurse. They can make special arrangements to give your child the vaccine safely.

For more information on immunisation visit www.hebs.com

Please find below a table of immunisation details for 3 to 5 year olds.

You will receive an appointment inviting you to bring your child for their pre-school immunisations. These are due three years after your child has completed the immunisations they had a two, three and four months old.

Diphtheria, tetanus and acellular pertussis (whooping cough) (Dtap)

One injection	This is a booster dose of a similar vaccine your child had as a baby

Polio

By mouth	This is a booster dose of a vaccine your child had as a baby

Measles, mumps and rubella (MMR)

One injection	This is a second dose of MMR vaccine. If your child has not had the first dose yet, then it should be given now, and they should have their second dose in three months time.

DTaP vaccine

The Dtap vaccine protects against diptheria, tetanus and pertussis (whooping cough).

What is the difference between the DtaP vaccine and the DTP vaccine that babies are given at two, three and four months old?
The pertussis (whooping cough) part of the DTP vaccine works well for babies but it causes a higher rate of mild reactions in older children. The acellular pertussis vaccine (aP) is more suitable for older children.

The information contained within *Vaccinations* was kindly supplied by:

THE GLASGOW GUIDE FOR PARENTS AND CARERS

2005 edition

NOTE TO ADVERTISERS

If you were not listed in ***The Glasgow Guide for Parents and Carers*** 2004 (2nd) edition, don't worry. Have your business or service listed in ***The Glasgow Guide for Parents and Carers*** 2005 (3rd) edition. Fill in your details below and return by the 30th September 2004 to:

Glasgow Under 6's Ltd
48 Flenders Avenue
Clarkston
Glasgow, G76 7XZ
Tel/Fax 0141 616 3661
E: glasgowunder6s@fsmail.net

Name of Business & Contact Name . . . .

Address . . . .

. . . .

Postcode . . . . Tel/Fax No. . . . .

Email . . . . www . . . .

PLEASE TICK BELOW

Free Listing ☐

Request advertising details ☐

NOTE TO READERS

We would like to hear your comments and suggestions for our 2005 edition. These should be sent to **Glasgow Under 6's Ltd** at the address above.

Restaurants (coffee & family eating out)

Please find included in the following section listings of:

- **Coffee Houses**
- **Family Eating Out**

For more Birthday Party ideas and venues *see* Birthday Parties, Days Out (places to visit), Community & Leisure (local authority)

RESTAURANTS (COFFEE & FAMILY EATING OUT)

Please find in this section below listings of child friendly coffee houses and restaurants in and around the Glasgow area.

Many of the restaurants will also cater for children's birthday parties, please check directly with the venue itself.

- **Agenda**
  15 Millbrae Road
  Glasgow
  G42 9UA
  ☎ 0141 649 6861

For family eating
Agenda also have a soft play area called Noiseland. Noiseland can also be booked for children's birthday parties *see* BIRTHDAY PARTIES (CHILDREN'S ACTIVITY & ADVENTURE CENTRES)

- **The Ashoka at the Mill**
  500 Corselet Road
  Darnley
  G53
  ☎ 0141 876 0458

Opening Times:
Mon – Thurs 5.00pm-11.00pm, Fri 12.00pm–11.00pm, Sat 4.00pm–11.00pm, Sun 4.00pm–11.00pm
Highchairs available
Children's menu & play area

- **Beanscene Shawlands**
  19 Skirving Street
  Glasgow
  G41 3AB
  ☎ 0141 632 8090
  Fax: 0141 632 9612
  www.beanscene.co.uk

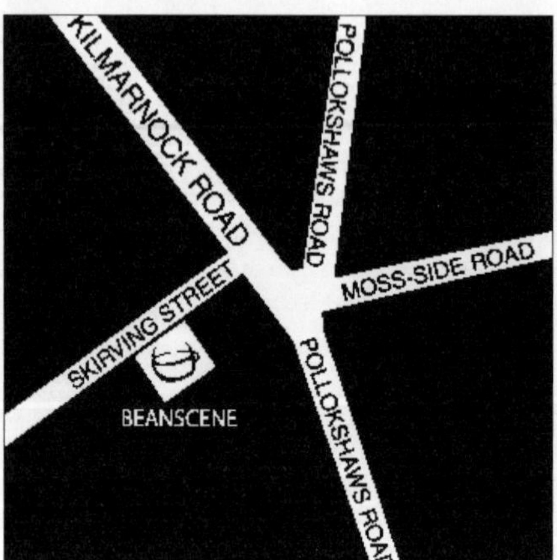

Opening Times:
Mon – Sat 8am – 11pm, Sun 10am – 11pm
Closed Christmas Day

Children welcome anytime
Non smoking

Facilities include
- Child play area
- Children's Food & Drinks. Scooby Snack & Big Deal, Babyccino & Chococcino
- Toy box
- Baby changing facilities and baby changing supplies
- High chairs
- Disabled toilets
- Food and bottle heating facilities
- Monthly prize draw

Setting the Scene

At **Beanscene** we aim to please. The whole gig is inspired by the Coffee Houses which predominate in the Italian Quarter of San Francisco, one of THE most happening neighbourhoods on this planet.

Beanscene is home from home and we want you to spend quality time here; morning, noon & night. For you to do that we must ensure that you have the widest possible choice. That means taking care of the SMALL BEANS.

Here @ Beanscene we're 110% committed to 'doing it for the kids'
– 3 steps to parental heaven

1. SMALL BEAN BAG: one stop refuelling and entertainment kit with; drink, sandwich, yoghurt, fruit and drawing kit.
2. ENTERTAINMENT: fully laden toys and games box.
3. COMFORT & JOY: fully equipped baby changing facilities and more than enough high chairs to go round.

So! Take a few moments away from the daily grind to get yourself up to speed with Beanscene. Smarter than your average Coffee House; read, digest and live the beautifully simple concept of coffee, music and conversation.

Opening Times:
Mon – Sat 8am–11pm, Sun 10am–11pm
Closed Christmas Day

Children welcome anytime
Non smoking

Facilities include
- Children's Food & Drinks. Scooby Snack & Big Deal, Babyccino & Chococcino
- Toy box
- Baby changing facilities and baby changing supplies
- High chairs
- Disabled toilets
- Food and bottle heating facilities
- Monthly prize draw

■ **Beanscene West End**
Cresswell Lane
Hillhead
Glasgow
G12 8AA
☎ 0141 334 6776
Fax: 0141 334 8361

Opening TImes:
Mon – Sat 8am–10pm
Sun 10am–10pm
Closed Christmas Day

Children welcome anytime
Non smoking

Facilities include
- Children's Food & Drinks. Scooby Snack & Big Deal, Babyccino & Chococcino
- Toy box
- Baby changing facilities and baby changing supplies
- High chairs
- Disabled toilets
- Food and bottle heating facilities
- Monthly prize draw

■ **Beanscene Parkgate**
10 Parkgate
Holyrood Road
Edinburgh
EH8 8AE
☎ 0131 557 6549
Fax: 0131 557 8316

- **Beanscene Nicolson Street**
  99 Nicolson Street
  Edinburgh
  EH8 9BY
  ☎ 0131 667 6549
  Fax: 0131 667 8630

Opening Times:
Mon – Sat 8am–10pm
Sun 10am–10pm
Closed Christmas Day

Children welcome anytime
Non smoking

Facilities include
- Children's Food & Drinks. Scooby Snack & Big Deal, Babyccino & Chococcino
- Toy box
- Baby changing facilities and baby changing supplies
- High chairs
- Disabled toilets
- Food and bottle heating facilities
- Monthly prize draw

- **Beanscene Stirling**
  40 King Street
  Stirling
  FK8 1AY
  ☎ 01786 451 472
  Fax: 01786 462 421

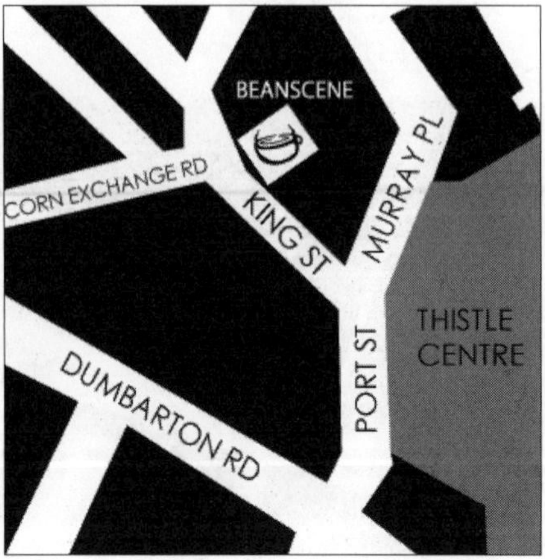

Opening Times:
Mon – Sat 8am–11pm
Sun 10am – 11pm
Closed Christmas Day

Children welcome anytime
Non smoking

Facilities include
- Children's Food & Drinks. Scooby Snack & Big Deal, Babyccino & Chococcino
- Toy box
- Baby changing facilities and baby changing supplies
- High chairs
- Disabled toilets
- Food and bottle heating facilities
- Monthly prize draw

- **Bistro Du Sud**
  Cambridge Street
  Glasgow
  ☎ 0141 332 2666

Opening Times:
8.00am–11.00pm daily, except Sunday's, which is open from 12.00pm–11.00pm
Children welcome

- **Bellziehill Farm**
  Brewsters & Travel Inn
  New Edinburgh Road
  Bellshill
  ML4 3HH
  ☎ 01698 740180
  Fax 01698 845969

Opening Times: Fun Factory (soft play)
Mon – Thurs 12.00pm–9.00pm,
Fri, Sat & Sun 12.00pm–10.00pm,
Family Restaurant, Mon – Sat 11.00am–10.00pm, Sun 12.00pm–10.00pm
Children's Birthday Parties available contact directly for further details
Highchairs available
Baby changing & disabled facilities

- **Broadwood Farm**
  Brewsters
  Back o'Hill,
  Craiglinn
  Cumbernauld
  G68 9AD
  ☎ 01236 737556
  Fax 01236 452970

Opening Times: Fun Factory (soft play)
Sun – Thurs 12.00pm–9.00pm,
Fri 12.00pm–10.00pm,
Sat 11.00am–10.00pm
Family Restaurant, Mon – Sat 11.30am–10.00pm, Sun 12.00pm–10.00pm
Children's Birthday Parties available contact directly for further details
Highchairs available
Baby changing & disabled facilities

- **Garvel Point**
  Brewsters & Travel Inn
  3 James Watt Way
  Greenock
  PA15 2AJ
  ☎ 01475 730911
  Fax 01475 730890

Opening Times: Fun Factory (soft play) Mon – Sat 11.30am – 9.00pm,
Sun 12.00pm – 9.00pm
Family Restaurant, Mon – Sat 11.30am – 10.00pm, Sun 12.00pm – 10.00pm
Children's Birthday Parties available contact directly for further details
Highchairs available
Baby changing & disabled facilities

- **Kingsgate Still Brewsters**
  Mavor Avenue
  East Kilbride
  G74 4QX
  ☎ 01355 232331

Opening Times: Fun Factory (soft play)
Mon – Sat 11.00am – 9.00pm,
Sun 12.00pm – 9.00pm
Family Restaurant, Mon – Sat 11.00am –10.00pm, Sun 12.00pm – 10.00pm
Children's Birthday Parties available contact directly for further details
Highchairs available
Baby changing & disabled facilities

- **Leven Valley Brewsters**
  7 Allerdyce Road,
  Great Western Retail Park,
  Glasgow
  G15 6SA
  ☎ 0141 944 3366

Opening Times: Fun Factory (soft play)
7 days, 11.00am – 9.00pm
Family Restaurant, Mon – Sat 11.30am – 10.00pm, Sun 12.00pm – 10.00pm
Children's Birthday Parties available contact directly for further details
Highchairs available
Baby changing & disabled facilities

- **Monkton Lodge Brewsters & Travel Inn**
  Kilmarnock Road
  Monkton,
  Prestwick
  KA9 2RJ
  ☎ 01292 678262
  Fax 01292 678248

Opening Times: Fun Factory (soft play)
Sun – Thurs 11.00am – 9.00pm,
Fri & Sat 11.00am – 10.00pm
Family Restaurant, Mon – Sat 11.00am – 10.00pm, Sun 11.30am – 10.00pm
Children's Birthday Parties available contact directly for further details
Highchairs available
Baby changing & disabled facilities
This is the only Brewsters in Scotland that has two Brewster Bears performing hourly

- **Newhaven Quay Brewsters & Travel Inn**
  51–3 Newhaven Place
  Newhaven,
  Edinburgh
  EH6 4TX
  ☎ 0131 555 1570

Opening Times: Fun Factory (soft play)
Mon – Sat 11.00am – 9.00pm,
Sun 12.00pm – 9.00pm
Family Restaurant, Mon – Sat 11.00am – 10.00pm, Sun 12.00pm – 10.00pm
Children's Birthday Parties available contact directly for further details
Highchairs available
Baby changing & disabled facilities

Opening Times: Fun Factory (soft play)
Sun – Thurs 11.00am – 9.00pm,
Fri & Sat 11.00am – 10.00pm
Family Restaurant, Mon – Sat 11.30am – 10.00pm, Sun 12.00pm – 10.00pm
Children's Birthday Parties available contact directly for further details
Highchairs available
Baby changing & disabled facilities

Opening Times: Fun Factory (soft play)
Mon – Thurs 11.00am – 9.00pm,
Fri & Sat 11.00am – 10.00pm, Sun 12.00pm – 10.00pm
Family Restaurant, Mon – Sat 11.00am – 10.00pm, Sun 12.00pm – 10.00pm
Children's Birthday Parties available contact directly for further details
Highchairs available
Baby changing & disabled facilities

Opening Times: Fun Factory (soft play)
Sun – Thurs 11.00am – 9.00pm,
Fri & Sat 11.00am – 10.00pm
Family Restaurant, Mon – Sat 11.30am – 10.00pm, Sun 12.00pm – 10.00pm
Childrens Birthday Parties available contact directly for further details
Highchairs available
Baby changing & disabled facilities

Opening Times:
Mon – Thurs 12.00pm–11.00pm,
Fri & Sat 12.00pm–midnight
Sun 12.30pm–11.00pm

- **Orion Way**
  Brewsters & Travel Inn
  Cambuslang Investment Park,
  Drumhead Place
  Glasgow
  G32 8EY
  ☎ 0141 764 2655
  Fax 0141 778 1703

- **Phoenix Park**
  Brewsters & Travel Inn
  Phoenix Park,
  Paisley
  PA1 2BH
  ☎ 0141 887 4865
  Fax 0141 887 2799

- **Stepps Brewsters**
  & Travel Inn
  Crowwood Roundabout
  Cumbernauld Road, Stepps, Glasgow
  G33 6HZ
  ☎ 0141 779 8040
  Fax 0141 779 8060

- **Di Maggios (Hamilton)**
  42 Gateside Street
  Hamilton
  ML3 7JQ
  ☎ 01698 891828

- **Di Maggios (East Kilbride)**
  Stroud Road
  East Kilbride
  Glasgow
  G75 0YA
  ☎ 01355 242222

  Opening Times:
  Mon – Thurs 12.00pm–11.00pm,
  Fri & Sat 12.00pm–midnight
  Sun 12.30pm–11.00pm
  This Di Maggios has a children's play area inside and outside

- **Di Maggios (City Centre)**
  21 Royal Exchange Square
  Glasgow
  ☎ 0141 248 2111

  Opening Times:
  6 Days 12.00pm–midnight,
  Sun 12.30pm–midnight

- **Di Maggios (Shawlands)**
  1038 Pollokshaws Road
  Shawlands
  Glasgow
  G41 3EB
  ☎ 0141 632 8888

  Opening Times:
  Mon – Thurs 12.00pm–3.00pm & 5.00pm–11.00pm,
  Fri 12.00pm–3.00pm & 5.00pm–12.00pm
  Sat 12.00pm–midnight
  Sun 12.30pm–11.00pm

- **Di Maggios (West End)**
  61 Ruthven Lane
  Glasgow
  G12 9BG
  ☎ 0141 334 6000

  Opening Times:
  Mon – Thurs 12.00pm–3.00pm & 5.00pm–11.00pm, Fri 12.00pm–3.00pm & 5.00pm–12.00pm, Sat 12.00pm–midnight
  Sun 12.30pm–11.00pm

- **Di Maggios (Pronto)**
  163 West Nile Street
  Glasgow
  ☎ 0141 333 4999

  Opening Times:
  6 Days 12.00pm–midnight,
  Sun 12.30pm–midnight

- **Di Maggios (Airdrie)**
  1 Rochsollock Road
  Airdrie
  ML6 9BG
  ☎ 01236 763853

  Opening Times:
  Mon – Thurs 12.00pm–11.00pm,
  Fri & Sat 12.00pm–midnight
  Sun 12.30pm–11.00pm

- **Di Maggios (Gibson Street)**
  18 Gibson Street
  Glasgow
  G12 8NX
  ☎ 0141 341 0999

  Opening Times:
  Mon – Thurs 12.00pm–11.00pm,
  Fri 12.00pm–midnight
  Sat 11.00pm–midnight
  Sun 11.00am–11.00pm

■ **The Eagle Lodge Homespreads**
(Funky Forest Soft Play)
2 Hilton Road
Bishopbriggs
G64
☎ 0141 772 5951

Family eating, children's menu, highchairs available
Indoor & outdoor play
The Funky Forest Soft Play Area is open
Mon – Thurs 12.00pm–9.00pm,
Fri 12.00pm–9.30pm,
Sat 12.00pm–9.30pm,
Sun 12.30pm–9.00pm
Birthday party bookings available 7 days, party bags included in price, birthday cakes not supplied

■ **Est Est Est**
21–5 Bothwell Street
Glasgow
G2
☎ 0141 248 6262

High chairs, baby-changing facilities
Children's menu available
Children can make there own pizza
Children's birthday parties available, max 12 children

■ **Fenwick Hotel**
Ayr Road
Fenwick
☎ 01560 600478

Sunday Special – Free entry to Bouncy Castle, Kids Activities & Helium balloons.
Casual menu served all day including Spit Roast Chicken and Free Salad Bar.
Roast of the Day & Kids menu & Pizzas

■ **Mother India**
28 Westminster Terrace
Glasgow
☎ 0141 221 2217

Opening Times:
Mon – Sat 5.30pm–10.30pm,
Sun 5.30pm–10.00pm
Lunches available Wed, Thurs & Fri 12.00pm–2.00pm

■ **Peel Park** (Funky Forest Soft Play)
Eaglesham Road
East Kilbride
Glasgow
G75 8LW
☎ 0870 700 1398

Family eating, highchairs available
Funky Forest Soft Play Area, height restriction 4ft 6
Available for children's birthday parties 7 days
Party bags included in price, birthday cakes not supplied

■ **Pizza Hut**
203–5 Argyle Street
Glasgow
G2 8BU
☎ 0141 221 0144

Opening Times:
Mon – Thurs 11.00am–11.00pm,
Fri, Sat 11.00am–midnight
Sun 12.00pm–11.00pm
Highchairs available
Children's menu & activities

■ **Pizza Hut**
85 West George Street
Glasgow
G2 1QG
☎ 0141 226 3633

Opening Times:
Mon – Thurs 11.00am–11.00pm,
Fri, Sat 11.00am–midnight,
Sun 11.30am–11.00pm
Highchairs available
Children's menu & activities

■ **Pizza Hut**
Restaurant Unit
Goodyear Leisure Park
Great Western Road
Glasgow
G15 6SA
☎ 0141 944 4800

Opening Times:
7 Days 11.00am–11.00pm
Highchairs available
Children's menu & activities

■ **Pizza Hut East Kilbride**
Unit 11 Kingsgate Retail Park
East Kilbride
Glasgow
☎ 01355 242 442

Opening Times:
7 days 11.30am–11.00pm
Highchairs available
Children's menu & activities

■ **Pizza Hut**
108 Renfield Street
Glasgow
G2 1NH
☎ 0141 332 4820

Opening Times:
Sun – Thurs 11.00am–11.00pm,
Fri, Sat 11.00am–midnight
Highchairs available
Children's menu & activities

■ **Pizza Hut**
32–4 Queen Street
Glasgow
G1 3DX
☎ 0141 248 5682

Opening Times:
Mon – Wed 11.00am–10.00pm,
Thurs & Sun 11.00am–11.00pm,
Fri 11.00am–11.30pm,
Sat 10.30am–11.30pm
Highchairs available
Children's menu & activities, Toy box

- **Pizza Hut**
  122 Braehead Shopping Centre
  Kings Inch Road
  Glasgow
  G51 4BS
  ☎ 0141 885 9393

  Opening Times:
  Mon – Fri 11.00am–9.00pm,
  Sat 11.00am–6.30pm,
  Sun 11.00am–6.00pm
  Highchairs available
  Children's menu & activities

- **Pizza Hut**
  Unit 3 Paisley Leisure Park
  Paisley
  PA1 2BH
  ☎ 0141 887 2345

  Opening Times:
  Mon – Fri 11.00am–9.00pm,
  Sat 11.00am–6.30pm,
  Sun 11.00am–6.00pm
  Highchairs available
  Children's menu & activities

- **Pizza Hut**
  The Forge Retail Park
  Parkhead Forge
  Glasgow
  G31 4BW
  ☎ 0141 550 0202

  Opening Times:
  7 days 11.30am–11.00pm
  Highchairs available
  Childrens menu & activities

- **TGI Friday's**
  113 Buchanan Street
  Glasgow
  G1 3HF
  ☎ 0141 221 6996

  Opening Times:
  Mon – Sat 12.00pm–11.30pm,
  Sun 12.00pm–11.00pm
  Birthday celebration for all ages encouraged
  Children's menu & colouring
  Highchairs available

T.G.I. FRIDAY'S®

Great food and fun

TGI's in the city centre gave itself a new look and is busier than ever. Friendly and well-trained staff ensure a meal at the restaurant meets the needs of all age groups.

Nominated category of

Family Outlet of the Year 2003 by the SLTN

THE GLASGOW GUIDE FOR PARENTS AND CARERS

2005 edition

NOTE TO ADVERTISERS

If you were not listed in ***The Glasgow Guide for Parents and Carers*** 2004 (2nd) edition, don't worry. Have your business or service listed in ***The Glasgow Guide for Parents and Carers*** 2005 (3rd) edition. Fill in your details below and return by the 30th September 2004 to:

Glasgow Under 6's Ltd
48 Flenders Avenue
Clarkston
Glasgow, G76 7XZ
Tel/Fax 0141 616 3661
E: glasgowunder6s@fsmail.net

Name of Business & Contact Name ....

Address ....

....

Postcode .... Tel/Fax No. ....

Email .... www ....

PLEASE TICK BELOW

Free Listing ☐

Request advertising details ☐

NOTE TO READERS

We would like to hear your comments and suggestions for our 2005 edition. These should be sent to **Glasgow Under 6's Ltd** at the address above.

SHOPPING

Please find included in the following section listings of:

- **Baby & Children's Clothes Shops**
- **Baby & Children's Traditional Furniture & Gifts / Nursery & Pram Shops**
- **Balloons & Fancy Dress**
- **Bookshops – Ottakar's**
- **Children's Footwear**
- **Cycle Shops**
- **Dancewear**
- **Maternity Wear**
- **School Outfitters**
- **Toy Shops**

For Cake Shops *see* BIRTHDAY PARTIES

Baby & Children's Clothes Shops

Please find in the section below listings of baby and children's clothes shops in and around the Glasgow area.

- **Apron Strings**
79 Main Street
Bothwell
Glasgow
G71 8ER
☎ 01698 854649

Opening Times:
Mon, Tues, Thurs, Fri & Sat
10.00am–5.00pm, Wed 10.00am–1.00pm,
Sun – closed

- **Baby Wear (Alladin's Indoor Mall)**
16 Motherwell Road
Bellshill
ML4 1RE
☎ 01698 844419

Opening Times:
Mon – Sat 9.00am–5.00pm, Sun – closed
Suppliers of baby wear from birth to 18 mnths

- **Babyspot (The)**
Unit 33–34 Savoy Centre
Sauchiehall Street
Glasgow
G2
☎ 0141 332 5184

Opening Times:
Mon, Tues & Wed 9.00am–5.30pm,
Thurs, Fri & Sat 9.00am–6.00pm,
Sun – closed

- **Bebe Bonito**
41 Westmuir Street
Parkhead
G31 5EL
☎ 0141 556 4511

Opening Times:
Mon – Sat 10.30am–5.00pm,
Sun – closed
Suppliers of baby designer wear & shoes up to age 6 yrs for girls and boys

- **Bebe Prema**
155 Union Street
Larkhall
ML9 1EB
☎ 01698 886123

Opening Times:
Mon – Sat 9.30am–5.00pm, Sun – closed
Suppliers of children's continental wear & shoes to 12 yrs

- **Bib & Tucker**
  97 Main Street
  Uddingston
  Glasgow
  G71 7EW
  ☎ 01698 812499

Opening Times:
Mon – Sat 9.00am–5.00pm, Sun – closed
Suppliers of designer children's clothes from birth to 6 yrs and suppliers of baby shoes

- **Bubbles**
  136 Merry Street
  Motherwell
  ML1 1NA
  ☎ 01698 264133

Opening Times:
Mon – Sat 10.00am–5.00pm, Sun – closed
Suppliers of designer continental children's wear and footwear from 1 to 6 yrs
Suppliers of christening and communion wear

- **Buttons & Bows**
  36 Langside Place
  Glasgow
  G41 3DL
  ☎ 0141 649 7437

Opening Times:
Mon – Sat 10.00am–5.00pm, Sun – closed
Suppliers of designer children's wear from birth to 12 yrs

- **Cradle Care**
  85 Main Street
  Coatbridge
  ML5 3EH
  ☎ 01236 422732

Opening Times:
Mon – Sat 9.30am–5.30pm, Sun – closed
Suppliers of children's wear from birth to 8 yrs, christening & communion wear, designer labels, Timberland, Kickers & Elle

- **Elizabeth's**
  4 Market Place
  Carluke
  ML8 4BP
  ☎ 01555 772057

Opening Times:
Mon, Tues, Fri, & Sat 9.00am–5.00pm,
Wed 9.00am–1.00pm, Sun – closed
Suppliers of baby & children's wear & soft toys

- **Girl Heaven**
  Buchanan Galleries
  200 Buchanan Street
  G1 2GF
  ☎ 0141 331 2500

Opening Times:
Mon, Tues, Wed, Fri & Sat 9.00am–6.00pm,
Thurs 9.00am–8.00pm,
Sun 11.00am–5.00pm
Suppliers of children's clothes, fashions & accessories, dressing up clothes
Birthday party bookings available
See BIRTHDAY PARTIES (CHILDREN'S ACTIVITY & ADVENTURE CENTRES)

■ **Golly Gosh**
258 Kilmarnock Road
Shawlands
Glasgow
☎ 0141 632 9889

Opening Times:
Mon – Sat 10.00am–5.00pm, Sun – closed
Suppliers of affordable continental children's wear, christening wear, shoes, soft toys, wooden toys & handmade cards & pictures

■ **Hippychick Ltd**

For Hippychick *see*
SHOPPING (BABY & CHILDREN'S TRADITIONAL FURNITURE & GIFTS / NURSERY & PRAM SHOPS)

■ **JoJo Maman Bébé** (mail order)
☎ 0870 241 0451 to request a catalogue

Maternity, baby/kids clothes, nursery products & toys

■ **Junior V I P**
155 High Street
Glasgow
G1 1PH
☎ 0141 552 0929

Opening Times:
Mon, Tues, Wed 10.00am–5.00pm
Thurs, Fri & Sat 10.00am–5.30pm,
Sun 12.00pm–4.30pm
Suppliers of baby & children's wear, shoes & christening wear

■ **Just Dawn**
(exclusive baby hat & pram set mfrs)
34 Castlemilk Arcade
Dougrie Drive
Glasgow
G45 9AA
☎ 0141 634 1600

Opening Times:
Mon – Sat 9.00am–5.00pm, Sun – closed

■ **Kids Plus**
1021 Shettleston Road
Glasgow
G32 7PB
☎ 0141 778 0771

Opening Times:
Mon – Sat 9.30am–5.00pm, Sun – closed
Suppliers of continental/designer wear & shoes for children age from birth to 12 yrs

■ **Kids Plus**
26 Main Street
Coatbridge
ML5 3AE
☎ 01236 440045

Opening Times:
Mon – Sat 10.00am–5.00pm, Sun – closed
Suppliers of continental/designer wear & shoes for children age from birth to 12 yrs

- **Little Darlings**
  273 Glasgow Road
  Hamilton
  ML3 0QG
  ☎ 01698 327145

Opening Times:
Mon, Tues, Thurs, Fri & Sat 9.00am–5.00pm,
Wed & Sun – closed
Suppliers of children's wear, christening wear, shoes & soft toys

- **Little Sweethearts**
  1006 Pollokshaws Road
  Glasgow
  G41 2HG
  ☎ 0141 649 8446

Opening Times:
Mon – Sat 9.30am–5.30pm, Sun – closed
Suppliers of continental children's wear from birth to 12 yrs
Suppliers of shoes & christening wear

- **Papillon**
  31 Farmeloan Road
  Rutherglen
  Glasgow
  G73 1DN
  ☎ 0141 647 1492

Opening Times:
Mon – Sat 9.30am–5.30pm, Sun – closed
Suppliers of continental children's wear from birth to 8 yrs for boys and to 10 yrs for girls

- **Paul's Baby Shop**
  124 Quarry Street
  Hamilton
  ML3 7AD
  ☎ 01698 286175

Opening Times:
Mon – Sat 10.00am–5.00pm, Sun – closed
Suppliers of designer & continental children's wear & baby's shoes

- **Piccolo**
  40 New kirk Road
  Bearsden Cross
  Glasgow
  G61 3SL
  ☎ 0141 942 2624

Opening Times:
Mon – Sat 9.15am–5.30pm, Sun – closed
Suppliers of designer clothes & shoes to 12 yrs
Specialists in christening wear

- **Shillinglaws Childrens Wear**
  27a Montgomery Street
  East Kilbride
  ☎ 01355 244535

Opening Times:
Mon – Fri 9.30am–5.00pm,
Sat, 9.30am–5.30pm, Sun – closed
Specialists in children's wear and footwear and suppliers of christening wear

- **Spoilt Rotten**
  489 Victoria Road
  Glasgow
  G44 8RW
  ☎ 0141 422 2528

  Opening Times:
  Mon – Sat 10.00am–5.00pm, Sun – closed
  Suppliers of designer continental children's wear & shoes from birth to 12 yrs
  Suppliers of christening wear

- **Strawberry Fields**
  517 Great Western Road
  Glasgow
  G12 8HN
  ☎ 0141 339 1121

  Opening Times:
  Mon – Sat 9.30am–5.00pm, Sun – closed
  Suppliers of designer continental children's wear from birth to 14 yrs

- **Tot Spot**
  104 Trongate
  Glasgow
  G1 5EP
  ☎ 0141 552 1178

  Opening Times:
  Mon – Sat 9.30am–5.30pm,
  Sun 11.00am–5.00pm
  Suppliers of baby/children's wear & nursery goods

- **Young Generation**
  90 Main Street
  Cambuslang
  G72
  ☎ 0141 641 3616

  Opening Times:
  Mon, Tues, Thurs & Sat 9.30am–5.00pm,
  Wed 9.30am–1.00pm, Sun – closed
  Suppliers of continental children's wear & shoes from birth to 6 yrs
  Suppliers of christening wear

Baby & Children's Traditional Furniture & Gifts / Nursery & Pram Shops

Please find in this section a list of baby and children's traditional furniture and gift shops & nursery and pram shops in and around the Glasgow area.
The shops below sell a variety of prams, cots, nursery equipment & furniture.
Some may also sell baby & children's clothing. *See also* SHOPPING (BABY & CHILDREN'S CLOTHES SHOPS)

■ **A & M Robinson Ltd**
1008 Pollokshaws Road
(in lane @ Buongiorno)
Shawlands
G41 2HQ
☎ 0141 632 1384
www.robinsonsbeds.co.uk

Opening Times:
Mon – Fri 9.00am–5.30pm,
Sat 9.00am–5.00pm, Sun 11.00am–5.00pm
After over 25 years, we're still at the end of a cobbled lane and we still manufacture top quality divan beds and mattresses in all sizes. However, we are now bettter known for being design leaders in the finest beds and bedroom furniture sourced from all over Europe. So come in for a browse.
A & M Robinson also have a branch in Edinburgh ☎ 0131 466 0000

■ **Baby Must Have**
☎ 01236 756607

Manufacturers of a safer baby bedding

■ **Baby World**
92 Brandon Parade East
Motherwell
☎ 01698 268505
www.babyworldscotland.co.uk

Opening Times:
Mon – Sat 9.30am–5.00pm,
Sun – closed

■ **Clydebank Pram Shop**
Clydebank Shopping Centre
Sylvania Way
Clydebank
☎ 0141 952 6777

Opening Times:
Mon – Sat 9.00am–5.30pm,
Sun – closed

■ **Cowans**
63–65 Templehill
Troon
Ayrshire
KA10 6BQ
☎ 01292 311211

Opening Times:
Mon – Sat 9.30am–5.00pm,
Sun 12.30pm–4.30pm
Suppliers of prams, nursery equipment, cots & fashions up to 3 yrs

- **Frank B Craig Discount Centre**
13–15 Union Street
Larkhall
☎ 01698 882029

Opening Times:
Mon – Sat 9.00am–5.30pm, Sun – closed
Suppliers of & Mamas & Papas

- **Glasgow Pram Centre**
25–29 Mcfarlane Street
Glasgow
G4 0TL
☎ 0141 552 3998

Opening Times:
Mon – Sat 9.00am–5.30pm, Sun 10.00am–5.30pm
Suppliers of all baby goods & nursery furniture

- **Hippychick Ltd**
1 Roberts Drive
Taunton Road
Bridgwater
Somerset
TA6 6BH
☎ 01278 434440
🖹 01278 434448
www.hippychick.com

Manufacturers and suppliers of practical, natural and fun products for children, including:
Child Hipseat: Innovative back-supporting belt with integral seat for carrying children (6 months–3 years). Endorsed by osteopaths.
Bed Protector: A soft, absorbent 100% waterproof bed mat made from two layers of brushed cotton sandwiching a polyurethane layer. Essential mattress protection for bed wetting.
Cotton Fleece Blanket: 100% natural cotton fleece baby blankets in two sizes and a wonderful array of colours.
Shoo Shoos: Imaginative and refreshingly different, soft leather and suede baby shoes (from 0–24 months).
Aromakids: Diverse range of essential-oil based toiletries for babies and toddlers.

The horses are handcrafted to order. Each one has its own unique character and shape, with the head and neck angled towards the rider.

Available in a range of sizes from 2 yrs to adult of up to 65kg. Genuine leather accessories with chrome leather for the padded saddle, real horsehair and solid brass stirrups and fittings. Have your clan tartan for a blanket. Optional extras include a mounting step and safety pommels.

Each limited edition rocking horse has been designed and constructed to comply with the UK Toy (Safety Regulations) 1995 (subject to any revised CE Regulations in 2004) and has a CE kite mark. A brass plate is inscribed with the unique number and date of construction of the horse and a further brass plate allows for a personal message to be displayed. You will also receive a framed **Certificate of Authenticity** about your horse and a fancy brass dress comb.

- **Home Craft of Helensburgh**
  24 Kildonan Drive
  Helensburgh
  Argyle & Bute
  G84 9SA
  ☎ 01436 671718

Rocking Horses by Shaun Hoey
Heirloom quality rocking horses in selected hardwoods ie walnut, yew, elm, rosewood, ash etc.

Prices range from £800 to £1950 depending on size and specification. Normally payments are staged ie
Stage 1 – £50 deposit,
Stage 2 and Stage 3 – 25% each stage,
Stage 4 – the balance payable on delivery.

Credit facilities are available with monthly payments at 0% APR plus admin fee of £25.

All customers receive a contract and agreed specifications. Occasionally complete rocking horses are available for that last minute gift. Please telephone for a brochure or an appointment at my premises.

■ **Jan Stewart**
16 Wilson Place
East Kilbride
Glasgow
G74 4QD
☎ 01355 222064

Opening Times:
Mon – Sat 10.00am–5.30pm, Tues closed
Sun 11.00am–5.30pm

■ **NCT** (maternity sales)
239 Shawbridge Street
Glasgow
G43 1QN
☎ orderline 0870 112 1120

For NCT (The National Childbirth Trust) *see* HEALTH (HELPLINES)

■ **Paisley Pram Shop**
20 Moss Street
Paisley
Renfrewshire
PA1 1BL
☎ 0141 889 0808

Opening Times:
Mon – Sat 9.30am–5.30pm,
Sun 11.00am–4.00pm

■ **Scottish Nappy Co Ltd**
☎ 0800 015 5570

The Scottish Nappy Company…a very special service for busy parents. Buying nappies can become a thing of the past!

Opening Times:
Mon – Sat 10.00am–5.30pm, Sun 12.00pm–5.00pm

We are an independent family business established in 1982 and operating from a large retail outlet on the A82 just 2 minutes from junction 17 on the M8 motorway in Central Scotland and a short walk west from St Georges Cross Underground.

We specialise in quality carved pine and painted children's furniture which is reminiscent of Snow White and the Seven Dwarfs and our painted nursery furniture is an exciting innovative concept of hand built funky furniture whose main characteristics are the unique applied three dimensional hand painted themed resin figures or the massive funky contrasting handles.

We also specialise in quality carved reclaimed and reproduction pine furniture for every room in the house.

■ **Something Special**
240 Great Western Road
Glasgow
G4 9EJ
☎ 0141 332 5677
Email: somethingspecial@supanet.com
Nursery furniture:
www.somethingspecial.info

Pine furniture: www.somethingspecial.sco.fm

- **Stork Exchange**
  ☎ 01698 252715

  As new nursery equipment bought & sold

- **Young Trend Nursery Centres**
  39–41 South Bridge Street
  Airdrie
  ML6 6JQ
  ☎ 01236 767 248

  Opening Times:
  Mon, Tues, Thurs, Fri & Sat 9.00am–5.00pm,
  Wed & Sun – closed

- **Young Trend Nursery Centres**
  30 Stewarton Street
  Wishaw
  ML2 8AN
  ☎ 01698 372161

  Opening Times:
  Mon, Tues, Thurs, Fri & Sat 9.00am–5.00pm,
  Wed & Sun – closed

Balloons & Fancy Dress

Please find in the following section listings of balloon suppliers, fancy dress shops and party accessory shops in and around the Glasgow area.

■ **And Sew Louise**
Aladdins 16 Motherwell Road
Bellshill
☎ 01698 748770

Opening Times:
Mon – Sat 9.00am–5.00pm, Sun – closed
Fancy dress, accessories, masks & make-up

■ **And Sew Louise**
Clyde Walk
Cumbernauld Shopping Centre
☎ 01236 455055

Opening Times:
Mon – Sat 9.00am–5.00pm, Sun – closed
Fancy dress, accessories, masks & make-up

■ **Balloon 2 U & Flowers 2**
Unit 1 Tweed Walk
Cumbernauld Shopping Centre
Cumbernauld
G67 1EN
☎ 01236 457632

Opening Times:
Mon – Sat 9.00am–5.00pm, Sun – closed
Florist and balloon decoration

■ **Balloon Elegance**
Unit 2 53 Love Street
Paisley
Renfrewshire
☎ 0141 848 6119

Opening Times:
Mon – Fri 9.00am–5.00pm,
Sat & Sun by order

■ **Balloons N Parties**
☎ 0141 649 7181

Opening Times:
24hrs, 7 days
Supplier of balloons & decorations
Clowns for children's birthday parties
For Animal Man & Pickles the Clown *see* Birthday Parties (Children's Enterainers)

■ **Celebrations**
15 London Street
Larkhall
☎ 01698 882000
www.celebrationspartyshop.co.uk

Opening Times:
Mon, Tues, Thurs, Fri & Sat 9.00am – 5.00pm, Sun & Wed – closed

■ **Fairy Funny Fancy Dress**
First Floor
52 St Enoch Square
Glasgow
G1 4AA
☎ 0141 248 4846

Opening Times:
Mon, Tues, Wed, Sat, 10.00am–5.30pm,
Thurs 10.00am–7.00pm, Sun – closed
Fancy dress, face paints, kids costumes & accessories

■ **Fun World**
350 Pollokshaws Road
Glasgow
G41
☎ 0141 423 1117

Opening Times:
Mon, Tues & Wed 10.00am–5.30pm,
Thurs 10.00am–7.00pm,
Sat 10.00am–5.00pm, Sun – closed

■ **Happy Talk**
25 Quarry Street
Hamilton
ML3 7AW
☎ 01698 282813
www.happytalkpartyshop.co.uk

Opening Times:
Mon – Fri 9.00am–5.30pm,
Sat 9.00am–5.00pm, Sun closed
Balloons, banners, confetti, party decorations

■ **Hi Flyers**
Unit 2 Moffat Street
Gorbals
G5 0PD
☎ 0141 420 6020

Opening Times:
Mon – Fri 9.30am–5.00pm,
Sat 10.00am–4.00pm, Sun – closed
Supplier of balloons & party wear

■ **Occasions Direct**
Unit 6 8 Meadow Road
Partick
Glasgow
G11 6HX
☎ 0141 337 3373

Opening Times:
Mon – Fri 9.00am–5.00pm
Sat 10.00am–4.00pm, Sun – closed
Suppliers of balloons & gas

■ **Party Props**
31 Murray Square
East Kilbride
☎ 01355 263117

Opening Times:
Mon – Sat 9.30am–5.00pm, Sun – closed
Party accessories, costumes & balloons

Bookshops – Ottakar's

Please find in the following section listings of Ottakar's book stores in Scotland

With thirteen branches, **Ottakar's** is now the largest dedicated book-selling chain in Scotland. The acquisition of the James Thin high street retail branches meant not only job security for the staff in those shops but an opportunity for Ottakar's to provide these towns and cities with a really great bookshop.

We have recently re-sited our branches in Inverness, East Kilbride and Dumfries and will be opening a brand new branch in Oban at the end of October 2003.

Some Authors that we have welcomed for events this year have been; Terry Pratchett, Jacqeline Wilson, Michael Palin, Mairi Hedderwick and Jamie Oliver as well as pop signings with David Sneddon and Darius.

We try to really get behind Scottish books and Scottish authors and have sponsored a ticket back voucher offer on the "Itchy Coo" imprint at the Edinburgh Book Festival and have a rolling monthy program of Scottish promotions.

As well as a fantastic selection of books, our Launch Pad stores also carry an exciting range of educational and fun toys for children of all ages, indeed whereas most bookshops generate about 10% of their sales from Children's books, at Ottakar's they account for almost 20%.

Ottakar's bookstores are about range, choice, personality, expertise, value and a passion for books.

For more information contact Bob McDevitt on 0141 554 8803 / 07980 788 819 / bob.mcdevitt@ottakars.co.uk.

- **ELEANOR LOGAN**
  1 Douglas Court
  Lenzie
  Glasgow
  G66 4NP
  ☎ 0141 776 4478/07980 788 815
  eleanor.logan@ottakars.co.uk

- **BOB McDEVITT**
  38 Circus Drive
  Dennistoun
  Glasgow
  G31 2JE
  ☎ 0141 554 8803/07980 788 819
  bob.mcdevitt@ottakars.co.uk

- 57 George Street
  Edinburgh
  EH2 2JQ
  ☎ 0131 225 3211
  🖹 0131 225 9626

- **ABERDEEN**
  3/7 Union Bridge
  Trinity Centre
  Aberdeen
  AB11 6BG
  ☎ 01224 592 440
  🖹 01224 592 442
  manager.abd@ottakars.co.uk
  www.ottakars.co.uk

  Vicky Dawson – MANAGER
  Oil and related industries, Academic, Children's, Scottish Business Accounts, School Accounts, Customer Orders, Costa Coffee

■ **AVIEMORE**
87 Grampian Road
Aviemore
PH22 1RH
☎ 01479 810 797
🖹 01479 812 274
manager.avi@ottakars.co.uk
www.ottakars.co.uk

Yvonne Rosie
Scottish, Walking/Climbing
Customer Orders

■ **AYR**
127–147 High Street
Ay
KA7 1QR
☎ 01292 262 600
🖹 01292 262 150
manager.ayr@ottakars.co.uk
www.ottakars.co.uk

Alex MacKinnon – MANAGER
Scottish/Local Interest
Customer Orders, Costa Coffee

■ **CAMERON TOLL – EDINBURGH**
Cameron Toll Shopping Centre
6 Lady Road
Edinburgh
Mid Lothian
EH16 5PB
☎ 0131 666 1866
🖹 0131 666 1873
manager.cto@ottakars.co.uk
www.ottakars.co.uk

Fiona Malcolm– MANAGER
Children's, Local Interest
Customer Orders

■ **DUMFRIES**
18–26 Church Crescent
Dumfries
DG1 1DQ
(Moving to a new site in High Street - Spring 2003)
☎ 01387 254 288
🖹 01387 257 242
manager.duf@ottakars.co.uk
www.ottakars.co.uk

Lorraine McLean – MANAGER,
(AM – Frances)
Artist Materials, Scottish, Stationery
Customer Orders

■ **DUNDEE**
7/8 High Street
Dundee
DD1 1SS
☎ 01382 223 999
🖹 01382 202 963
manager.dun@ottakars.co.uk
www.ottakars.co.uk

Gordon Dow – MANAGER
(AM – Kevin)
Academic, Scottish/Local Interest
Customer Orders, Author Events

■ **EAST KILBRIDE**
38A The Plaza
East Kilbride
G74 1LW
☎ 01355 271 835
🖹 01355 271 840
manager.eki@ottakars.co.uk
www.ottakars.co.uk

Camilla Wootten – MANAGER
Children's, Crime Fiction
Customer Orders

■ EDINBURGH

57 George Street
Edinburgh
EH2 2JQ
☎ 0131 225 4495
🖹 0131 225 9626
manager.gst@ottakars.co.uk
www.ottakars.co.uk

Duncan Furness – MANAGER
Biography, Children's, Crime Fiction, History, Scottish/Local Interest, Travel
Customer Orders, Author Events, School Accounts, Brodies Coffee

■ ELGIN

Unit 10–11, St Giles Centre
Elgin
IV30 1EA
☎ 01343 547 321
🖹 01343 545 799
manager.elg@ottakars.co.uk
www.ottakars.co.uk

Judith Craib – MANAGER
Children's, Scottish/Local Interest
Customer Orders

■ GLASGOW

Unit 6, Buchanan Galleries
Buchanan Street
Glasgow
G1 2FF
☎ 0141 353 1500
🖹 0141 353 0649
manager.gla@ottakars.co.uk
www.ottakars.co.uk

Ian Owens – MANAGER
Children's (Launch Pad), Crime Fiction, Fiction, Scottish/Local Interest, Travel
Customer Orders, School Accounts, Author Events, Costa Coffee

■ INVERNESS

Unit 69, Eastgate Centre
Inverness
IV2 3PR
☎ 01463 233 500
🖹 01463 711 474
manager.inv@ottakars.co.uk
www.ottakars.co.uk

Brid McKibbon – MANAGER,
Grainne Cooney – CHILDREN'S REGIONAL SUPPORT MANAGER
Academic, Children's, Scottish/Local Interest, Stationery
Mail Order Service, Customer Orders, School/Business Accounts, Ordnance Survey sub agent

■ KIRKCALDY

175 High Street
Kirkcaldy, Fife, KY1 1JA
☎ 01592 263 755
🖹 01592 263 811
manager.kir@ottakars.co.uk
www.ottakars.co.uk

Kate Ewing –MANAGER,
(AM – Carole-Anne)
Children's, Scottish/Local Interest
Customer Orders

■ NEWTON MEARNS

38 Avenue Centre
Newton Mearns
Glasgow, G77 6EY
☎ 0141 616 3933
🖹 0141 616 3255
manager.nme@ottakars.co.uk
www.ottakars.co.uk

Shelley Naughton – MANAGER
Children's, Scottish/Local Interest
Customer Orders

Children's Footwear

Please find in the following section listings of children's footwear shops in and around the Glasgow area.

For suppliers of Bridesmaid & Communion Shoes *see* SHOPPING (DANCE & BALLET WEAR)

- **Bellini Footwear**
  578 Clarkston Road
  Glasgow
  G44 3SQ
  ☎ 0141 633 1784

  Opening Times:
  Mon – Sat 9.30am–5.30pm, Sun – closed
  Suppliers of continental children's footwear from tots to teens

- **Brantano**
  9 Douglas Park Lane
  Hamilton
  ML3 0DF
  ☎ 01698 459140
  www.brantano.co.uk

  Opening Times:
  Mon, Tues, Wed & Fri 10.00am–7.00pm,
  Thurs, 10.00am–8.00pm,
  Sat 9.00am–6.00pm &
  Sun 11.00am–5.00pm
  A fitting service for Hush Puppies available

- **Brantano**
  Livingstone Street
  Clydebank
  Dunbartonshire
  G81 2XA
  ☎ 0141 951 8363
  www.brantano.co.uk

  Opening Times:
  Mon, Tues & Wed 10.00am–6.00pm,
  Thurs 10.00am–8.00pm,
  Fri 10.00am–7.00pm, Sat 9.00am–6.00pm
  & Sun 11.00am–5.00pm
  A fitting service for Hush Puppies available

- **Famous Feet**
  6 North Court Lane
  Royal Exchange Square
  Glasgow
  G1 2PD
  ☎ 0141 227 2727

  Opening Times:
  Mon – Sat 9.30am–5.30pm
  Sun 12.00pm–5.00pm
  Suppliers of continental children's footwear.
  Pre-walkers to size 40

- **Flossie's**
  3 Bank Street
  Coatbridge
  ML5 1AJ
  ☎ 01236 426310

  Opening Times:
  Mon – Sat 10.00am–5.00pm, Sun – closed
  Suppliers of continental children's footwear

- **Happy Feet Shoes**
  4a Neva Place
  Main Street
  Bridge of Weir
  ☎ 01505 610600

Opening Times:
Mon – Sat 9.30am–5.00pm, Sun – closed
Suppliers of start-rite shoes & continental children's footwear

- **Zapatitos**
  80 Cadzow Street
  Hamilton
  ML3 6DS
  ☎ 01698 891808

Opening Times:
Mon – Sat 10.00am–5.00pm, Sun – closed
Suppliers of continental children's footwear

Cycle shops

Please find in the following section listings of cycle shops in and around the Glasgow area.

- **Alpine Bikes**
116 Great Western Road
Glasgow
G4 9AD
☎ 0141 353 2226
www.alpinebikes.co.uk

Opening Times:
Mon – Sat 9.00am–6.00pm &
Sun 12.00pm–5.00pm
Bikes from 6 yrs, accessories & servicing

- **The Bicycle Chain**
1417 Dumbarton Road
Scotstoun
Glasgow
☎ 0141 958 1055

Opening Times:
Mon – Sat 9.30am–5.30pm, Sun – closed

- **The Bicycle Chain**
3 Collier Street
Johnstone
☎ 01505 335551

Opening Times:
Mon – Sat 9.30am–5.30pm, Sun – closed

- **Bike Wise**
15 Townhead
Kirkintilloch
Glasgow
G66 1NG
☎ 0141 775 3722

Opening Times:
Mon – Fri 8.00am–5.00pm, Sat 10.00am–5.00pm, Sun – closed

- **Billy Bilsland**
15 Main Street
Cumbernauld
Glasgow
G67 2RR
☎ 01236 452632

Opening Times:
Mon – Sat 9.00am–5.00pm,
Sun 12.00pm–4.00pm

- **Billy Bilsland Cycles**
176 Saltmarket
Glasgow
G1 5LA
☎ 0141 552 0841

Opening Times:
Mon – Sat 9.00am–5.00pm, Sun – closed

■ **City Cycles** 261 High Street Glasgow G4 0QR ☎ 0141 552 0961	Opening Times: Tues – Sun 11.00am–5.00pm, Mon – closed
■ **The Clarkston Cycle Centre** 681 Clarkston Road Netherlee Glasgow G44 3SE ☎ 0141 633 1152	Opening Times: Mon – Sat 9.30am–5.30pm, Sun – closed Traditional cycle shop & accessories
■ **Craig MacMartin Cycles** 924 Pollokshaws Road Shawlands Glasgow G41 1ET ☎ 0141 632 2733	Opening Times: Mon – Sat 10.00am–6.00pm, Tues & Sun – closed
■ **Cycle Lane** 193 Clarkston Road Clarkston Glasgow G44 3BS ☎ 0141 637 2439	Opening Times: Mon – Sat 9.30am–5.30pm, Sun – closed Delivery service available
■ **Cycle Lane** 5 Westwood Square Westwood East Kilbride G75 8JQ ☎ 01355 228225	As above
■ **Dales Cycles Ltd** 150 Dobbies Loan Glasgow G4 0JE ☎ 0141 332 2705 www.dalescycles.com	Opening Times: Mon, Tues, Wed, Fri & Sat 9.00am–6.00pm, Thurs, 9.00am–7.00pm, Sun 12.00pm–4.00pm

- **Glasgow Bicycle Co**
  1274 Paisley Road West
  Glasgow
  G52 1DF
  ☎ 0141 427 6030

  Opening Times:
  Mon – Sat 9.30am–5.30pm, Sun – closed

- **Kinetics**
  54 Switchback Road
  Bearsden
  Glasgow
  G61 1AE
  ☎ 0141 942 2552

  Opening Times:
  Tues – Sat 9.00am–5.00pm,
  Sun & Mon – closed

- **Magic Cycles**
  Arch 4 & 5
  Bowling Harbour
  Bowling
  Glasgow
  G60 5AF
  ☎ 01389 873433

  Opening Times:
  Mon, Wed, Thurs, Fri, Sat, Sun
  9.00am–6.00pm, Tues – closed

- **Rutherglen Cycles**
  73 Mill Street
  Rutherglen
  Glasgow
  G73 2LD
  ☎ 0141 647 2001

  Opening Times:
  Mon – Sat 9.15am–5.15pm, Sun – closed

- **West End Cycles**
  16-18 Chancellor Street
  Glasgow
  G11 5RQ
  ☎ 0141 357 1344

  Opening Times:
  Mon – Sat 10.00am–6.00pm, Sun – closed
  Cycles & accessories
  Cycle hire available (seasonal)

Dancewear

Please find in the following section listings of dancewear shops in and around the Glasgow area.

For Dancing Schools *see* Activities for Children

- **Backstage Dancewear**
  192 Quarry Street
  Hamilton
  ML3 6QR
  ☎ 01698 420957

  Opening Times:
  Mon – Sat 9.30am–4.30pm, Sun – closed
  All dancewear
  Bridesmaid & communion shoes

- **Clarkston Dancewear Centre**
  Unit 1 Busby Road
  Clarkston
  Glasgow
  ☎ 0141 638 2488

  Opening Times:
  Mon – Fri 9.45am–5.15pm,
  Sat 9.45am–5.00pm, Sun – closed
  All dancewear

- **Dance Apparel**
  Unit 6 Kirky Arcade
  15 Cowgate
  Kirkintilloch
  Glasgow
  G66 1HW
  ☎ 0141 578 0078

  Opening Times:
  Mon – Sat 9.00am–5.00pm, Sun – closed
  All dancewear

- **Fitness Fashions**
  13 Cambuslang Road
  Rutherglen
  Glasgow
  G73
  ☎ 0141 647 6746

  Opening Times:
  Mon, Wed, Thurs, Fri & Sat 9.30am–5.00pm,
  Sun & Tues – closed
  Leotards, cat suits, jazz pants, sweat pants, ballet, tap & jazz shoes

- **Total Dance Supplies**
  53 Kelvin Road North
  Lenziemill
  Cumbernauld
  ☎ 01236 611771

  Opening Times:
  Mon, Tues, Thurs, Fri & Sat 9.00am–5.00pm,
  Wed & Sun – closed
  All dancewear & shoes
  Bridesmaid & communion shoes

Opening Times:
Mon – Sat 9.30am–5.00pm
(except Thurs to 7.00pm),
Sun 12.00pm–4.00pm
Dancewear & footwear

- **West End Dance Boutiques**
  1018 Dumbarton Road
  Glasgow
  G14 9UJ
  ☎ 0141 959 0922

Maternity Wear

Please find in the following section listings of maternity wear shops & maternity wear mail order companies in and around the Glasgow Area.

- **Blooming Marvellous**
  22 Albion Court
  Albion Place
  London
  W6 0QT

  Head Office
  ☎ 020 87480025
  Maternity wear, babywear & orders
  ☎ 0870 751 8944
  For a Blooming Marvellous catalogue
  ☎ 0870 751 8977
  www.bloomingmarvellous.co.uk
  See also SHOPPING (BABY & CHILDREN'S CLOTHES SHOPS)

- **Bumpsadaisy**
  103 Byres Road
  Glasgow
  G11 5HW
  ☎ 0141 339 8344

  Opening Times:
  Mon – Sat 10.00am–5.00pm, Sun – closed

- **Formes**
  28 Gordon Street
  Glasgow
  ☎ 0141 221 6633
  www.formes.com
  Free catalogue ☎ 020 86891122

  Opening Times:
  Mon – Sat 9.30am–5.30pm
  (Thurs till 7.00pm),
  Sun closed

- **Hippychick Ltd**
  1 Roberts Drive
  Taunton Road
  Bridgwater,
  Somerset
  TA6 6BH
  ☎ 01278 434440
  www.hippychick.com

  For Hippychick *see* SHOPPING (BABY & TRADITIONAL FURNITURE & GIFTS / NURSERY & PRAM SHOPS)

- **JoJo Maman Bébé** (mail order)
  ☎ 0870 241 0451
  www.jojomamanbebe.co.uk

  Maternity, baby/kids clothes, nursery products & toys

■ **NCT** (maternity sales)
239 Shawbridge Street
Glasgow
G43 1QN
☎ orderline 0870 112 1120

Opening Times:
Mon – Fri 9.00am–5.00pm
Baby's room, pregnancy essentials, feeding your baby, bras for breastfeeding, bath and change, safe and sound, out and about, first play, play and learn, personalised items, book, videos and music

For NCT (The National Childbirth Trust) *see* HEALTH (HELPLINES)

■ **Nursing Underwear**
Rainbows End
246 Stonelaw Road
Rutherglen
Glasgow
G73 2SA
☎ 0141 647 8106

Opening Times:
Mon – Sat 9.30am–5.30pm, Sun – closed

SCHOOL OUTFITTERS

Please find in the following section listings of School Outfitters in and around the Glasgow area.

- **A P Alston**
  84 Quarry Street
  Hamilton
  ML3 7AX
  ☎ 01698 283852

Opening Times:
Mon – Sat 9.00am–5.30pm,
Sun – closed

- **Academy Uniforms Ltd**
  Glenwood Business Park
  Glenwood Place
  Glasgow
  G45 9UH
  ☎ 0141 630 9300
  0141 630 9200

Academy Uniforms specialise in the direct supply of Nursery, Primary and Secondary school uniforms. Our comprehensive range of clothing consists of items such as painting tabards, sweatshirts, polo shirts, school bags and blazers. All items can be embroidered with your school logo. Academy only supply quality products suitable for the rough and tumble within the play ground. All items of clothing are fully machine washable, manufactured from top quality fabrics and are always competitively priced.

Through years of experience, in this competitive market, Academy understands the importance of supplying good quality uniforms with accurate delivery dates. The service that we offer meets the individual needs of each school.

Academy have a wealth of experience in creating new uniforms. This is particularly beneficial to either new nursery schools or schools that are amalgamating or even when schools are moving into a new building.

Please contact Academy Uniforms for a price comparison on your existing uniform, or to see our extensive range of school uniforms that are available or even for new ideas to help PTAs and School Boards raise valuable school funds.

Opening Times:
Mon – Fri 9.00am–5.00pm

■ **Campbell Boys & Girls Shops Ltd**
358 Victoria Road
Glasgow
G42 8YW
☎ 0141 423 1455

Opening Times:
Mon, Wed, Thurs & Fri 9.00am–5.30pm,
Tues & Sat 9.00am–5.00pm, Sun – closed

■ **Le Mirage**
77 Manse Road
Motherwell
(nr Firpark)
☎ 01698 252990

Opening Times:
Mon – Sat 9.30am–5.00pm, Sun – closed
Closed on Wed afternoon after schools return in August

■ **Mans World**
157–159 Byres Road
☎ 0141 357 0400

Opening Times:
Mon – Sat 9.00am–5.30pm, Sun – closed

204 Fenwick Road
Giffnock
☎ 0141 638 7689

Opening Times:
Mon – Sat 9.00am–5.30pm, Sun – closed

Mans World
13 Eaglesham Road
Clarkston
☎ 0141 644 4118

Opening Times:
Mon – Sat 9.00am–5.30pm, Sun – closed

- **Mayor's Sport & Menswear**
1606 Dumbarton Road
Scotstoun
Glasgow
☎ 0141 959 9003

Opening Times:
Mon – Sat 9.00am–5.30pm, Sun – closed
Suppliers of schoolwear

- **National Schoolwear Centres**
174 Saltmarket (beside High Court)
Glasgow
☎ 0141 552 0102

Opening Times:
Mon – Sat 10.00am–4.45pm, Sun – closed

- **R W Stevens & Co**
83 Deanston Drive
Shawlands
Glasgow
G41
☎ 0141 632 8617

Opening Times:
Mon – Fri 9.00am–6.00pm, closed Tues
except July & August

Toy Shops

Please find in the following section listings of toy shops, traditional toy shops and mail order toy shops in and around the Glasgow area.
Many of the opening times are subject to change nearer to Christmas.

- **Arkworks**
  21 Old Coach Road
  East Kilbride
  Glasgow
  G74 4DS
  ☎ 01355 579292

  Opening Times:
  Tues – Sat 10.00am–4.15pm,
  Sun & Mon– closed

- **The Bear Factory**
  Unit 17 Buchanan Galleries
  Buchanan Street
  Glasgow
  ☎ 0141 331 2173

  Opening Times:
  Mon, Tues, Wed, Fri & Sat 9.00am–6.00pm,
  Thurs 9.00am–8.00pm,
  Sun 11.00am–5.00pm
  All types of teddy bears
  Make your own teddy, start with the teddy's skin, stuff your bear, dress your bear & then name your bear

■ **The Big Top**
26 Charing Cross Mansions
St Georges Road
Glasgow
G3 6UJ
☎ 0141 332 3300

Opening Times:
Mon – Sat 10.30am–5.00pm, Sun – closed
THE SHOP All the things you wish you had been given as a child and can't find now -we have them! Circus equipment, tin toys, puppets, kites, unicycles, sailing boats, face paints, old-fashioned toys, parachutes, earth-balls, play equipment, garages, dolls houses, stilts, castles, Russian dolls, rocking horses, – the variety is endless – but no batteries or computers!
FUNSHOPS Schools, play-groups, galas, corporate days, shopping centres, etc. are just some of the venues for our funshops. Funshops are either 'structured' (with the same children for the duration of the funshop) or 'come-and-try' which is informal (participants stay for as long as they want and 'have a go') so numbers vary. We can customize each workshop to satisfy the needs of your group. Structured funshops are based on a ratio of 2 leaders to 30 participants. You provide the venue and participants, we provide the rest!
PERFORMERS Stilt walkers, jugglers, puppet shows, clowns, clownshows, unicyclists, balloon-modellers, magicians, face painters and even Santa Claus! – whatever your needs The Big Top can fit the bill. We provide: clown shows for schools & nurseries, birthday parties, christmas parties etc. We organise events for councils, police forces, stately homes, major companies, etc linking workshops, shows and entertainers to provide a full day of events. Our professional entertainers have public liability insurance.
EQUIPMENT We supply schools, nurseries, community centres, councils, etc with a wide range of workshop trunks, bubble materials, earth-balls, parachutes, outdoor games equipment, face paints, etc. We supply and despatch on purchase order.

■ **Centre for Under 5's +**
50 Parnie Street
Glasgow
☎ 0141 552 4006

Opening Times:
Mon – Thurs 10.00am–4.00pm,
The bright pink shop at 50 Parnie Street is the new home for **The Centre for Under 5's+**. Based for a number of years in St Vincent Street, it is an established charity and voluntary organisation, which specialises in providing toys on loan for children with special needs, playgroups, toddlers, voluntary and statutory organisations (childminders etc).
It also has a craft shop selling a wide range of craft materials, which is open to all. For further info please contact the Centre for Under 5's + on 0141 552 4006.
Parking: Candleriggs car park (access off Albion Street), High Street car park, King Street car park, Ingram Street car park, Glassford Street car park. There is limited meter parking in surrounding streets. There are also a number of bus routes and High Street and Argyle Street rail stations are within a 10-minute walk.

■ **Early Learning Centre**
26 Buchanan Street
Glasgow
G1 3LB
☎ 0141 248 2589

Opening Times:
Mon, Tues, Wed 9.00am–6.00pm,
Thurs 9.00am–8.00pm,
Sat 9.00am–6.00pm, Sun 11.00am–5.00pm

Early Learning Centre
Forge Shopping Centre
1221 Gallowgate
Glasgow
G31 4EB
☎ 0141 554 5818

Opening Times:
Mon – Fri 9.30am–5.30pm,
Sat 9.00am–5.30pm, Sun 11.00am–5.00pm

Early Learning Centre
148 Braehead Shopping Centre
Kings Inch Road
Glasgow
G51 4BS
☎ 0141 885 9408

Opening Times:
Mon – Fri 10.00am–9.30pm,
Sat 9.00am–6.00pm,
Sun 11.00am–6.00pm

Early Learning Centre
Unit 3 The Avenue
Newton Mearns
Glasgow
G77 6EY
☎ 0141 616 2772

Opening Times:
Mon – Wed 9.00am–5.30pm,
Thurs 9.00am–7.00pm,
Fri 9.00am–5.30pm,
Sat 9.00am–5.30pm,
Sun 10.00am–5.00pm

Early Learning Centre
17 Moss Street
Paisley
PA1
☎ 0141 848 1571

Opening Times:
Mon – Sat 9.00am–5.30pm, Sun – closed

- **Formative Fun**
Unit 3 Bearsden Shopping Centre
Milngavie Road
Glasgow
G61 2TX
☎ 0141 942 9578

Opening Times:
Mon – Sat 9.30am–5.30pm,
Sun 12.00pm–5.00pm
Sells educational toys & games

- **Funasaurus Shoppers Créche**

For **Funasaurus** *see* SHOPPING BIRTHDAY PARTIES (CHILDREN'S ACTIVITY & ADVENTURE CENTRES)

- **Girl Heaven**

See SHOPPING (BABY & CHILDREN'S CLOTHES SHOPS)

- **Lomond Activities**
Hope Street
Drymen
Glasgow
G63 0BG
☎ 01360 660066
www.lomondactivities.co.uk

Opening Times:
Mon – Sat 9.00am–5.00pm,
Sun 10.00am–5.00pm
Sells traditional toys, bikes & outdoor play equipment

For NCT (The National Childbirth Trust) *see* HEALTH (HELPLINES)

- **NCT** (toy sales)
  239 Shawbridge Street
  Glasgow
  G43 1QN
  ☎ orderline 0870 112 1120

Opening Times:
Tues – Sat 9.30am–5.30pm,
Sun & Mon – closed
(Sun opening from Oct – Dec for Christmas)

- **Pause For Bears**
  199 Crow Road
  Glasgow
  G11 7PD
  ☎ 0141 339 5236

Precious Moments Stationery is a family-based business specialising in printed card designs for all occasions. We create beautiful cards, which can include a photograph. We pride ourselves on personal attention to detail and our flexible approach to customer's requests. Christening and 1st birthdays a speciality.
For **Precious Moments Stationery** *see* BIRTHDAY PARTIES (STATIONERY)

- **Precious Moments Stationery**
  ☎ 0141 639 0429
  www.preciousmomentsstationery

Opening Times:
Tues – Sat 10.00am–5.00pm,
Sun, Mon – closed

- **The Sentry Box**
  175 Great George Street
  Glasgow
  G12 8AQ
  ☎ 0141 334 6070

- **Toy Master**
  A Real Toy Shop
  16–18 New Street
  Paisley
  PA1
  ☎ 0141 887 2395

  Opening Times:
  Mon – Sat 9.00am–5.30pm, Sun – closed
  (Sun opening nearer to Christmas)

- **Toystop**
  Cowglen Road
  Glasgow
  G53 6EQ
  ☎ 0141 891 4919
  www.thetoystop.co.uk

  Opening Times:
  Mon – Sat 9.00am–5.00pm, Sun – closed

Toystop
Savoy Centre
Sauchiehall Street
Glasgow
☎ 0141 332 4868

Opening Times:
Mon, Tues & Wed 9.00am–5.30pm,
Thurs, Fri & Sat 9.00am–6.00pm
Sun – closed

Toystop
Premier Markets
Parkhead Forge
Glasgow
☎ 0141 554 7004

Opening Times:
Mon – Sat 9.00am–5.00pm,
Sun, 11.00am–5.00pm

INDEX